INTRODUCTION TO THE TEXT OF THE NEW TESTAMENT

FROM THE AUTHORS AND SCRIBES TO THE MODERN CRITICAL TEXT

Edward D. Andrews

INTRODUCTION TO THE TEXT OF THE NEW TESTAMENT

From the Authors and the Scribes to the Modern Critical Texts

Edward D. Andrews

Christian Publishing House

Cambridge, Ohio

CHRISTIAN PUBLISHING HOUSE

FOUNDED 2005

INTRODUCTION TO THE TEXT OF THE NEW TESTAMENT: *From the Authors and the Scribes to the Modern Critical Texts* by Edward D. Andrews

ISBN-10: 1949586782

ISBN-13: 978-1949586787

Table of Contents

Edward D. Andrews

Book Description

Introduction to the Text of the New Testament" provides a comprehensive guide to the complex world of New Testament textual criticism. Delving into the history, transmission, and analysis of the New Testament text, this book offers an in-depth exploration of the various factors that have shaped the biblical text throughout the centuries.

From the origins of the New Testament canon and the materials used by ancient scribes to the emergence of critical texts and modern methodologies, the book covers a wide range of topics. Readers will gain an understanding of the significance of paleography, the role of ancient translations and church fathers, the development of textual families, and the impact of the printing press on the biblical text.

The book also examines the various approaches to New Testament textual criticism, including the coherence-based genealogical method, Aland's local-genealogical method, and Metzger's evaluation of variant readings based on text-types. With insightful discussions on collation and classification of manuscripts, this work serves as a valuable resource for scholars, students, and anyone interested in the history and development of the New Testament text. Discover the fascinating journey of the New Testament text from its ancient origins to the cutting-edge scholarship of the 21st century.

Preface

The New Testament, as a foundational document for millions of Christians around the world, has been the subject of intense study and scrutiny throughout history. Its text has been passed down through generations, copied by scribes, translated into numerous languages, and analyzed by scholars seeking to understand the original meaning and message of its authors. This book, "Introduction to the Text of the New Testament: From the Authors and the Scribes to the Modern Critical Texts," aims to provide readers with a comprehensive overview of the rich and complex journey that the New Testament text has taken from its inception to the present day.

This work is not meant to be a mere repetition of existing scholarship; instead, it strives to synthesize the wealth of knowledge that has been accumulated on this subject and present it in a clear, accessible, and engaging manner. The chapters are organized in a logical progression, guiding readers through the various stages of the New Testament's development, including the materials used by ancient scribes, the transmission of the text, the emergence of textual families, and the various methodologies employed by scholars in their quest to recover the original text.

In writing this book, we have endeavored to strike a balance between depth and accessibility, ensuring that both newcomers to the field and experienced scholars will find value in its pages. We have also made a conscious effort to be inclusive of different perspectives and methodologies, highlighting the ongoing debates and discussions within the field of New Testament textual criticism.

As you embark on this journey through the history and development of the New Testament text, we hope that you will not only gain a deeper appreciation for the intricate process of textual transmission but also be inspired by the dedication and passion of the many scholars who have devoted their lives to preserving and understanding this sacred text. Ultimately, our aim is for this book to serve as a valuable resource and guide, illuminating the fascinating story behind the text that continues to shape the lives and beliefs of millions of people around the world.

Edward D. Andrews

Chief Translator of the Updated American Standard Version

Introduction

The New Testament, a collection of 27 books written by various authors in the first century CE, has had a profound impact on the lives of countless individuals and communities throughout history. It has inspired great works of art, shaped the course of nations, and provided solace and guidance to believers in times of joy and sorrow. As one of the most widely-read and influential texts in human history, it is essential to understand the process by which this sacred collection has been preserved, transmitted, and interpreted over the centuries.

This book seeks to explore the fascinating story behind the text of the New Testament, delving into the world of scribes, scholars, and translators who have worked tirelessly to ensure that the message of the New Testament remains accessible to future generations. The objective of this introduction is to provide a brief overview of the main themes and topics that will be discussed throughout the book, setting the stage for a more in-depth examination of the various aspects of New Testament textual criticism.

First, we will explore the historical and cultural context in which the New Testament was written, examining the use of Koine Greek as the medium of communication and the materials and tools employed by ancient scribes. This background information will help to contextualize the challenges and issues that have arisen in the transmission and preservation of the New Testament text.

Next, we will delve into the study of paleography, the art and science of deciphering ancient manuscripts, which has played a crucial role in the analysis and understanding of New Testament texts. From the development of Greek script to the dating of manuscripts and the insights gained through the study of scribal habits, paleography offers a wealth of information that helps to illuminate the complex process of textual transmission.

The book will then examine the various sources of the New Testament text, including the formation of the canon, the role of autographs and early manuscripts, the significance of textual families, and the influence of ancient translations and church fathers on the transmission of the text.

Following this, we will discuss the factors that have contributed to the introduction of textual variants into the New Testament text, as well as the methods and approaches employed by scholars in evaluating and interpreting these variants. The advent of the printing press and its impact on the dissemination and study of the New Testament will also be examined, highlighting the shift from handwritten manuscripts to printed editions.

Finally, the book will explore the period of the critical text and the development of modern textual criticism methodologies, including the work of notable scholars and the ongoing efforts to determine the original reading of the New Testament text.

As you begin this exploration of the New Testament text, we invite you to immerse yourself in the rich history, diverse perspectives, and cutting-edge scholarship that have shaped the study and understanding of this sacred collection of writings. By engaging with the material presented in this book, we hope that you will gain a newfound appreciation for the intricate process of textual transmission and the enduring legacy of the New Testament.

CHAPTER 1 Introduction: The Text of the New Testament

Explanation and Definition of New Testament Textual Criticism

What lies below is a very basic overview that will be taken up in greater detail later. New Testament textual criticism is an academic discipline that aims to analyze and reconstruct the original text of the New Testament by examining the vast number of surviving manuscripts and other historical sources. The field of textual criticism is crucial because the original autographs (i.e., the initial handwritten documents) of the New Testament books have not survived, and there are thousands of copies containing numerous variations in the text. Scholars in this field endeavor to determine the most authentic reading of the text, which is considered to be closest to the original.

The term "textual criticism" encompasses various methods and principles that scholars use to evaluate the textual evidence and make decisions about which readings are most likely to reflect the original wording. These methods and principles include documentary evidence (i.e., the manuscripts themselves), transcriptional evidence (i.e., the types of errors scribes made while copying texts), and internal evidence (i.e., the content and style of the text).

Manuscript Evidence

The New Testament was originally written in Greek, and the primary sources of textual criticism are the surviving Greek manuscripts. Over 5,800 Greek manuscripts have been discovered, dating from the 2nd century CE to the late medieval period. These manuscripts vary in size, content, and quality; some are complete books or compilations, while others are fragments of single pages or even just a few verses.

In addition to Greek manuscripts, there are also thousands of early translations of the New Testament into other languages such as Latin, Syriac, Coptic, Armenian, and Georgian. These translations, called versions, can provide valuable insights into the Greek text that was used in their creation. Furthermore, the writings of the early Christian authors, known as the Church Fathers, often quote or paraphrase portions of the New Testament, which can help scholars reconstruct the text.

Types of Manuscripts

There are two main types of Greek manuscripts: uncials and minuscules. Uncials are characterized by large, capital letters and were the predominant script used from the 3rd to the 9th centuries AD. Minuscules, written in a smaller, more compact script, emerged in the 9th century and became the standard form of Greek writing.

Manuscripts are also categorized based on their textual character or the way the text has been copied and transmitted over time. The major text-types are the Alexandrian, the Western, the Byzantine, and the Caesarean. Each text-type represents a group of manuscripts that share common characteristics and readings.

Methods and Principles

Textual critics use various methods and principles to analyze the manuscript evidence and make decisions about the original text. These can be grouped into two main categories: external evidence and internal evidence.

External evidence involves examining the manuscripts themselves, considering factors such as age, geographical distribution, and the relationship between manuscripts. Generally, earlier manuscripts are considered more reliable because they are closer to the original text in time. However, later manuscripts that belong to a well-established text-type or have a clear lineage may also be considered valuable.

Internal evidence focuses on the content and style of the text itself. This includes an analysis of the author's vocabulary, grammar, and style, as well as the context and the historical background of the text. Textual critics also examine various types of scribal errors that may have occurred during the transmission of the text, such as omissions, additions, or alterations.

One of the key principles in textual criticism is "lectio difficilior potior," which means "the more difficult reading is preferable." This principle is based on the assumption that scribes were more likely to change a difficult or obscure reading to something more familiar or easier to understand.

Eclecticism and Textual Criticism

Eclecticism is an approach in textual criticism that involves examining individual variants on a case-by-case basis rather than relying solely on the overall character of a manuscript or text-type. Eclectic critics weigh both external and internal evidence when evaluating variant readings and make decisions based on a combination of factors. This method seeks to balance the importance of manuscript evidence with an understanding of the textual context and the tendencies of scribes.

Eclecticism has been particularly influential in the development of critical editions of the New Testament, such as the Nestle-Aland and United Bible Societies (NU) Greek New Testaments. These editions represent a carefully considered synthesis of manuscript evidence and scholarly judgment, aiming to present the most reliable reconstruction of the original text.

However, eclecticism has its critics, who argue that the method can lead to inconsistency and overreliance on internal evidence. Some scholars advocate for a more rigorous focus on manuscript evidence and text-types, prioritizing the testimony of the earliest and most reliable witnesses to the text.

The Goal of New Testament Textual Criticism

The ultimate goal of New Testament textual criticism is to reconstruct the original text, or the "autograph," of each book as accurately as possible. While the task is complex and scholars recognize that we may never fully recover the exact wording of the autographs, the discipline of textual criticism has made significant progress in understanding the transmission history of the New Testament and identifying the most reliable readings.

It is important to note that the variations found in the manuscript tradition do not significantly affect core Christian beliefs or the overall message of the New Testament. The vast majority of textual variants involve minor differences in spelling, word order, or grammar, which have little to no impact on the meaning of the text.

In conclusion, New Testament textual criticism is a vital discipline that seeks to reconstruct the original text of the New Testament using the wealth of manuscript evidence and scholarly methods available. By examining both external and internal evidence and employing principles such as eclecticism, textual critics work to produce the most accurate and reliable text possible. While the task is challenging and ongoing, the discipline has made substantial progress in understanding the history and transmission of the New Testament text, ensuring that its message remains accessible and relevant to future generations.

Introductory Comments Why We Need New Testament Textual Criticism

New Testament textual criticism is essential for several reasons, as it helps scholars, theologians, and readers alike in understanding and preserving the original message of the New Testament. The necessity for this discipline stems from the following factors:

1. **Absence of original manuscripts**: The autographs, or original manuscripts, of the New Testament books have been lost over time. What we have today are copies of copies, which were produced and transmitted by scribes through the centuries. As a result, the textual transmission process has inevitably introduced variations into the text. Textual criticism seeks to recover the original wording of the text as accurately as possible by analyzing and comparing the available manuscript evidence.

2. **Numerous manuscript copies**: The New Testament is one of the most well-documented ancient texts, with over 5,800 Greek manuscripts and tens of thousands of translations in other languages, such as Latin, Coptic, and Syriac. The sheer number of these manuscripts has led to a wealth of textual variants. Textual critics meticulously study these variants to determine the most probable original reading.

3. **Scribe errors and intentional changes**: Throughout history, scribes have made unintentional errors while copying the text, such as misspellings, omissions, or duplications. Sometimes, scribes even made intentional changes to clarify the text, harmonize passages, or emphasize particular theological views. Textual criticism aims to identify and correct these alterations by examining the tendencies and habits of scribes and evaluating the internal and external evidence for each variant.

4. **Ensuring accurate translations**: Translations of the New Testament into modern languages rely on the most reliable and accurate Greek text. Textual criticism helps establish the best possible Greek text, which in turn, ensures that translations convey the original message as faithfully as possible.

5. **Strengthening the historical reliability of the New Testament**: By reconstructing the original text and understanding the history of its transmission, textual criticism strengthens the historical reliability of the New Testament. This is crucial for both scholarly research and the faith of those who consider the New Testament as a sacred text.

6. **Enhancing our understanding of early Christianity**: Studying the textual variants and the manuscript evidence sheds light on the beliefs, practices, and challenges faced by early Christians. Textual criticism not only helps us understand the New Testament better but also provides valuable insights into the development of Christianity in its formative years.

In conclusion, New Testament textual criticism is an indispensable discipline that strives to reconstruct the original text of the New Testament, despite the challenges posed by the absence of autographs, numerous manuscript copies, and scribal errors. This academic pursuit not only ensures accurate translations and bolsters the historical reliability of the New Testament but also enhances our understanding of early Christianity and its development.

The Place of the New Testament in Textual Criticism

The New Testament holds a unique and significant place in the field of textual criticism, particularly because it is considered the Word of God by millions of people worldwide. As such, the accuracy, reliability, and faithfulness of the text to its original form are of utmost importance. Here are some factors that highlight the unique position of the New Testament in textual criticism:

1. **The sacred nature of the text**: For Christians, the New Testament is the inspired Word of God, a collection of sacred writings that convey divine revelation and guidance. This belief elevates the importance of textual criticism, as it seeks to ensure that the text remains as close as possible to the original manuscripts, thereby preserving the intended message.

2. **The wealth of manuscript evidence**: The New Testament has a vast number of manuscript copies, far surpassing any other ancient text. This extensive manuscript evidence provides a solid foundation for textual criticism and allows scholars to examine and compare various readings, ultimately working towards reconstructing the original text.

3. **The early origin of the manuscripts**: Many of the New Testament manuscripts date back to within a few centuries of the original writings. This early origin provides a relatively short gap between the autographs and the extant copies, increasing the likelihood of recovering the original text and ensuring the preservation of the early Christian message.

4. **The historical and cultural context**: Understanding the New Testament's historical and cultural context is crucial for textual criticism. Scholars consider the world in which the New Testament was written and transmitted – including the social, political, and religious landscape – to gain insights into the reasons behind textual variants and to make informed decisions about the most plausible readings.

5. **The impact on theology and interpretation**: Since the New Testament is foundational for Christian theology, any textual variants can have a significant impact on how believers understand and interpret the text. Textual criticism plays a crucial role in examining these variants and determining the most likely original readings, thus minimizing the potential for misinterpretation and maintaining the integrity of Christian doctrine.

6. **The transmission of the text through history**: The New Testament has been transmitted through diverse communities,

languages, and cultural contexts throughout history. Textual criticism helps trace this transmission process, revealing how the text has been preserved, adapted, and understood by different Christian communities over time.

In conclusion, the New Testament holds a unique and prominent place in the field of textual criticism due to its sacred nature, the wealth of manuscript evidence, its early origin, historical context, and its impact on theology and interpretation. Textual criticism plays a vital role in ensuring the accuracy and reliability of the New Testament text, upholding its sacred status and preserving the divine message for generations to come.

The Area of Textual Criticism That Needs Focus

While the New Testament manuscripts exhibit a high degree of agreement (around 80-85%), there are still textual variants that require attention from textual scholars. These variants, which constitute the remaining 15-20% of the text, are crucial for ensuring the accuracy and reliability of the New Testament. Here are some areas of textual criticism that need focus:

1. **Identifying significant textual variants**: Among the numerous textual variants, only a small percentage significantly impact the meaning or interpretation of the text. Textual scholars need to focus on identifying these significant variants and determining the most likely original readings.

2. **Analyzing scribal habits and transmission**: To better understand the reasons behind textual variants, scholars must analyze the habits of scribes who copied the manuscripts and the processes of textual transmission. This includes studying intentional and unintentional scribal errors, as well as the influence of theological, cultural, or linguistic factors on the copying process.

3. **Evaluating manuscript witnesses**: Given the vast number of New Testament manuscripts, scholars need to carefully

evaluate the quality and reliability of each witness. This involves considering factors such as the age, geographical origin, and textual affiliation of the manuscripts, as well as the overall character and tendencies of the scribes who produced them.

4. **Understanding the historical and cultural context**: As mentioned previously, the historical and cultural context of the New Testament plays a significant role in textual criticism. Scholars must continue to investigate the social, political, and religious landscape in which the text was written and transmitted to gain insights into the reasons behind textual variants and make informed decisions about the most plausible readings.

5. **Developing and refining critical methods**: Textual criticism relies on various methodologies to assess and compare textual variants. Scholars should continue to develop and refine these methods, incorporating advances in technology and research to improve the accuracy and efficiency of their work.

6. **Collaborating with interdisciplinary fields**: Textual criticism can benefit from collaboration with other fields of study, such as linguistics, archaeology, history, and theology. By engaging with scholars from diverse disciplines, textual critics can gain new insights and perspectives that enrich their understanding of the New Testament text and its transmission.

By focusing on these areas, textual scholars can continue to address the remaining textual variants in the New Testament, working towards reconstructing the most accurate and reliable text possible. This, in turn, helps to preserve the integrity of the New Testament and maintain its status as the sacred and authoritative Word of God for Christians worldwide.

The Importance of Textual Criticism

Textual criticism is essential for several reasons, particularly when it comes to understanding and interpreting ancient texts like the New Testament. Its importance can be seen through the following aspects:

1. **Preserving the integrity of the text**: Textual criticism aims to reconstruct the original wording of ancient texts, ensuring their accuracy and reliability. By examining various manuscripts and identifying textual variants, scholars can work to preserve the integrity of the texts, which is crucial for maintaining their historical, literary, and theological significance.

2. **Enhancing our understanding of the text**: Textual criticism helps scholars gain a deeper understanding of the historical and cultural context of the texts. By analyzing the reasons behind textual variants, scholars can uncover valuable insights about the social, political, and religious landscape in which the texts were written and transmitted.

3. **Guiding accurate translations**: The process of textual criticism provides a foundation for accurate translations of ancient texts. By determining the most likely original readings, translators can create translations that closely reflect the intended meaning of the authors. This is particularly important for religious texts like the New Testament, which serve as the basis for the beliefs and practices of millions of people worldwide.

4. **Informing biblical interpretation**: Textual criticism plays a crucial role in biblical interpretation and exegesis. By identifying and evaluating textual variants, scholars can make informed decisions about the most plausible readings, which can significantly impact the interpretation and application of biblical passages.

5. **Fostering interdisciplinary collaboration**: Textual criticism encourages collaboration between scholars from diverse fields, such as linguistics, archaeology, history, and theology. By engaging with experts from various disciplines, textual critics

can gain new insights and perspectives that enrich their understanding of the texts and their transmission.

6. **Supporting historical and theological research**: Textual criticism contributes to the broader field of historical and theological research by providing essential data on the development, transmission, and reception of ancient texts. This information can inform a wide range of studies, from historical inquiries into the origins of Christianity to theological investigations into the development of Christian doctrines and beliefs.

In summary, textual criticism is of paramount importance to the study of ancient texts, particularly those with significant religious, historical, and cultural value like the New Testament. By reconstructing the most accurate and reliable text possible, textual criticism helps to preserve the integrity of these texts, enhance our understanding of their context, and support the ongoing study and interpretation of their contents.

The Medium of Koine (Common Greek)

The period of Classical Greek, also known as Classical Attic Greek, dates roughly from the 5th to the 4th century BCE. This period coincides with the height of Greek civilization, particularly in Athens, where political, philosophical, artistic, and literary achievements flourished. Classical Greek is primarily associated with the works of famous authors and philosophers such as Homer, Herodotus, Thucydides, Sophocles, Euripides, Aristophanes, Socrates, Plato, and Aristotle.

Koine Greek, also known as Common Greek or Hellenistic Greek, developed around the late 4th century BCE and continued to be widely used until around the 4th century CE. The emergence of Koine Greek can be traced back to the conquests of Alexander the Great, which led to the spread of Greek culture and language throughout the Mediterranean and the Near East.

As a result of the increased interaction between different Greek-speaking communities, regional dialects began to merge, leading to the development of a more simplified and standardized form of Greek. Koine Greek became the lingua franca in the Hellenistic world, used for communication, commerce, and administration across the diverse territories under Greek influence.

Koine Greek is of particular significance for the study of early Christianity and the New Testament, as it was the language in which the Christian Bible was written. The use of Koine Greek allowed the New Testament to be more widely accessible to the diverse populations of the Mediterranean world at the time.

Koine Greek came into general use as a result of the conquests of Alexander the Great in the late 4th century BCE. Alexander's campaigns led to the spread of Greek culture and language across the Mediterranean and the Near East, including regions such as Egypt, Persia, and Asia Minor. As people from various regions and linguistic backgrounds began to interact more frequently, the need for a common language arose. This led to the development of Koine Greek, a simplified and more standardized form of the Greek language that incorporated elements of different regional dialects.

The widespread use of Koine Greek facilitated communication, trade, and administration throughout the Hellenistic world. As the lingua franca of the eastern Mediterranean and the Near East, Koine Greek was spoken and understood by a diverse range of people, making it an ideal language for the dissemination of ideas, literature, and religious texts.

The Bible, particularly the New Testament, testifies to the use of Koine Greek in the time of Jesus and his apostles. The New Testament was written primarily in Koine Greek, ensuring that its message could be understood by a wide audience across the Mediterranean region. Several passages in the New Testament also reflect the multilingual environment of the time. For instance, Jesus and his apostles likely spoke Aramaic as their native language, but they would have been familiar with Koine Greek to communicate with non-Aramaic-speaking communities. This is evident in passages like Acts 21:37-40, where the apostle Paul addresses a crowd in Greek, and John 19:20, which mentions that the sign placed on Jesus' cross was written in Hebrew, Latin, and Greek, signifying the linguistic diversity of the area.

In summary, the extensive use of Koine Greek during the time of Jesus and his apostles can be attributed to the influence of Alexander the Great's conquests and the need for a common language to facilitate communication, trade, and administration throughout the Hellenistic world. The New Testament, written in Koine Greek, serves as testimony to the widespread use of this language and its importance in the early Christian movement.

Nomina sacra IC XC, from the Greek ΙΗΣΟΥΣ ΧΡΙΣΤΟΣ (Jesus Christ - the letter C on the icon being koine Greek Σ).

Koine Greek was well suited for communicating God's Word for several reasons:

1. **Widespread use**: As the lingua franca of the eastern Mediterranean and Near East during the Hellenistic period, Koine Greek was spoken and understood by a diverse range of people across various regions. This widespread use allowed for

the message of the New Testament to be accessible to a large audience, transcending geographical and cultural boundaries.

2. **Simplicity and clarity**: Koine Greek was a simplified and more standardized form of the Greek language that incorporated elements of different regional dialects. This made it easier for people from various linguistic backgrounds to learn and understand the language, which in turn facilitated the dissemination of the Christian message.

3. **Flexibility**: Koine Greek was a versatile language with a rich vocabulary and a flexible grammatical structure. This allowed for nuanced expression of theological concepts and ideas, making it an ideal language for conveying the teachings of the New Testament.

4. **Existing literature and translation tradition**: By the time the New Testament was being written, the Hebrew Bible (Old Testament) had already been translated into Greek in the form of the Septuagint. This meant that there was a tradition of using Greek for religious texts, making it a natural choice for the authors of the New Testament.

5. **Continuity with the wider cultural context**: The use of Koine Greek connected the New Testament to the broader Hellenistic world and its intellectual, philosophical, and literary traditions. This allowed the early Christian movement to engage with contemporary thought and ideas, making the teachings of Christianity more relatable and appealing to a wider audience.

In summary, Koine Greek was well suited for communicating God's Word due to its widespread use, simplicity, clarity, flexibility, existing translation tradition, and continuity with the wider cultural context. The use of Koine Greek allowed the message of the New Testament to reach a vast audience and facilitated the spread of Christianity throughout the Mediterranean and beyond.

CHAPTER 2 Tracing the Script: Paleography and the Text of the New Testament

Materials for Receiving Writing

Introduction to Writing Materials in the Ancient World

Paleography, the study of ancient handwriting, is an essential discipline for understanding and analyzing the text of the New Testament. By examining the styles, materials, and techniques used in creating manuscripts, paleography allows scholars to date and categorize the texts, establish their authenticity, and trace the development and transmission of the New Testament over time. This knowledge is crucial for textual criticism, as it helps identify variations and potential scribal errors in the manuscripts.

In the ancient world, various materials were used for writing purposes, each with its unique properties and limitations. The choice of material depended on factors such as availability, cost, and the intended purpose of the document. Here, we provide an overview of the primary writing materials used during the time of the New Testament's composition and transmission.

1. **Papyrus**: Papyrus was the most common writing material in the ancient Mediterranean world, particularly in Egypt, where it was made from the pith of the papyrus plant. Papyrus sheets were created by placing strips of pith side by side and overlaying them with another layer of strips laid perpendicularly. The two layers were then pressed and dried, forming a sturdy writing surface. Papyrus was relatively cheap and widely available, making it an ideal material for the dissemination of the New Testament texts.

2. **Parchment and Vellum**: Parchment, made from animal skins (usually calf, sheep, or goat), provided a more durable and expensive alternative to papyrus. Vellum, a term often used interchangeably with parchment, specifically refers to a high-quality, fine-grained parchment made from the skins of young animals. Parchment and vellum were more resilient to moisture and wear, which made them suitable for preserving valuable texts, such as copies of the New Testament intended for long-term use.

3. **Ostraca**: Ostraca, or potsherds, were broken pieces of pottery or limestone used for writing short notes, receipts, or informal correspondence. While they were not typically used for writing New Testament texts, they provide valuable insight into the everyday language and writing practices of the ancient world.

4. **Inscriptions on Stone and Metal**: Permanent records or commemorations, such as monumental inscriptions or public decrees, were often engraved on stone or metal surfaces. These materials were not used for writing New Testament texts but do serve as important sources for understanding the historical and cultural context in which the New Testament was written and transmitted.

In conclusion, the study of writing materials in the ancient world is an essential component of paleography and the analysis of the New Testament text. Understanding the properties and limitations of these materials helps scholars to better interpret the manuscripts and reconstruct the history of the New Testament's transmission.

Papyrus: The Most Common Material for Early New Testament Texts

Papyrus, the most prevalent writing material in the early centuries of the New Testament's composition and transmission, played a crucial role in the preservation and dissemination of its texts. Derived from the pith of the papyrus plant (Cyperus papyrus), this material was especially popular in Egypt due to its abundance and cost-effectiveness. Papyrus' widespread use, coupled with its durability under the region's dry climate, enabled a substantial number of early New Testament manuscripts to survive, allowing scholars to study and analyze these ancient texts.

Papyrus Manufacturing: Creating papyrus sheets involved several steps. First, the pith of the papyrus plant was cut into thin strips. These strips were then placed side by side, with their edges slightly overlapping, to form a layer. Another layer of strips was laid perpendicularly over the first, and the two layers were soaked in water, pressed, and dried to create a firm, flat surface. The final product was polished using a smooth stone or shell to create a more uniform writing surface. Papyrus sheets could be joined together by gluing their edges to form a continuous roll (known as a scroll) or by stacking and binding them to create a codex, an early form of the modern book.

Papyrus in New Testament Manuscripts: The majority of the earliest surviving New Testament manuscripts are written on papyrus. Some of these papyri date back to the 2nd and 3rd centuries CE, providing valuable insight into the early transmission and textual history of the New Testament. Among the most significant papyrus collections are the Chester Beatty Papyri, which include portions of the Gospels, Acts, Pauline Epistles, and Revelation, and the Bodmer Papyri, containing substantial sections of the Gospels of John and Luke, as well as other New Testament writings.

Writing on Papyrus: Scribes typically wrote on the recto (front) side of papyrus sheets, where the horizontal fibers provided a smoother writing surface. The ink was made from a mixture of soot or other pigments, gum, and water. Scribes used reed pens with split nibs to write, and the script could vary from formal, carefully executed styles to more informal and rapidly written cursive hands. In some instances, scribes wrote on both the recto and verso (back) sides of the papyrus, known as an opisthograph. This practice was more common in the case of codices than scrolls.

Limitations and Preservation of Papyrus: While papyrus was relatively inexpensive and widely available, it had its limitations. Papyrus sheets were susceptible to damage from humidity, insects, and physical wear. Consequently, many papyrus manuscripts have only partially survived or are fragmented. The dry climate of Egypt, however, has helped preserve numerous papyrus texts, including early New Testament manuscripts, which are invaluable resources for textual scholars.

In conclusion, papyrus played a significant role in the early transmission of the New Testament texts. Its widespread use and accessibility facilitated the copying and circulation of these writings throughout the ancient world. The surviving papyrus manuscripts provide essential evidence for the textual history of the New Testament and offer scholars a window into the early Christian communities and their practices.

Parchment and Vellum: Durable Alternatives to Papyrus

As the study of the New Testament manuscripts progressed, two additional writing materials, parchment and vellum, emerged as important alternatives to papyrus. These materials offered greater durability, making them suitable for preserving sacred texts and other significant writings for posterity.

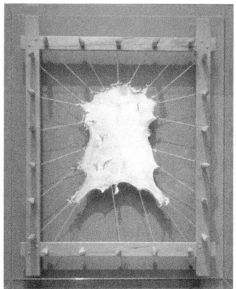

Parchment: A Durable Writing Material Parchment, made from the cleaned and treated skins of animals, such as sheep, goats, and calves, was a more resilient alternative to papyrus. The production process involved soaking the animal skins in lime, stretching them on a wooden frame, and scraping off any remaining hair and tissue. The skins were then treated with a pumice stone to create a smooth writing surface.

The advantages of parchment over papyrus included its greater flexibility, strength, and resistance to moisture. Parchment could also be written on both sides, making it more efficient for creating larger volumes. Due to its durability, parchment eventually became the preferred writing material for many scribes, particularly for copying and preserving religious texts such as the New Testament.

Vellum: A High-Quality Form of Parchment: Vellum is a refined form of parchment made from the skins of young, often stillborn, animals, typically calves. The manufacturing process was similar to that of parchment, but the result was an even smoother, finer, and more supple writing surface. Vellum was considered a luxury material due to its high quality and the scarcity of suitable skins. Consequently, it was often reserved for the most important texts, including illuminated manuscripts and deluxe editions of sacred works.

Parchment and Vellum in New Testament Manuscripts: Some of the most well-known New Testament manuscripts, including Codex Sinaiticus, Codex Vaticanus, and Codex Alexandrinus, were written on parchment. These codices contain substantial portions or even the entirety of the New Testament and have been essential for understanding the textual history of these writings.

The transition from papyrus to parchment and vellum took place gradually, as scribes recognized the benefits of these more durable materials. By the 4th century CE, parchment had become the dominant writing material for New Testament texts, with vellum reserved for the most exquisite copies.

In conclusion, parchment and vellum provided more durable and long-lasting alternatives to papyrus in the production and preservation of New Testament manuscripts. Their use allowed for the creation of high-quality, resilient copies of sacred texts, which have become invaluable resources for textual scholars and paleographers studying the history and development of the New Testament.

Ostraca: Potsherds as Writing Surfaces

In the context of the New Testament and paleography, ostraca provide another form of writing material, distinct from papyrus, parchment, and vellum. Ostraca are broken pieces of pottery or ceramic, known as potsherds, used as a writing surface in ancient times. Though not as common or prestigious as papyrus, parchment, or vellum, ostraca held unique advantages and has contributed valuable insights into the textual history of the New Testament.

The Lachish Ostraca

Lachish, 605–539 BC

Ostracon: potsherd with writing

Found in the Israelite city of Lachish

Written before Nebuchadnezzar's Judah conquest

The Use of Ostraca in Antiquity: Ostraca were widely used in the ancient world, particularly in Egypt, Greece, and the Near East. They were an affordable and readily available alternative to more expensive writing materials. Pottery was a common household item, and broken pieces were easily repurposed for writing.

In ancient societies, ostraca were utilized for various purposes, such as receipts, tax records, lists, letters, and even literary texts. These fragments often contained brief texts or notes, and their durability ensured they could survive for centuries.

Ostraca and the New Testament: While the majority of New Testament manuscripts were written on papyrus, parchment, or vellum, some New Testament texts have been discovered on ostraca. These instances are relatively rare, but they offer additional evidence for the textual history of the New Testament and the dissemination of its message.

For example, a 3rd-century ostracon from Egypt contains a portion of the Gospel of John (John 2:11-22), providing valuable insight into the text's transmission during this period. Another ostracon, dated to the 5th century, features a fragment of the Gospel of Matthew (Matthew 27:62-64).

Although ostraca are not as common as other writing materials for preserving New Testament texts, their existence demonstrates the wide variety of materials used by ancient scribes to record and transmit the Christian message. Ostraca also provide paleographers with unique opportunities to study ancient handwriting styles, as the texts inscribed on these potsherds were often more informal and less polished than those found on more expensive writing materials.

In conclusion, ostraca serve as a crucial resource in the study of the New Testament's textual history and paleography. These potsherds, though less common than other writing materials, offer unique insights into the transmission and dissemination of the New Testament in antiquity. They reveal how ancient scribes used various materials to ensure the preservation and communication of the Christian message, and they provide valuable information for scholars studying the development of ancient handwriting styles.

Inscriptions on Stone and Metal: Permanent Records

In the study of the New Testament and paleography, inscriptions on stone and metal hold a significant place as enduring records from antiquity. Although such inscriptions are not as common as papyrus, parchment, or vellum for preserving New Testament texts, they offer valuable insights into the cultural, historical, and linguistic context in which the early Christian texts were produced and circulated.

Inscriptions on Stone: Stone inscriptions were widely used in the ancient world for various purposes, including commemorative monuments, public records, legal documents, and religious texts. Because stone is a durable material, many inscriptions have survived the ravages of time and offer scholars important information about the societies that created them.

In the context of the New Testament, stone inscriptions are particularly useful for understanding the linguistic environment in which the texts were written. For instance, inscriptions featuring the

Greek language and Koine dialect provide essential background information for the study of the New Testament, as they help scholars understand the vocabulary, grammar, and syntax employed by the authors.

Potsherd with an Aramaic inscription mentioning allocation of barley to a person named Hașt for a camel and two donkeys
Baked clay, ink | Tel Arad, Israel | 5th–4th century BCE
AA 1967 1887

חרס עם כתובת ארמית
המצ יינת הקצאת שעורה
לאדם בשם חן עבור גמל
ושני חמורים

Moreover, stone inscriptions related to early Christianity, such as epitaphs, dedicatory inscriptions, and monumental texts, shed light on the beliefs, practices, and social dynamics of the early Christian communities. Although direct quotations from the New Testament are rare in stone inscriptions, they do provide indirect evidence for the circulation and impact of the Christian message.

Edward D. Andrews

Inscriptions on Metal: Metal inscriptions, though less common than those on stone, also hold significance for the study of the New Testament and paleography. Metals such as bronze, silver, and gold were used for inscribing important texts, often for ceremonial or religious purposes.

In the context of the New Testament, metal inscriptions offer valuable insights into the social and cultural milieu of the early Christian communities. For example, inscriptions on metal objects like cups, plates, or plaques provide information about the religious practices and rituals of the early Christians. Additionally, metal inscriptions may also offer clues about the linguistic environment and the transmission of Christian texts.

In conclusion, inscriptions on stone and metal, while not directly preserving New Testament texts, play a crucial role in the study of the New Testament's historical and linguistic context. These permanent records offer valuable information about the ancient societies that produced and circulated the Christian message, and they provide essential background knowledge for scholars examining the text and paleography of the New Testament.

Other Writing Materials: Wax Tablets and Wooden Boards

Besides papyrus, parchment, vellum, ostraca, and inscriptions on stone and metal, other writing materials such as wax tablets and wooden boards also played a role in the ancient world, including in the context of the New Testament and early Christian communities. While these materials may not have been commonly used for preserving the biblical text, they were essential for everyday communication, education, and record-keeping in antiquity.

Wax Tablets: Wax tablets were a popular and reusable writing surface in the ancient Mediterranean world. These tablets consisted of a wooden frame filled with a layer of beeswax. Using a stylus, writers could inscribe their messages onto the wax surface, and the text could be easily erased by smoothing the wax for reuse.

34

Wax tablets were frequently employed for various purposes, such as taking notes, composing drafts, keeping records, and teaching children to write. In the context of the New Testament, it is likely that some of the authors and their scribes may have used wax tablets for composing drafts or taking notes before transcribing the final version onto more durable materials like papyrus or parchment.

Although no New Testament texts have been preserved on wax tablets, these materials provide valuable insights into the writing practices and the educational system of the ancient world. Furthermore, the use of wax tablets illustrates the importance of writing and literacy in the early Christian communities and the broader Greco-Roman society.

Wooden Boards: Wooden boards, also known as wooden tablets, were another writing material used in antiquity. These boards were typically made of thin, smooth wooden panels, often joined together by cords or hinges to form a booklet or diptych. The wooden surface could be used for writing directly with ink, or it could be covered with a thin layer of gesso or another material to create a more receptive surface for writing.

Wooden boards were employed for a variety of purposes, such as legal documents, personal correspondence, and literary texts. Some early Christian texts, known as the "wooden codices," have been found written on wooden boards, although none of them are part of the New Testament canon.

In the study of the New Testament and paleography, the use of wooden boards demonstrates the variety of writing materials available in antiquity and provides insights into the writing practices of the early Christian communities. While papyrus, parchment, and vellum were the primary materials for preserving the biblical text, wax tablets and wooden boards played essential roles in everyday communication, education, and record-keeping in the ancient world.

Writing Utensils

The Reed Pen: The Main Writing Tool for Papyrus and Parchment

In the ancient world, the reed pen was the primary writing tool used for inscribing texts on papyrus and parchment. The pen's widespread use and its role in the transmission of the New Testament text make it an essential element to consider when studying paleography and the textual history of the biblical writings.

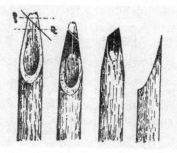

The Reed Pen: The reed pen was typically made from the stem of a reed plant, such as the Phragmites or Arundo species, which grew abundantly in the marshy areas around the Mediterranean, especially in Egypt. The reed's hollow stem would be cut, shaped, and sharpened at one end to form a nib. The nib was split, allowing it to hold ink, which would then be transferred onto the writing surface when pressure was applied.

The reed pen was a versatile and durable writing tool, and its nib could be sharpened and reshaped multiple times before the pen was discarded. These pens were relatively cheap and easy to produce, making them the preferred writing instrument for the majority of scribes and writers in the ancient world.

Using the Reed Pen for Writing on Papyrus and Parchment: The reed pen was well-suited for writing on both papyrus and parchment due to its flexibility and adaptability. When writing on papyrus, scribes would use the pen to apply ink along the horizontal fibers of the papyrus sheet, which allowed for smooth and even writing. On parchment, the pen could be used to write on both the smooth, flesh side and the rougher, hair side of the animal skin.

In the context of the New Testament, it is likely that the authors and their scribes used reed pens to inscribe the biblical text onto papyrus and parchment manuscripts. The use of the reed pen contributed to the unique features of ancient handwriting, such as letterforms and ligatures, which are essential aspects of paleographical analysis.

The reed pen played a crucial role in the transmission of the New Testament text and the broader world of ancient writing practices. Its widespread use and adaptability to various writing surfaces, including papyrus and parchment, make it an indispensable element in the study of paleography and the textual history of the New Testament.

The Metal Stylus: For Inscriptions and Wax Tablets

While the reed pen was the primary writing tool for papyrus and parchment, the metal stylus played a significant role in the ancient world for inscribing texts on other surfaces, such as stone, metal, and wax tablets. Understanding the metal stylus's use and its impact on writing practices is essential in the study of paleography and the textual history of the New Testament.

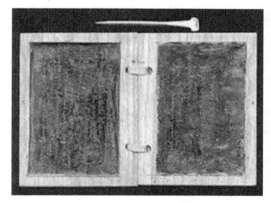

The Metal Stylus: The metal stylus was a writing instrument typically made of bronze, iron, or sometimes bone. It had a pointed end for writing and a flat end, called a spatula, for erasing or smoothing the writing surface. The pointed end of the stylus was used to inscribe or engrave text onto surfaces like stone, metal, or wax-covered wooden tablets.

Inscriptions on Stone and Metal Inscriptions on stone and metal were common forms of communication and record-keeping in the ancient world. They were used to create permanent records, such as commemorative inscriptions, official documents, and epitaphs. The metal stylus was the primary tool for engraving these inscriptions. Although the New Testament texts were not typically inscribed on stone or metal, studying these inscriptions can provide insights into the broader context of writing practices and language usage in the ancient world.

Wax Tablets: Wax tablets were another popular writing surface in the ancient world, especially for temporary records or drafts. These tablets typically consisted of a wooden frame filled with a layer of wax, and the metal stylus was used to write on the wax surface. The flat end of the stylus could be used to smooth the wax and erase the text, allowing the tablet to be reused multiple times.

While wax tablets were not commonly used for transmitting the New Testament text, they may have been employed for drafting or taking notes before the final text was written on papyrus or parchment. Studying the use of wax tablets can provide valuable insights into the writing practices and methodologies of the authors and scribes involved in producing the New Testament.

In conclusion, the metal stylus played a crucial role in the transmission of written texts in the ancient world, particularly for inscriptions and writing on wax tablets. Although it was not the primary writing tool for the New Testament, understanding its use and impact on writing practices enhances our knowledge of paleography and the textual history of the biblical writings.

Ink: Composition and Varieties

In the context of paleography and the textual history of the New Testament, understanding the composition and varieties of ink used in ancient writings is essential. Ink played a crucial role in the transmission of the New Testament texts, as it was the primary medium used to write on materials like papyrus and parchment.

Ink Composition: Ancient ink was typically composed of two main components: a colorant and a binder. The colorant provided the ink with its distinctive color, while the binder helped the ink adhere to the writing surface.

Colorants were usually derived from natural sources, such as minerals, plants, and even animal byproducts. The most common colorant for ink in the ancient world was carbon black, which was produced by grinding soot or charcoal into a fine powder. Other colorants, such as red ochre, were also used occasionally.

Binders were typically derived from plant gums or other organic materials, such as egg whites, animal glues, or honey. These substances helped to bind the colorant particles together and ensure that the ink adhered to the writing surface.

Ink Varieties: There were several different types of ink used in the ancient world, depending on the specific requirements of the writing project and the materials available.

1. **Carbon Ink:** This was the most common type of ink used in the ancient world, particularly for writing on papyrus and parchment. Carbon ink was made by combining carbon black with a binder, such as gum arabic or another plant gum. The ink was water-soluble, which made it relatively easy to produce and use. Most of the New Testament manuscripts were written using carbon ink.

2. **Iron Gall Ink:** Iron gall ink was another popular ink variety, especially in later periods. It was made by combining iron salts with tannic acids derived from oak galls or other plant materials. The resulting ink was dark blue-black and had a higher resistance to fading and water damage than carbon ink. However, iron gall ink could be corrosive, causing damage to

the writing surface over time. Some later New Testament manuscripts were written using iron gall ink.

3. **Metal-based Inks**: Inks made from metal compounds, such as copper or lead salts, were occasionally used in ancient writings. These inks were more durable and resistant to fading but were less common due to their higher cost and limited availability.

Understanding the composition and varieties of ink used in ancient writings is crucial for paleography and the study of the New Testament textual history. The choice of ink and its properties could impact the longevity, readability, and preservation of the biblical texts, providing valuable insights into the writing practices and transmission of the New Testament manuscripts.

Brushes and Chisels: Tools for Stone and Metal Inscriptions

While the primary focus of New Testament textual criticism is on manuscripts written on papyrus, parchment, and other organic materials, stone and metal inscriptions also played a role in the transmission and preservation of texts in the ancient world. These inscriptions were created using different tools and techniques than those employed on more fragile writing surfaces. Brushes and chisels were the primary tools used for creating inscriptions on stone and metal surfaces.

1. **Brushes**: For inscriptions on stone, brushes were often used to apply paint or ink to the surface. These brushes were typically made from animal hair, plant fibers, or reeds, and were attached to wooden or bone handles. The brushes allowed scribes to create smooth, flowing lines, making them suitable for a wide range of lettering styles. Although the paint or ink used for inscriptions on stone would eventually fade or wear away over time, the brushstrokes could leave subtle traces in the stone's surface, providing valuable evidence for paleographers studying ancient writing practices.

2. **Chisels**: For more permanent inscriptions on stone or metal surfaces, chisels were employed to carve the text directly into the material. These chisels were made of metal, typically bronze or iron, and had a sharp, wedge-shaped tip. To create an inscription, the chisel was placed against the surface, and a mallet was used to strike the handle, driving the chisel into the material and carving out the desired letter forms.

There were various types of chisels used for different purposes. For example, flat chisels were used for creating straight lines and broad strokes, while curved chisels were used for carving rounded letters and intricate designs. In some cases, a scribe would first sketch the outline of the letters using a brush or a sharp stylus, then use the chisel to carve the final inscription.

Stone and metal inscriptions played a significant role in preserving texts and commemorating important events, laws, or religious dedications in the ancient world. While the New Testament was primarily transmitted through manuscripts on papyrus and parchment, the study of inscriptions on stone and metal can provide valuable insights into the wider context of ancient writing practices, scripts, and languages. Understanding the tools and techniques used to create these inscriptions, such as brushes and chisels, is essential for paleographers and New Testament textual scholars as they seek to reconstruct the history of the biblical text.

Book Forms

The Scroll: The Ancient Standard

Before the advent of the codex, the most common book form in the ancient world was the scroll. Scrolls were used for literary, religious, and official documents, and were a prominent feature of the cultural and intellectual life of the ancient Mediterranean world. Understanding the nature and role of scrolls in antiquity is essential for a comprehensive understanding of the textual transmission and history of the New Testament.

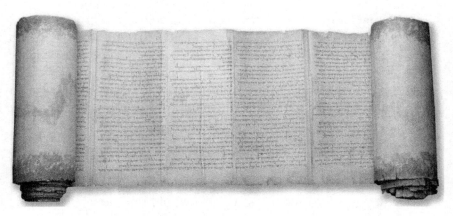

1. **Composition of Scrolls**: Scrolls were made by attaching sheets of writing material, such as papyrus or parchment, together in a long strip. Papyrus scrolls were the most common type in the eastern Mediterranean, while parchment scrolls were more common in the western regions. The sheets were typically glued or sewn together, and the completed scroll could range from a few inches to several feet in length, depending on the content.

2. **Writing and Reading Scrolls**: Text was written on one side of the scroll, in columns running parallel to the short edges of the sheets. The reader would unroll the scroll with one hand while rolling it up with the other, exposing the text column by column. This method of reading limited the reader's ability to access specific parts of the text easily, making scrolls less convenient for reference purposes than the later codex format.

3. **Storage and Preservation**: Scrolls were typically stored in protective cylindrical containers, often made of leather, wood, or metal. They were shelved or stacked horizontally in libraries and archives, with labels attached to the containers to identify the contents. Scrolls were susceptible to damage from moisture, insects, and general wear and tear, which is why so few ancient scrolls have survived to the present day.

4. **Scrolls in Early Christianity**: The New Testament documents were initially written and circulated as scrolls,

although the exact form and size of these scrolls remain a matter of scholarly debate. The use of scrolls in early Christianity is confirmed by several New Testament passages (e.g., Luke 4:17, 2 Timothy 4:13, Revelation 5:1). The transition from scrolls to the codex format, which eventually became the standard for Christian texts, occurred gradually over the course of the second and third centuries CE.

The study of ancient scrolls is crucial for understanding the early transmission of the New Testament text. By examining the physical characteristics, writing techniques, and methods of production and circulation of scrolls, paleographers and textual scholars can gain valuable insights into the origins and development of the New Testament documents and the broader literary culture in which they were produced.

The Codex: A Revolutionary Format Developed by Christians

The codex, which eventually replaced the scroll as the primary form of book in the ancient world, had a significant impact on the preservation and transmission of the New Testament text. Developed by early Christians, the codex provided numerous advantages over the scroll, ultimately leading to its widespread adoption throughout the Christian world and beyond.

1. **Origins and Development of the Codex**: The codex format emerged in the first and second centuries CE, with early Christians being among the first to adopt and popularize its use. The exact reasons for this adoption remain debated among scholars; however, it is likely that the codex offered practical advantages for the compilation, organization, and accessibility of Christian texts, such as the Gospels and the letters of Paul.

2. **Structure and Composition of the Codex**: The codex consists of individual sheets of writing material, such as papyrus or parchment, which are folded and bound together along one edge. The sheets, known as leaves or folios, are then cut or trimmed to create a book with pages that can be easily

turned and accessed. Text is written on both sides of the leaves, maximizing the use of available writing space.

3. **Advantages of the Codex**: The codex format offers several significant advantages over the scroll, including easier navigation and reference, greater durability, and more efficient use of writing materials. The codex allows for random access to specific passages or sections, making it an ideal format for studying, teaching, and preaching. Furthermore, the bound structure of the codex provides better protection for the written text, contributing to the improved preservation of many early Christian manuscripts.

4. **Impact on the Transmission of the New Testament**: The adoption of the codex format by early Christians had a lasting impact on the preservation and transmission of the New Testament text. As the codex became the standard format for Christian texts, it facilitated the compilation and organization of the various New Testament writings into a single volume. This not only aided in the development of the New Testament canon but also contributed to the widespread dissemination and standardization of the text throughout the Christian world.

The codex format, developed and popularized by early Christians, played a crucial role in shaping the textual history of the New Testament. By examining the physical characteristics, writing techniques, and production methods of early Christian codices, paleographers and textual scholars can gain valuable insights into the early transmission and reception of the New Testament documents, as well as the broader development of the book as a cultural and technological innovation.

EXCURSION: The Early Christian Codex

Before the advent of the printed book, literary works were recorded on scrolls made of either animal skins or papyrus sheets. These scrolls were long and narrow, measuring around 20-30 feet in length and 9-10 inches in height. To form a scroll, multiple sheets were fastened together and written on in columns, which formed the pages.

The word "volume" comes from the Latin word for something that is rolled up or revolves around rollers. Jesus himself would have been familiar with this form of book, as he was handed a scroll of the prophet Isaiah in the synagogue of Nazareth.

However, over time, a new format for recording information emerged called the codex. The word "codex" comes from the Latin word for "tree trunk," as early versions of the codex were made of wooden tablets with raised rims, coated in wax and written on with a stylus. By the fifth century BCE, these wooden tablets had evolved into multi-leaf tablets bound together with strings passing through pierced holes. Because they looked like a tree trunk when bound together, they were called a codex.

Carrying around these heavy and unwieldy wooden tablets was not ideal, and so the search began for a lighter and more flexible material. The Romans developed the parchment notebook, an intermediate step between the tablet and the later book-form codex. As the style and material of the original tablet changed, it became a problem to know what to call the new format. The Latin word "membranae" was used to describe the parchment notebook, and Paul even used this word when requesting "the scrolls, especially the parchments [membranas]." It is believed that Paul used a Latin word because there was no Greek equivalent to describe what he was calling for. Later, the word "codex" was transliterated into the Greek language to refer to the book.

Christians Develop the Codex: The development of the codex, a book format that replaced the traditional scroll, is a topic of much interest to scholars. Evidence gathered to date places the rise of the codex alongside the increasing use of vellum in the fourth century CE, according to F.G. Kenyon, a manuscript keeper at the British Museum. However, until the discovery of numerous papyrus manuscripts in Egypt and the Dead Sea region in recent years, there was little evidence of papyrus codices, as papyrus requires a dry climate to survive.

Most striking is the fact that nearly all the Christian-era Bible manuscripts found on papyrus are in codex form, suggesting that the codex was regarded as especially suitable for Christian writings. This is in contrast to classical writings, which continued to be circulated in scrolls for a long time. A survey of pagan literature from the second century CE revealed only about 2.4% codices to rolls, with only one later manuscript of the Psalms in roll form. In contrast, all Biblical manuscripts assigned to the second century are codices.

Today, over a hundred and forty-four Bible codices on papyrus, some just fragments, written before the end of the fourth century, are scattered throughout museums and collections worldwide. This evidence suggests that Christians abandoned the roll form early on, in favor of the more versatile and practical codex format.

Second Century Bible Manuscripts: Determining the age of an ancient manuscript can be challenging, as very few dates are prominently displayed on the manuscript. However, paleography, the art of studying the writing, form, and style of a manuscript, can provide clues to its age. Minute features such as spaces between words, punctuation, and abbreviations can help experts date a manuscript to within forty or fifty years. Tables of typical letters have been drawn up from non-literary papyri, such as receipts, letters, petitions, and leases, that give exact dates and provide a good basis for comparison.

For example, the fragment of John's Gospel known as P52 has distinctive features such as a hook or flourish added to some strokes, certain marks omitted, a special type of cross-stroke, and rounded letters that are all typical of early second-century writers. While not all experts agree, most of them have assigned two dozen papyrus codices to the second century CE based on paleography.

These early Greek New Testament papyri and Septuagint Greek version of the Hebrew Scriptures are recognized internationally and given numbers on the Gregory-von Dobschütz and Rahlfs lists, respectively. Each manuscript also bears a collection name and number to identify where it was found or to whom it belongs. These second-century codices are of great importance due to their early date and early codex form.

Making a Codex: When examining early codices, several interesting features can be noticed. Early codices were often made up of one enormous quire, or a group of sheets folded together, resulting

46

in narrow columns of writing compared to the wider outer leaves. However, it was later found that quires consisting of four or five sheets, or eight to ten leaves, were more convenient.

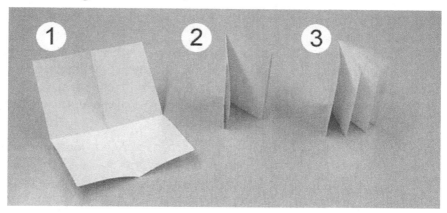

Different methods of laying down the sheets reveal personal preferences. Each sheet consists of two layers of papyrus fiber glued together crosswise, so the side showing the horizontal layer is known as the recto, while the side displaying the vertical layer of fibers is the verso. The method of laying down the sheets would alter the appearance when the codex was opened. A recto page might face a verso page, but some might prefer to have recto facing recto and verso facing verso.

Some early codices with two narrow columns of writing to a page were likely copied from rolls with as little disarrangement of the original layout as possible. Conversely, when the back of an old roll containing an epitome of Livy was reused, an economical Christian copied from a codex of Hebrews and even inserted the page numbers. Such a reused roll is called an opisthograph. These factors reveal the personal preferences and practical considerations of those making codices.

Why the Codex Was Preferred: The codex, or book format, was preferred over the traditional roll for several reasons. First, the codex allowed for convenient compilation of texts, such as putting all four Gospels in one book, which would not be practical as a single roll due to its length. Additionally, the codex allowed for quick reference to specific texts, which was important to early Christians who used their Scriptures extensively. Even pocket-sized codices have been discovered, demonstrating the value of portability.

Another benefit of the codex was its protection of the inspired books of Scripture. When several of Paul's epistles were bound together in one codex, it established a link between the various writings and made it more difficult for unrecognized works to be inserted into the collection. The adoption of the codex for the Septuagint version of the Hebrew Scriptures also shows that it was frequently used and not considered inferior to newer writings.

The universal use of the codex in Christian circles in the second century suggests that its adoption must have gone back to the first century. This could explain the loss of the ending of Mark's Gospel, which could have been lost with the last leaf of a codex, whereas in a roll, the beginning would be more likely to suffer damage. Additionally, the codex was cheaper, as both sides of the papyrus sheet were used. These factors demonstrate why the codex was preferred and became the dominant book format over the traditional roll.

As the Greek New Testament began to take shape, it is possible to imagine the scene. Matthew, known for his meticulous record-keeping as a tax collector, likely continued this habit when he began writing his Gospel. His notes may have initially been made in a parchment notebook, which would then be compiled into a codex. As other Gospels were completed, they would be added to Matthew's Gospel to form a collection.

As demand for copies of the Gospels grew, the codex format would become more prevalent. Copies would be widely circulated, with pocket codices making it possible for traveling ministers like Paul, Timothy, and Titus to carry the Scriptures with them. Upon returning to congregations, these ministers would likely commend those using the newly received codices while still encouraging those using the traditional roll format.

The prevalence of the second-century codex provides important insights into the early Christian community. Firstly, it supports the authenticity of the Bible as the gap between the time of the apostles and the earliest surviving manuscripts is greatly reduced. Secondly, it highlights the eagerness of early Christians to make the Scriptures widely available, reducing the cost of books so that everyone could have access to them. Lastly, the codex shows us how important it was for early Christians to be able to quickly and easily locate specific passages within their copies of the Scriptures. As modern believers, we can learn from the example of these enthusiastic early Christians by regularly studying our own Bibles and carefully examining them to confirm our faith.

END OF EXCURSION

The Transition from Scroll to Codex: Factors and Implications

The transition from the scroll to the codex format played a pivotal role in the preservation and transmission of the New Testament text. This shift involved a complex interplay of cultural, technological, and religious factors, ultimately leading to widespread adoption of the codex by early Christians and transforming the way texts were produced, circulated, and consumed in the ancient world.

1. **Technological Advancements**: The development of the codex format was facilitated by advances in the production of writing materials, such as papyrus and parchment. These materials were more durable and flexible than those used for scrolls, making them better suited for folding, binding, and cutting into the pages of a codex.

2. **Practical Benefits**: The codex format offered several practical advantages over the scroll, including easier navigation and reference, more efficient use of writing materials, and greater durability. These benefits made the codex an appealing option for early Christians, who were eager to share and study their sacred texts.

3. **The Role of Early Christians**: Early Christians played a crucial role in popularizing the codex format. They were among the first to recognize its potential for organizing, preserving, and disseminating their sacred writings, such as the

49

Gospels and the letters of Paul. The adoption of the codex by early Christians helped to establish it as the standard format for Christian texts and contributed to its eventual acceptance by other religious and secular communities.

4. **Canonical Implications**: The transition from scroll to codex facilitated the compilation and organization of the various New Testament writings into a single volume. This process not only aided in the development of the New Testament canon but also contributed to the standardization and widespread dissemination of the text throughout the Christian world.

5. **Impact on Textual Scholarship**: The shift from scroll to codex had significant implications for the study of the New Testament text. The increased durability and accessibility of the codex format contributed to the preservation of many early Christian manuscripts, providing valuable resources for modern textual scholars. Furthermore, the codex format allowed for the development of more consistent and standardized methods of copying and transmitting the text, which can help scholars reconstruct the original wording of the New Testament and trace its textual history.

In conclusion, the transition from scroll to codex was a transformative event in the history of the New Testament text, driven by a combination of technological advancements, practical benefits, and the influence of early Christians. By embracing the codex format, early Christians played a crucial role in shaping the textual history of the New Testament and laid the groundwork for the development of the book as a cultural and technological innovation.

Other Book Forms: Tablets, Diptychs, and Collections

In addition to scrolls and codices, the ancient world saw the development and use of various other book forms for preserving and transmitting texts. These alternative formats played a role in shaping the textual history of the New Testament and provided insight into the diverse methods of communication and documentation during that time.

1. **Tablets**: Before the widespread use of papyrus and parchment, clay and wax tablets were commonly used for writing in the ancient world. These tablets were often made of wooden boards covered with a layer of wax, providing a reusable surface for inscribing text with a metal stylus. Tablets were used for various purposes, including recording notes, legal documents, and even literary works. While not directly related to the New Testament, tablets demonstrate the diversity of writing materials and methods available in the ancient world.

2. **Diptychs**: Diptychs consisted of two hinged tablets, typically made of wood, ivory, or metal, and often adorned with intricate carvings or artwork. These were used for various purposes, such as writing letters, creating lists, or commemorating important events. Some early Christian texts, like letters and homilies, might have been written on diptychs before being copied onto more permanent materials like parchment or papyrus.

3. **Collections**: In addition to individual book forms, collections of texts were also common in the ancient world. These could include sets of scrolls, bundles of codices, or even groups of inscriptions or ostraca. Collections played an essential role in the development and organization of the New Testament canon, as early Christians gathered and compiled various sacred writings into a coherent body of literature.

4. **The Relationship to the New Testament**: While the New Testament was primarily transmitted through scrolls and codices, these other book forms provide valuable context for understanding the broader literary and cultural environment of early Christianity. By examining these alternative formats, scholars can gain insight into the diverse methods of documentation, communication, and textual transmission available to early Christians, shedding light on the ways in which the New Testament texts were produced, circulated, and preserved.

In summary, the diverse range of book forms, including tablets, diptychs, and collections, played a role in shaping the textual history of the New Testament and provided valuable context for understanding the literary and cultural environment of early Christianity. By examining these alternative formats, scholars can better appreciate the variety of methods and materials used for communication and documentation in the ancient world, offering important insights into the development and transmission of the New Testament texts.

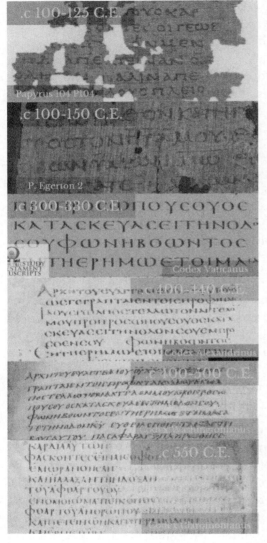

Handwriting Styles

The Professional Bookhand: Some of the early manuscripts of the New Testament were produced by skilled professionals who were able to create literary texts. One such example is the Gospel codex known as P4+64+67, which displays expert calligraphy, paragraph markings, double-columns, and punctuation. The papyrologist C. H. Roberts noted that the text was divided into sections according to a system found in other manuscripts, indicating that this characteristic was not specific to

Egypt. Other professionally produced manuscripts with skilled calligraphy include P30, P39, P46, P66, P75, P77+P103, P95, and P104. These manuscripts demonstrate the high level of skill and attention to detail required to create such works, and attest to the importance and value placed on the written word by early Christians. The existence of these manuscripts also confirms the authenticity of the biblical text and its importance in the early Christian community.

Reformed Documentary Hand: Many of the early New Testament manuscripts were written in what is called "the reformed documentary hand," indicating that the scribe knew they were working on a manuscript that was not just a legal document but a literary work. The style of writing exhibits a competent level of calligraphy that was likely the work of experienced scribes, whether Christian or not. It is assumed that these scribes may have been employed to make copies for individual Christians or for a Christian congregation. Among the extant papyri that predate 300 CE, there are at least fifteen "reformed documentary" New Testament manuscripts, according to estimation. These manuscripts include P1, P30, P32, P35, P38, P45, P52, P69, P87, P90, P100, P102, P108, P109, and P110.

Documentary Hand: It seems that a number of the earliest New Testament manuscripts were not produced by professionals in the book trade, but by people within communities who were used to writing documents. Manuscripts with a "documentary" hand are less uniform in appearance than those produced by professionals, with letters on each line not necessarily keeping an even line across the page. Documentary texts will often have larger letters at the beginning of each line or section, sporadic punctuation, numerical abbreviations, and spaces between words or groups of words.

Many of these manuscripts were likely produced by churchmen or women who had been trained in writing documents and then applied those skills to making copies of Scripture for specific individuals or for their congregations. It's possible that many of these scribes were church lectors, whose job was to keep copies of Scripture, make new ones as needed, and prepare the text for reading to the congregation.

Nearly half of the early New Testament papyri (27 in total) are "documentary," according to my study. These include P5, P13, P15+P16, P17, P20, P23, P27, P28, P29, P37, P47, P48, P49+65, P50, P53, P70, P80, P91, P92, P101, P106, P107, P108, P111, P113, and P114.

Common Hand: The "common" hand refers to a writing style that indicates the scribe had little to no formal training in writing Greek. It can be difficult to distinguish between a "documentary" hand and a "common" hand, but a common hand is usually more crude and less uniform in appearance. Examples of manuscripts produced in a common hand include P9, which contains a portion of 1 John, and P78, which is an amulet. Interestingly, many of the manuscripts containing the book of Revelation exhibit a common hand, such as P18, P24, and P98. It is unclear if this is simply a coincidence or if it indicates that Revelation was not being read in the churches and therefore not being copied by trained scribes.

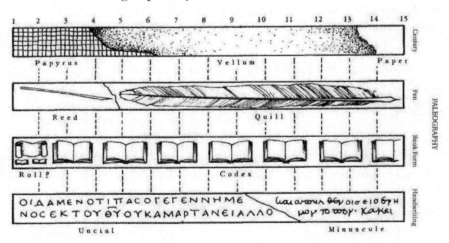

Uncial Script: The Early Majuscule Style

The development of different handwriting styles played a significant role in the transmission and preservation of the New Testament texts. One of the earliest and most significant writing styles employed in the copying of the Greek New Testament was the uncial script, which emerged as the predominant majuscule (or uppercase) style.

1. **Characteristics of Uncial Script**: Uncial script was characterized by its clear and distinct letterforms, written with a rounded, capital style. The letters were usually separated from each other and did not have connecting strokes or ligatures. This made the text easier to read, as each letter was distinct and stood on its own. Uncial script also lacked punctuation, word spacing, and diacritical marks, which were later added to the text by scholars to aid in reading and understanding.

2. **Development and Use**: Uncial script developed around the 3rd century CE and continued to be widely used until the 9th century CE. The script was especially popular among Christian scribes, who used it for copying biblical texts, including the Greek New Testament. The earliest and most important uncial manuscripts of the New Testament, such as Codex Vaticanus, Codex Sinaiticus, and Codex Alexandrinus, were written in this script.

3. **Significance for New Testament Textual Criticism**: The uncial script played a crucial role in the transmission and preservation of the New Testament texts. The script's clarity and distinct letterforms facilitated accurate copying, reducing the likelihood of transcriptional errors. Additionally, the uncial script's widespread use among early Christian scribes means that many of the oldest and most valuable New Testament manuscripts were written in this style. These manuscripts serve as vital sources for scholars engaged in textual criticism, helping to reconstruct the original text and trace the development of variant readings.

In conclusion, the uncial script was an essential handwriting style employed in the early transmission of the New Testament. Its clear and distinct letterforms facilitated accurate copying, and its widespread use among early Christian scribes resulted in the preservation of many important manuscripts. The study of uncial script and its use in New Testament manuscripts is crucial for understanding the development and transmission of the biblical text and remains a vital area of focus for textual criticism.

Minuscule Script: The Emergence of Lowercase Letters

The evolution of handwriting styles had a significant impact on the transmission and preservation of the New Testament texts. As the uncial script began to decline, a new writing style known as minuscule script emerged and became the primary script for Greek manuscripts from the 9th century CE onwards. The minuscule script introduced lowercase letters to the Greek alphabet and greatly influenced the way texts were copied and read.

1. **Characteristics of Minuscule Script**: Minuscule script is characterized by its smaller, more compact letterforms, which were written using a combination of uppercase (majuscule) and lowercase (minuscule) letters. The script utilized ligatures, connecting letters to form a continuous flow of text, resulting in a more efficient and faster writing style. Minuscule script also introduced word spacing, punctuation, and diacritical marks, making the text more accessible and easier to read.

2. **Development and Use**: Minuscule script developed around the 9th century CE and quickly gained popularity due to its efficiency and readability. The script became the standard for Greek manuscripts, including those of the New Testament. Notable minuscule manuscripts of the New Testament include Minuscule 1 (also known as Codex Basiliensis) and Minuscule 2 (also known as Codex Angelicus).

3. **Significance for New Testament Textual Criticism**: The minuscule script played a vital role in the transmission and preservation of the New Testament texts during the Byzantine period. Its efficient and readable nature allowed for the production of a large number of manuscripts, which increased the availability of the biblical texts to a broader audience. As a result, the majority of surviving New Testament manuscripts are written in minuscule script. These manuscripts serve as important sources for textual critics, enabling them to

reconstruct the original text and identify the development of variant readings.

In summary, the minuscule script was a significant handwriting style in the transmission of the New Testament. Its efficiency and readability facilitated the production of numerous manuscripts and contributed to the widespread dissemination of biblical texts. The study of minuscule script and its use in New Testament manuscripts is essential for understanding the development and transmission of the biblical text and remains an important area of focus for textual criticism.

Cursive Script: A Faster Writing Style

Cursive script, also known as cursiva, is another handwriting style that emerged in the ancient world and played a role in the transmission of the New Testament texts. This script was developed primarily for speed and efficiency, and it was often used for everyday writing, including personal letters, business transactions, and informal documents.

1. **Characteristics of Cursive Script**: Cursive script is characterized by its rapid, flowing letterforms that are connected to each other, allowing the scribe to write quickly without lifting the writing instrument from the surface. The script exhibits a high degree of ligatures, abbreviations, and shorthand symbols, which further increased its writing speed. However, this efficiency came at the cost of legibility, making cursive script more challenging to read than other handwriting styles such as uncial or minuscule script.

2. **Development and Use**: Cursive script developed alongside other handwriting styles, such as uncial and minuscule scripts, and was used predominantly for informal and everyday writing purposes. It was not commonly used for copying the New Testament texts, but some cursive manuscripts have been identified, such as 𝔓66 (Papyrus 66), a fragmentary copy of the Gospel of John dating from around the 2nd century CE. This

manuscript is written in a semi-cursive script, exhibiting both cursive and formal letterforms.

3. **Significance for New Testament Textual Criticism**: Although cursive script is not as prevalent in New Testament manuscripts as uncial or minuscule script, it still offers valuable insights into the transmission and preservation of the biblical texts. The study of cursive script can help textual critics understand the writing practices, scribal habits, and abbreviations used in the ancient world, which can aid in identifying and evaluating variant readings in the New Testament manuscripts.

In conclusion, cursive script is an important handwriting style in the study of the New Testament's textual history. Although it was not as widely used for copying biblical texts, its use in certain manuscripts and everyday writing offers insights into the scribal practices and the transmission of the New Testament. The study of cursive script remains a valuable area of focus for textual criticism, contributing to our understanding of the development and preservation of the biblical text.

Ligatures and Abbreviations: Space-saving Techniques

Ligatures and abbreviations are important aspects of ancient handwriting styles, including those used in the transmission of the New Testament text. These techniques served as space-saving methods that allowed scribes to fit more content onto limited writing surfaces, such as papyrus, parchment, or ostraca.

1. **Ligatures**: A ligature is the combination of two or more letters into a single, connected character. Ligatures were employed to save space and increase writing speed by reducing the number of strokes needed to form each word. They are commonly found in various ancient scripts, including uncial, minuscule, and cursive writing styles. Ligatures can sometimes make reading ancient texts more difficult, as the combination of letters can alter the appearance of individual characters.

2. **Abbreviations**: Abbreviations were widely used in ancient manuscripts to conserve space on writing materials and to increase writing efficiency. They were especially common in the New Testament texts, where certain words or phrases appeared frequently. One notable example is the use of nomina sacra, sacred names or terms that were abbreviated in the manuscripts by writing the first and last letters of a word, followed by a horizontal line above the letters to indicate the abbreviation. Common examples of nomina sacra include abbreviations for words such as "God," "Jesus," "Christ," and "Lord."

3. **Significance for New Testament Textual Criticism**: The study of ligatures and abbreviations in the ancient handwriting styles is crucial for textual critics working with New Testament manuscripts. Understanding these space-saving techniques helps scholars to accurately decipher, transcribe, and analyze the text. Additionally, the analysis of ligatures and abbreviations can provide insights into the scribal habits, practices, and preferences of the scribes who copied the New Testament texts. This information can contribute to the process of evaluating and comparing different manuscripts and assessing the reliability of the transmitted text.

In summary, ligatures and abbreviations are essential aspects of ancient handwriting styles that played a crucial role in the transmission of the New Testament texts. The study of these space-saving techniques is vital for textual critics, as it helps to accurately read and analyze the manuscripts, providing valuable insights into the scribal practices and preferences of the ancient scribes. By understanding these techniques, textual critics can make more informed decisions when evaluating and comparing different manuscripts, ultimately contributing to our knowledge of the history and preservation of the New Testament text.

Decorative Elements and Illuminations: The Artistry of Manuscripts

While the primary purpose of New Testament manuscripts was to preserve and transmit the sacred text, the artistry and craftsmanship involved in their production were also significant. Decorative elements and illuminations added beauty, elegance, and visual impact to the manuscripts, demonstrating the reverence and devotion of the scribes and patrons who commissioned them.

1. **Decorative Elements**: Decorative elements in New Testament manuscripts could include ornamental designs, such as intricate patterns, flourishes, or borders that adorned the text. These embellishments often enhanced the appearance of the manuscript, making it more aesthetically pleasing and engaging. Decorative elements could also serve practical purposes, such as helping to organize the text by visually separating sections, chapters, or paragraphs.

2. **Illuminations**: Illuminated manuscripts are those that feature elaborate illustrations, often in gold, silver, or vibrant colors, which were intended to enhance the text and its meaning. These illuminations could depict scenes from the biblical narrative, portray religious figures, or represent symbolic imagery. Illuminated manuscripts were typically produced for wealthy patrons or religious institutions, as the materials and labor required for their creation were expensive and time-consuming. The level of skill and artistry involved in creating illuminations reflected the importance placed on the sacred text and its preservation.

3. **Significance for New Testament Textual Criticism**: The study of decorative elements and illuminations in New Testament manuscripts provides insight into the cultural, artistic, and religious contexts in which these texts were created. Examining these artistic features can help scholars to better understand the motivations and intentions of the scribes and patrons responsible for producing the manuscripts.

Furthermore, the presence of unique decorative elements or illuminations can sometimes aid in the identification of specific scribal traditions or artistic schools, which can be useful for dating and attributing manuscripts.

In conclusion, decorative elements and illuminations in New Testament manuscripts represent the artistry and devotion that went into preserving and transmitting the sacred text. These artistic features not only added visual appeal to the manuscripts but also provided valuable context and meaning to the biblical narrative. The study of these elements is essential for textual critics, as it sheds light on the cultural, artistic, and religious influences that shaped the production and preservation of the New Testament text, ultimately enriching our understanding of its history and development.

Evolution of Handwriting Styles: Regional and Chronological Variations

The study of handwriting styles in New Testament manuscripts is an essential aspect of paleography, as it helps scholars to date, classify, and trace the development of the text through time and space. Handwriting styles in the New Testament manuscripts evolved over centuries, reflecting regional and chronological variations that offer valuable insights into the cultural, artistic, and linguistic contexts in which these texts were created.

1. **Regional Variations**: Throughout the history of New Testament textual transmission, different regions developed distinct handwriting styles due to geographical, cultural, and linguistic factors. For example, Byzantine minuscule script was prevalent in the Eastern Mediterranean, while Insular script was characteristic of manuscripts produced in the British Isles. Studying these regional variations can help scholars to trace the movement of manuscripts, identify scribal traditions, and understand the cultural influences that shaped the transmission of the New Testament text.

2. **Chronological Variations**: Over time, handwriting styles in New Testament manuscripts evolved, reflecting changes in

artistic trends, writing materials, and tools. For instance, the transition from uncial to minuscule script occurred around the 9th century, coinciding with the rise of the Carolingian Renaissance and the spread of parchment as a writing material. These chronological variations can be crucial for dating manuscripts, as well as tracing the development of scribal practices and textual traditions over time.

3. **Interactions Between Regional and Chronological Variations**: Regional and chronological variations in handwriting styles often intersected and influenced one another. For example, the development of minuscule script in the Byzantine Empire eventually spread to other regions, where it was adapted and modified to suit local artistic and linguistic preferences. By analyzing these interactions, scholars can better understand the complex processes of cultural exchange and adaptation that shaped the transmission and preservation of the New Testament text.

In summary, the evolution of handwriting styles in New Testament manuscripts is a critical aspect of paleography that provides insight into the regional and chronological variations that influenced the text's development. By examining these variations, scholars can trace the movement of manuscripts, identify scribal traditions, and gain a deeper understanding of the cultural, artistic, and linguistic contexts that shaped the New Testament text. This knowledge is essential for textual critics, as it helps to illuminate the history and development of the sacred text, ultimately enriching our understanding of its origins and transmission.

Introduction to Paleography: The Art and Science of Deciphering Ancient Manuscripts

Paleography is the study of ancient handwriting, which involves the art and science of deciphering, analyzing, and understanding ancient manuscripts. It plays a crucial role in the field of New Testament textual criticism, as it aids scholars in determining the age, origin, and authenticity of manuscripts. By examining the scripts, styles, and materials used in ancient documents, paleographers can piece together the historical context and development of New Testament texts.

1. **Analyzing Handwriting Styles**: Paleographers closely examine the handwriting styles, letterforms, and other distinctive features in manuscripts to identify specific periods and regions. By studying the evolution and variations of writing styles, they can establish a relative chronology for the manuscripts and, in some cases, narrow down the possible dates of composition.

2. **Identifying Scribal Practices**: Scribes often had their unique habits, including spelling, punctuation, and abbreviations. Paleographers can identify individual scribes or scriptoria (writing centers) by recognizing these patterns, which can provide insight into the transmission and provenance of New Testament texts.

3. **Understanding Manuscript Materials and Techniques**: Analyzing the writing materials (such as papyrus, parchment, or ink) and techniques (like the use of pens, brushes, or chisels) can offer valuable information about the production and conservation of ancient manuscripts. It can also reveal the social, economic, and cultural context of the time and place in which the texts were created.

4. **Deciphering Damaged or Obscured Texts**: Paleographers employ various methods to read damaged or faded manuscripts, including the use of advanced imaging technology, chemical treatments, or digital enhancements. By recovering lost or hidden text, they can contribute to a more accurate reconstruction of the original New Testament writings.

5. **Assessing Authenticity and Reliability**: Paleographical analysis can help scholars differentiate between authentic manuscripts and forgeries or determine the reliability of a text by evaluating the competence and care of the scribe. This is

particularly important when comparing different manuscript traditions or weighing the value of variant readings in the process of textual criticism.

In conclusion, paleography plays an essential role in the study of the New Testament by providing a deeper understanding of the manuscripts' historical context, development, and transmission. By deciphering ancient manuscripts, paleographers contribute invaluable information to the field of New Testament textual criticism, helping scholars reconstruct the most accurate text possible and understand the rich history of these sacred writings.

The Development of Greek Script: From Uncials to Severe Style

There are four distinct styles of handwriting used in early Christianity that are relevant to New Testament paleography. These styles include the Roman Uncial, Biblical Uncial, Decorated Rounded Uncial, and Severe (or Slanted) style. It should be noted, however, that these styles are not always clearly distinct, and there is often a blending of features between them. Additionally, it is difficult to pinpoint exactly when each style emerged, as there was a lot of overlap and evolution between them. Nonetheless, each style has its own unique features and a general chronology for their popularity and eventual disappearance.

The Emergence and Characteristics of the Roman Uncial Script

Paleography scholars have determined that the Roman Uncial script emerged shortly after the conclusion of the Ptolemaic period in 30 BC. Consequently, the early Roman Uncial can be traced back to around 30 BC, and its usage can be observed throughout the first two to three centuries of the Common Era. When examining the Roman Uncial script, one can identify specific attributes that set it apart from the manuscripts of the preceding Ptolemaic period.

In contrast to the Ptolemaic manuscripts, the Roman Uncial script exhibits a more rounded and smoother appearance in the formation of its letters. Additionally, the script tends to be larger in size. Another distinguishing feature of the Roman Uncial script is the presence of decorative serifs in several, but not all, letters. This is in contrast to the Decorated Rounded style, which focuses on ensuring that the decorations are uniformly rounded and abundant.

The Evolution from Roman Uncial to Biblical Uncial The Roman Uncial script is considered a precursor to the Biblical Uncial script, with the latter evolving from the former. Consequently, some paleographers may use the terms "Roman Uncial" and "Biblical Uncial" interchangeably. However, there are subtle differences between the two styles. The Biblical Uncial script typically displays minimal or no decoration and exhibits noticeable shading, which is characterized by the deliberate alternation of thick and thin pen-strokes in relation to the angle at which the pen contacts the writing surface.

An Exemplary Roman Uncial Manuscript: P46 Sir Frederic Kenyon, a renowned paleographer, identified P46 as a prime example of a New Testament manuscript written in the Roman Uncial script. According to Kenyon, the editor of the editio princeps, the letters in P46 demonstrate an early Roman Uncial style characterized by well-formed lettering consistent with the Roman period. For further information, refer to the discussion on P46 in a future chapter.

The Biblical Uncial Handwriting Style (AKA Biblical Majuscule)

The Biblical Uncial, also known as the Biblical Majuscule, is a type of handwriting characterized by large, separate, unconnected uncial letters. This term was first used by Grenfell and Hunt to describe the handwriting found in specific biblical texts but was later extended to include any manuscript exhibiting this particular style, regardless of content. In this form of writing, letters maintain a bilinear appearance, conforming to imaginary upper and lower lines, and there is a purposeful alternation of thick vertical and thin horizontal strokes. Rectangular strokes exhibit right-angled shapes, while circular letters are truly circular rather than oval. The Biblical Uncial style does not include ligatures (connected letters) or ornamentation at the end of strokes, such as serifs and blobs.

This writing style began to emerge in the first century CE. Some paleographers have identified P. Herculaneum 1457, a manuscript from Herculaneum dated before 79 CE, as an early example of the Biblical Uncial. Other notable instances of this style can be seen in P. London II 141, a document dated to 88 CE, and in several Roman Uncial manuscripts from the second century. G. Cavallo, in his extensive work *Richerche sulla Maiuscola Biblica*, argues that the Biblical Uncial style took definitive shape in the middle to late second century CE, based on the dating of several significant manuscripts.

Early New Testament manuscripts written in the Biblical Uncial style include P4+64+67, P30, P35, P39, P40, P70, P95, 0162, and 0189. Each of these manuscripts exhibits the key features of the Biblical Uncial style, such as bilinearity, the alternation of thick and thin strokes, and the absence of ligatures and ornamentation. As paleographers continue to study these texts and their handwriting, our understanding of the development and significance of the Biblical Uncial style in the broader context of ancient manuscript production will only deepen.

Decorated Rounded Uncial: A Handwriting Style in Early Christian Manuscripts

The Decorated Rounded Uncial is a distinct handwriting style that was prevalent during the early period of the Christian church. This style features serifs or decorative roundels at the end of each vertical stroke. Some scholars, such as Schubart, believe that this style dates back to the last century of the Ptolemaic period (first century BC) and lasted until the end of the first century CE. Others, like Turner, argue that the style extended to the end of the second century, and possibly even into the early third century.

The debate over whether the Decorated Rounded Uncial represents a single style, or a single feature of multiple styles continues, but the fact remains that manuscripts featuring this style of handwriting are easily recognizable. Several existing examples of dated manuscripts (i.e., manuscripts with specific dates) showcasing this style fall within the period of 100 BC to 150 CE.

A notable concentration of dated manuscripts featuring the Decorated Rounded Uncial style can be found between 100 BC and 100 CE, with evidence suggesting that this time frame may extend to 150 CE. However, there are few dated documents beyond 150 CE that display this style. E. G. Turner points to P. Oxyrhynchus 3093 (dated 217 CE) and P. Oxyrhynchus 3030 (dated 207 or 211 CE) as rare late examples of this style.

While the Decorated Rounded Uncial may have been more common in the late first century and the second century, many scholars have hesitated to assign these dates to New Testament manuscripts featuring the style. Nevertheless, several New Testament manuscripts displaying the Decorated Rounded Uncial style, such as P32, P66, P90, and P104, likely belong to the period prior to 150 CE.

In conclusion, the Decorated Rounded Uncial is an important handwriting style that significantly influenced early Christian manuscripts. By examining the historical context and time frames of these manuscripts, scholars can gain valuable insights into the development and transmission of early Christian texts.

The Development and Characteristics of the Severe Style in Greek Handwriting

Over time, formal Greek handwriting experienced a transition from its traditional upright form during the Ptolemaic and Roman periods to a more slanted style. When the handwriting is upright, it features right angles and rounded curves. However, when the handwriting is slanted, the broad letters emphasize angularity, and the curves resemble ellipses. This style also combines both narrow and broad letters. As such, Turner referred to it as Formal Mixed, while Schubart named it Strenge Stil, or Severe Style. Turner believed that no effort was made in documents to differentiate between broad and narrow letters before Hadrian's age (117-138 CE). Nonetheless, G. Cavallo's work, "Libri scritture scribi a Ercolano," contradicts this view by demonstrating that documents exhibiting wide and narrow letters were present in Herculaneum prior to the second century.

Several second-century, third-century, and early fourth-century manuscripts with established dates showcase the Severe Style:

1. **P. Giss. 3 (117 CE)**: Celebratory libretto for Hadrian's accession, displaying the broad, slanting style that later became popular.

2. **P. Michigan 3 (second half of the second century)**: Dated solidly due to the verso's documentary text with a 190 CE date.

3. **P. Oxyrhynchus 2341 (202 CE)**: A legal proceeding record with a certain date.

4. **P. Florentine II. 108 (circa 200 CE)**: A manuscript of Homer's Iliad III, part of the Heroninos archive, dating to around 260 AD, with literary texts written approximately 50 years earlier.

5. **P. Rylands I. 57 (circa 200 CE)**: A Demosthenes manuscript, De Corona, also from the Heroninos archive.

6. **P. Florentine II. 259 (circa 260 CE)**: A letter in the Heroninos archive written in a professional hand resembling the common literary style of the time.

7. **P. Oxyrhynchus 2098 (first half of the third century)**: A manuscript featuring Herodotus, book 7, with a verso land survey dated to Gallienus' reign (253-268 CE).

8. **P. Oxyrhynchus 1016 (early to middle third century)**: A difficult-to-date Phaedres manuscript, written on the verso of a land register with an uncertain Roman emperor's 13th year.

9. **P. Oxyrhynchus 223 (early third century)**: A Homer manuscript (Iliad V), written on the verso of a document with Oxyrhynchite provenance, dated 186 CE.

10. **P. Herm. Rees 5 (circa 325 CE)**: A letter addressed to a known scholasticus (government official) from the 320s of the fourth century.

Early New Testament manuscripts that display the Severe (slanted) style include P13, P45, P48, P49, P110, and P115.

Dating New Testament Manuscripts: Methods and Challenges

Determining the Age of Manuscripts: Criteria and Considerations

Before delving into the identification of the earliest New Testament manuscripts, it is essential to establish the criteria used for dating these manuscripts. These criteria include archaeological evidence, codicology, comparative palaeography, and the evolution of nomina sacra. Among these, comparative palaeography is the most intricate, warranting a more in-depth discussion. In this context, the focus will be on determining the dates for literary texts based on dated documentary manuscripts and examining comparative morphology, which refers to the study of comparable handwriting styles.

1. **Archaeological Evidence**: This criterion involves assessing the physical context in which a manuscript was discovered, such as the location, associated artifacts, and stratigraphic information. These factors can provide valuable information about the manuscript's age.

2. **Codicology**: Codicology is the study of ancient manuscripts as physical objects, including their construction, materials, and format. Examining these aspects can reveal clues about the

time and place of a manuscript's creation, as well as its cultural and historical context.

3. **Comparative Palaeography**: Comparative palaeography is the study of ancient handwriting styles and their development over time. By comparing the script of a manuscript with other known examples from various periods, scholars can narrow down the time frame in which it was likely written. This approach comprises two main aspects:

a. **Dating Literary Texts Based on Documentary Manuscripts**: Literary texts can be challenging to date because they often lack explicit historical or chronological context. However, scholars can estimate their age by comparing them with documentary manuscripts that have known dates, such as legal documents or official records. By identifying similarities in handwriting styles between the literary and documentary texts, researchers can establish a more accurate date for the literary work.

b. **Comparative Morphology**: This aspect of comparative palaeography involves analyzing and comparing the specific forms and shapes of letters used in different manuscripts. By identifying similarities and differences in handwriting styles across various texts, scholars can trace the evolution of these styles and establish a more precise chronology for the manuscripts in question.

4. **Evolution of Nomina Sacra**: Nomina sacra refers to the abbreviated forms of sacred names used in early Christian manuscripts. These abbreviations evolved over time, with distinct patterns emerging during specific periods. By analyzing the nomina sacra used in a manuscript, scholars can gain insight into its age and context.

In conclusion, determining the age of ancient manuscripts is a complex task that requires careful consideration of various criteria, including archaeological evidence, codicology, comparative palaeography, and the evolution of nomina sacra. By taking these factors into account, scholars can arrive at a more accurate and comprehensive understanding of the historical context and chronology of these important texts.

Assessing Manuscript Ages through Archaeological Evidence and Other Criteria

The initial method employed in dating a manuscript involves examining archaeological evidence. External and circumstantial factors can aid scholars in determining the age of manuscripts. For instance, the terminus ante quem (latest possible date) for the Herculaneum manuscripts is 79 CE, corresponding to Mount Vesuvius' eruption, while for the Dead Sea Scrolls, it is 70 CE, when the Qumran caves were abandoned. As Scanlin notes, the Qumran community was destroyed during the Jewish war and Roman invasion around 70 CE. Assuming that the Dead Sea Scrolls discovered near the Qumran settlement were products of this community, the latest possible date for the manuscripts hidden in the nearby caves would be 70 CE. However, it is important to acknowledge that not all Dead Sea Scroll manuscripts may have originated from the Qumran community, as the caves could have been utilized by other Jews to hide manuscripts at different times. Nevertheless, very few scholars would date any of the Dead Sea Scrolls beyond the mid-first century AD, based on both archaeological and paleographical grounds.

The New Testament papyrus manuscript P4+P64+P67 cannot be dated later than 200 CE, as it was used in strips (potentially as binding) for a third-century codex of Philo. A certain period must be allowed for a well-crafted codex to have been used extensively before being torn up and repurposed as binding. The Gospel harmony manuscript 0212 cannot be dated later than 256 CE and is likely dated around 230 CE, as it was found in the filling of an embankment constructed in 256 CE. A nearby Christian house, which existed from 222 to 235 CE, was destroyed when the embankment was built.

Regrettably, most manuscripts cannot be dated based on archaeological evidence alone, as the surrounding circumstances are often unclear or ambiguous. Therefore, when dating the majority of biblical manuscripts, paleographers rely on additional criteria, such as codicology and comparative palaeography, which also encompass comparative stylistics and morphology.

Codicology and Its Influence on Manuscript Dating

Codicology, as explored in a previous chapter, refers to the study of codices, which were in use before the end of the first century AD. The codex was the exclusive book form employed by Christians for copying biblical texts. As such, any New Testament codex manuscript could date as far back as the late first century. The understanding of the codex's dating grew more refined during the latter half of the twentieth century, as an increasing number of papyri were published. Paleographers in the early twentieth century often regarded the codex as a late second-century or early third-century invention, which led them to hesitate in dating Christian manuscripts earlier than the third century. This was the case with Grenfell and Hunt, who assigned numerous third- and fourth-century dates to Christian Old Testament and New Testament manuscripts, despite the handwriting clearly belonging to an earlier era.

Advancements in knowledge about the codex's origins have prompted paleographers to reconsider and redate many of these manuscripts to earlier periods. This redating process is examined on a manuscript-by-manuscript basis in the following discussion.

Comparative Paleography: A Comprehensive Overview

Comparative paleography plays a crucial role in dating biblical manuscripts, which are primarily literary texts. Unlike documentary texts, which often contain explicit or implicit dates, literary manuscripts rarely, if ever, bear dates. Thus, paleographers rely on comparative analysis to determine the dates of these manuscripts.

One method involves examining literary texts written on the recto (the primary, higher-quality side of a papyrus or parchment leaf) with dated documentary texts on the verso (the secondary side). The date of the documentary text serves as the terminus ante quem (latest possible date) for the literary text. The time difference between the two could be significant, as the literary text would have likely been in use for an extended period before being repurposed for documentary use.

Conversely, if a literary text is written on the verso of a dated documentary text, the date of the documentary text serves as the terminus post quem (earliest possible date) for the literary text. The time between the two is typically shorter, as the document would have been deemed less valuable and quickly repurposed for literary use.

The primary method for dating New Testament manuscripts is comparing their handwriting with that of dated documentary texts. A secondary method involves comparing the handwriting of undated literary texts with literary manuscripts bearing dates due to their association with documentary texts on either the recto or verso. Since several New Testament papyrus manuscripts feature a documentary hand, it is possible to find comparable dated documentary manuscripts.

While dating literary texts by comparing them to other literary texts involves a degree of subjectivity, it remains an essential practice in paleography. The proposed date for the earliest New Testament manuscripts is often based on a comparative analysis of various dated documentary manuscripts and literary texts. However, factors such as the scribe's age or the time of a particular writing style's emergence can influence the date of a manuscript, potentially altering it by 25 to 50 years.

To account for such factors, it is advisable to date manuscripts within a 50-year range, offering both an early and a later date. Despite the inherent subjectivity in comparative analysis, paleographers seek to determine a manuscript's date by employing comparative morphology—a study of letter forms. This approach focuses on the overall resemblance between texts rather than matching individual letter forms, as was the practice in the past.

Comparative Stylistics: A Basic Analysis

Paleographers also employ comparative stylistics to date manuscripts by identifying the prevalent handwriting style during a specific time period. By comparing a manuscript to others with established dates, a paleographer can determine whether the manuscript exhibits early or late features of that period. In the following discussion, we will examine four distinct styles: Roman Uncial, Biblical Uncial, Decorated Rounded, and Severe (Slanting) Style. Several Christian manuscripts from both the Old Testament and New Testament display one of these styles.

Renowned papyrologists like Roberts and Turner have identified scribal tendencies during the first three centuries AD. They note that scribes in the first and second centuries tended to align their letters with an imaginary top line. Most bookhands exhibit bilinearity, striving to align letters with both imaginary top and bottom lines. Slanting handwriting emerged in the second century, while other second-century features include the final nu on a line replaced with an extending overbar over the last letter, a small omicron in documentary hands becoming prominent in third-century literary hands, and angular letters in the late second and early third centuries. There was also a tendency for documentary scribes to enlarge the first letter of each line or each new section in documentary and Greek biblical manuscripts from the first century CE onwards.

Additional Features for Dating Manuscripts: Paleographers may consider ink color when estimating a manuscript's date. Lustrous black ink, or carbon ink, is typically earlier than brown ink, which often derives from an iron salt or other chemical compound and usually indicates a date post-300 CE. The distinction between black and brown ink is significant for dating P15 and P16. Meanwhile, metallic ink typically suggests a later date, though P. Oxyrhynchus 2269, written in metallic ink, is dated 269 CE.

Turner also identified another feature that emerged in the early third century: the use of a separating apostrophe between double consonants. Some paleographers have taken this observation as fact, using it to date manuscripts with this feature as post-200 CE. However, it is important to consider that the presence of this specific feature could actually indicate an earlier date for its emergence, rather than redating the manuscript itself.

For instance, the Egerton Gospel, initially dated by many scholars to around 150 CE, should maintain that date despite the presence of the separating apostrophe. Similarly, the date for P52 should remain as early second century. Other manuscripts dated before 200 CE also exhibit the apostrophe or hook between double consonants, such as BGU iii 715.5 (101 CE), P. Petaus 86 (= P. Michigan 6871) (185 CE), SPP xxii 3.22 (second century), and P. Berol. 9570 + P. Rylands 60 (dated by the editors of the editio princeps to around 200, and by Cavallo to around 50). These examples serve as further evidence that the presence of this specific feature could predate the early third century.

Evolution of Nomina Sacra and Dating New Testament Manuscripts

The nomina sacra, or sacred names, underwent an evolutionary process. Initially, the divine names Kurios (Lord), Iesous (Jesus), Christos (Christ), and Theos (God) were given special written representations. As will be discussed later, the divine title Pneuma (Spirit) was also included early in the textual transmission process. Other early nomina sacra included Stauros (cross) and Stauromai (crucify). Over time, additional nomina sacra were incorporated, such as Huios (Son), Pater (Father), Anthropos (man), Israel, Ierosalem (Jerusalem), and Ouranos (heaven).

One might assume that fewer nomina sacra indicate an earlier manuscript. T. C. Skeat, for instance, used this rationale to date P4+64+67 to the second century. However, the second-century manuscript P66 contains more nomina sacra, similar to those found in the Chester Beatty VI, dated to the early to mid-second century. Hunger used the similarity of nomina sacra in P66 and Chester Beatty VI to argue for P66's second-century date.

English Meaning	Greek Word	Nominative (Subject)	Genitive (Possessive)
God	Θεός	Θ͞Σ	Θ͞Υ
Lord	Κύριος	Κ͞Σ	Κ͞Υ
Jesus	Ἰησοῦς	Ι͞Σ	Ι͞Υ
Christ/Messiah	Χριστός	Χ͞Σ	Χ͞Υ
Son	Υἱός	Υ͞Σ	Υ͞Υ
Spirit/Ghost	Πνεῦμα	Π͞Ν͞Α	Π͞Ν͞Σ
David	Δαυὶδ	Δ͞Α͞Δ	
Cross/Stake	Σταυρός	Σ͞Τ͞Σ	Σ͞Τ͞Υ
Mother	Μήτηρ	Μ͞Η͞Ρ	Μ͞Η͞Σ
God Bearer *i.e.* Mother of God	Θεοτόκος	Θ͞Κ͞Σ	Θ͞Κ͞Υ
Father	Πατήρ	Π͞Η͞Ρ	Π͞Ρ͞Σ
Israel	Ἰσραήλ	Ι͞Η͞Λ	
Savior	Σωτήρ	Σ͞Η͞Ρ	Σ͞Ρ͞Σ
Human being/Man	Ἄνθρωπος	Α͞Ν͞Ο͞Σ	Α͞Ν͞Ο͞Υ
Jerusalem	Ἰερουσαλήμ	Ι͞Λ͞Η͞Μ	
Heaven/Heavens	Οὐρανός	Ο͞Υ͞Ν͞Ο͞Σ	Ο͞Υ͞Ν͞Ο͞Υ

Using nomina sacra to date New Testament manuscripts is challenging because their evolution began in the first century, possibly when the New Testament books were first written, and continued into the second century. By the mid-second century, many divine names were represented as nomina sacra. Some names were consistently written as nomina sacra, while others, like Son and Father, were inconsistently represented in the same manuscript. This inconsistency suggests an ongoing evolutionary process for these titles, which became more fixed as nomina sacra in the third century.

Nomina Sacra Mark 1.1 Codex Sinaiticus

For instance, the second-century manuscript P4+64+67 does not use nomina sacra for Son and Father. In other notable second-century manuscripts, such as P46, P66, and P75, "Son" and "Father" are sometimes written as nomina sacra and other times not. In most third-century manuscripts, these titles are consistently treated as nomina sacra. Consequently, a manuscript with inconsistent representation of Father and Son or without nomina sacra for these titles should be considered for a second-century date, such as P45.

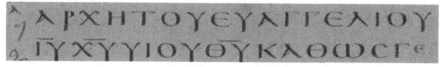

Nomina Sacra Mark 1.1 Codex Vaticanus

Another example is P46, which displays both nomina sacra and full written forms for all names of the Trinity (Father, Son, and Spirit). Notably, the scribe did not consistently use the nomen sacrum for Pneuma (Spirit) as expected. This suggests that the title was not yet fixed as a nomen sacrum when P46 was created and may indicate an early date for the manuscript.

Additionally, the suspended and short contracted forms likely preceded the longer contracted form. The question remains whether the fuller form developed later or concurrently with the shorter form. Some scholars believe the suspended form of Iesous (Jesus), IH, was the earliest, but this is uncertain.

In conclusion, using nomina sacra forms to date manuscripts is challenging. However, the presence or absence of specific nomina sacra and fluctuations in usage within a manuscript (as seen in P46) can provide valuable insights for dating purposes.

The Role of Paleography in Textual Criticism: Establishing Manuscript Relationships

Paleography, the study of ancient handwriting, plays a crucial role in textual criticism, the field of analyzing and evaluating the manuscripts of a text to establish its most accurate and reliable version. In the context of biblical studies, textual criticism involves examining the thousands of handwritten copies of biblical texts to reconstruct the original text as closely as possible. Paleography is essential in this process for several reasons:

1. **Dating Manuscripts**: One of the primary objectives of paleography is to date manuscripts based on their handwriting styles. By analyzing the evolution of letter shapes, ligatures, punctuation, and other scribal features, paleographers can estimate the age of a manuscript. Accurate dating of manuscripts is crucial for textual criticism, as it helps scholars establish a chronological order and determine which manuscripts are closer to the original text.

2. **Identifying Scribes and Scriptoria**: Paleography enables scholars to identify the scribes who copied manuscripts or the scriptoria (writing centers) where they were produced. Analyzing specific scribal habits, such as spelling tendencies, letter formations, and decorative elements, can reveal connections between different manuscripts. Identifying scribes and scriptoria helps textual critics understand the transmission of texts and trace the lineage of various manuscript families.

3. **Establishing Manuscript Relationships**: Paleography can uncover relationships between manuscripts by highlighting similarities in handwriting styles, layouts, and other scribal features. These similarities may suggest that two or more manuscripts share a common ancestor or belong to the same textual tradition. Establishing manuscript relationships is essential for creating a stemma (family tree) of the manuscripts, which allows textual critics to reconstruct the original text more accurately.

4. **Detecting Corrections and Alterations**: Paleographers can identify corrections, alterations, or additions made by scribes or later editors by examining the manuscript's handwriting. These changes can offer insights into the textual history and the scribes' understanding of the text. Identifying such alterations aids textual critics in determining which readings are more likely to be original and which are later modifications.

5. **Evaluating Manuscript Authenticity**: Paleography can help determine the authenticity of a manuscript. Forgeries or modern reproductions may exhibit anachronistic handwriting features or other inconsistencies that reveal their true nature. By analyzing the handwriting of a manuscript, paleographers can confirm or disprove its authenticity, ensuring that textual critics only work with genuine manuscripts in their analysis.

6. **Contributing to the Critical Apparatus**: The critical apparatus is an essential tool for textual critics, presenting variant readings from different manuscripts and providing information about their sources. Paleography contributes to the apparatus by offering detailed descriptions of the manuscripts' handwriting, enabling textual critics to make informed decisions about the weight and reliability of specific readings.

In summary, paleography plays a vital role in textual criticism by dating manuscripts, identifying scribes and scriptoria, establishing manuscript relationships, detecting corrections and alterations, evaluating manuscript authenticity, and contributing to the critical apparatus. Through these functions, paleography enables textual critics to reconstruct the original text more accurately and gain a deeper understanding of the textual history and transmission.

Analyzing Scribal Habits and Tendencies: Insights into the Transmission of the Text

Textual criticism, the discipline of studying and evaluating the manuscripts of a text to establish its most accurate and reliable version, relies heavily on understanding the habits and tendencies of the scribes who copied these manuscripts. By analyzing scribal habits, textual critics can gain valuable insights into the transmission of the text, manuscript relationships, and the reliability of specific readings. This essay will discuss various aspects of scribal habits and tendencies and their significance in the field of textual criticism.

Scribal Tendencies: An Overview

Scribes were responsible for manually copying texts before the invention of the printing press. During the process of copying, scribes could introduce unintentional errors or deliberate changes to the text. Some of the common scribal habits and tendencies include:

1. **Spelling and Orthography**: Scribes often had personal preferences or regional variations in spelling, which can help identify their origin or distinguish between different manuscript traditions. Consistent spelling mistakes or deviations from standard orthography may indicate a scribe's level of education or familiarity with the language of the text.

2. **Letter Formation and Abbreviations**: The way a scribe forms individual letters or employs abbreviations can provide clues about their training, scriptorium, or the time period in which they were active. Certain letter formations or abbreviations can be characteristic of specific regions or periods, helping to date and localize a manuscript.

3. **Punctuation and Layout**: Punctuation marks and layout choices, such as paragraph divisions, line breaks, and indentation, can reveal a scribe's understanding of the text or their adherence to a specific textual tradition. Consistent patterns in punctuation and layout across multiple manuscripts may suggest a common ancestor or shared scribal training.

4. **Corrections and Alterations**: Scribes sometimes corrected their work or made alterations to the text, either while copying or after completing the manuscript. These corrections can offer insights into the textual history and the scribes' comprehension of the text.

5. **Marginal Annotations and Glosses**: Scribes occasionally added annotations, glosses, or other supplementary material in the margins or between lines of the text. These additions can provide valuable context for understanding the text or reveal the scribe's interpretation of specific passages.

6. **Decorative Elements and Colophons**: Scribes often included decorative elements, such as initial letters, illustrations, or ornamental borders, in their manuscripts. Colophons, or notes at the end of a manuscript containing information about the scribe, date, or place of production, can also provide essential information about the manuscript's history and provenance.

Significance of Scribal Habits in Textual Criticism

1. **Dating Manuscripts**: By examining scribal habits and tendencies, textual critics can approximate the age of a manuscript. Certain letter formations, abbreviations, or decorative elements can be characteristic of specific time periods, helping scholars to date manuscripts more accurately.

2. **Identifying Scribes and Scriptoria**: Analyzing scribal habits can reveal the identity of individual scribes or the scriptoria where they were trained or worked. Recognizing specific scribal tendencies across different manuscripts can help scholars trace the lineage of various manuscript families and better understand the transmission of the text.

3. **Establishing Manuscript Relationships**: Scribal habits and tendencies can highlight similarities between manuscripts, suggesting that they share a common ancestor or belong to the same textual tradition. Establishing manuscript relationships allows textual critics to create stemmata (family trees) of the manuscripts, contributing to a more accurate reconstruction of the original text.

4. **Evaluating the Reliability of Readings**: By examining scribal habits, textual critics can assess the reliability of specific readings. For instance, if a scribe consistently makes certain types of errors, a textual critic can determine whether a variant reading in a manuscript is likely the result of an error or an intentional alteration. Understanding the tendencies of a particular scribe can help scholars weigh the evidence for

different readings and make more informed decisions about the most likely original text.

5. **Identifying Intentional Changes and Editorial Practices**: Analyzing scribal habits and tendencies can help distinguish between unintentional errors and deliberate changes to the text. Scribes sometimes made purposeful alterations to clarify, harmonize, or otherwise modify the text. Recognizing these intentional changes can provide valuable information about the editorial practices and theological perspectives of the scribes or their communities, which in turn can shed light on the broader context of the text's transmission and reception.

6. **Tracing the Evolution of Textual Features**: Scribal habits can offer insights into the development of specific textual features, such as punctuation, orthography, or abbreviations. By studying the patterns of these features in different manuscripts, scholars can trace their evolution over time and better understand the history of the text and its transmission.

7. **Understanding the Social and Cultural Context of Manuscript Production**: Studying scribal habits and tendencies can also reveal information about the social and cultural context of manuscript production. For example, analyzing the materials, techniques, or artistic styles employed by scribes can help scholars uncover information about the economic and cultural conditions of the time, the influence of different artistic and intellectual traditions, or the educational background of the scribes themselves.

In conclusion, the analysis of scribal habits and tendencies is a crucial aspect of textual criticism, providing valuable insights into the transmission of the text, the reliability of specific readings, and the relationships between manuscripts. By examining the various characteristics of scribes and their work, scholars can better understand the history, context, and evolution of the texts they study. This knowledge, in turn, allows textual critics to reconstruct the most accurate and reliable version of the text, ensuring its continued preservation and understanding for future generations.

Notable New Testament Manuscripts: A Paleographic Perspective

The study of New Testament manuscripts from a paleographic perspective allows scholars to analyze the physical features of these manuscripts, such as the style of handwriting, ink, and parchment, in order to date them and establish their relationships to one another. Throughout the centuries, numerous notable New Testament manuscripts have been discovered, each possessing unique characteristics that provide insights into the text's transmission and development. This essay will examine several of these significant manuscripts and their implications from a paleographic viewpoint.

1. **P52 (Rylands Library Papyrus P52)**: P52 is a small fragment of the Gospel of John, discovered in Egypt and dated to the first half of the 2nd century CE. It is currently the earliest known New Testament manuscript, with its early date offering important evidence for the early circulation of the Gospel of John. Paleographically, P52 is written in a script known as Roman uncial, characterized by its use of capital letters with minimal separation between words. Its early date and script type highlight the rapid spread of Christianity and its texts during the 2nd century.

2. **P66 (Bodmer Papyrus II)**: P66 is dated to 110-150 CE. It is a papyrus codex containing a large portion of the Gospel of John. It is an essential witness to the text, as it predates many other manuscripts containing the same gospel. Paleographically, P66 displays a professional and elegant style of Greek handwriting, showcasing the scribe's skill and the importance placed on the production of Christian texts. Its well-preserved state provides essential information on the text's early form and offers insights into the scribal practices of the time.

3. **P45 (Chester Beatty I)**: P45 is dated to 175-225 CE. It is a papyrus codex containing portions of the four canonical gospels and Acts of the Apostles. It is one of the earliest

witnesses to the text of these books, offering a glimpse into the early stages of the New Testament canon. Paleographically, P45 exhibits a script known as severe (slanting) style, characterized by its slanted, angular letterforms. The scribe's use of this particular style suggests a high level of skill and emphasizes the manuscript's importance within the Christian community.

4. **P46 (Chester Beatty II)**: P46 is a papyrus codex from 110-150 CE, containing a majority of Paul's letters, making it one of the oldest and most extensive collections of these texts. Paleographically, P46 is written in a professional and elegant script, with carefully executed letterforms and ligatures. The high quality of the script indicates the value placed on the Pauline epistles and their role within the early Christian community.

5. **P75 (Bodmer Papyrus XIV–XV)**: P75 is a papyrus codex from 175-225 CE, containing substantial portions of the Gospels of Luke and John. It is considered one of the most important witnesses to these texts, as it predates many other manuscripts and provides crucial information about their early form. Paleographically, P75 displays a careful and deliberate script, with the scribe taking great care to ensure the accuracy and legibility of the text. This attention to detail speaks to the importance of these gospels within the Christian community and the care taken to preserve them.

6. **Codex Sinaiticus (ℵ)**: Codex Sinaiticus, discovered in the 19th century at the Monastery of Saint Catherine in Sinai, is a 4th-century Greek codex (330-360 CE) that contains the earliest complete copy of the New Testament, as well as a substantial portion of the Greek Old Testament. Paleographically, Codex Sinaiticus is written in a script known as biblical uncial, characterized by its use of large, rounded capital letters and clear separation between words. The high quality of the script and the care taken in its production suggest the significant role that the codex played within the early Christian community. The Codex Sinaiticus is of immense

value to textual critics, as it offers a complete and early witness to the New Testament text and sheds light on the development of the canon.

7. **Codex Vaticanus (B)**: Codex Vaticanus, housed in the Vatican Library, is another 4th-century Greek codex (300-330 CE), containing almost the entire Bible. Like Codex Sinaiticus, it is an essential witness to the text of the New Testament and the development of the canon. Paleographically, Codex Vaticanus is written in a script similar to that of Codex Sinaiticus, utilizing biblical uncial with well-executed and rounded letterforms. The elegance and care displayed in its production highlight the importance of the text to the Christian community of the time.

8. **Codex Alexandrinus (A)**: Codex Alexandrinus, now in the British Library, is a 5th-century Greek codex containing the entire Bible. It is considered one of the most important witnesses to the text of the New Testament, alongside Codex Sinaiticus and Codex Vaticanus. Paleographically, Codex Alexandrinus is written in a script known as decorated rounded style, which is characterized by its use of large, rounded letterforms with decorative elements. The style and quality of the script emphasize the manuscript's significance within the Christian tradition.

9. **Codex Bezae (D)**: Codex Bezae, housed in Cambridge University Library, is a 5th-century Greek and Latin diglot (dual-language) codex containing the Gospels and Acts of the Apostles. It is known for its unique and variant readings, providing valuable insights into the transmission and development of the New Testament text. Paleographically, Codex Bezae is written in a script known as Latin uncial, characterized by its use of capital letters, decorative elements, and occasional ligatures. The bilingual nature of the manuscript and the care taken in its production underscore the significance of the text within the Christian community.

10. **Codex Ephraemi Rescriptus (C)**: Codex Ephraemi Rescriptus, housed in the Bibliothèque nationale de France, is a 5th-century Greek palimpsest (a manuscript in which the original text has been overwritten) containing portions of the Bible. The overwritten text includes substantial sections of the New Testament, making it an important witness to the early text. Paleographically, Codex Ephraemi Rescriptus is written in a script similar to that of Codex Sinaiticus and Codex Vaticanus, utilizing biblical uncial with rounded letterforms. The manuscript's status as a palimpsest highlights the challenges faced in preserving ancient texts and the lengths to which scribes went to conserve valuable materials.

In conclusion, the study of notable New Testament manuscripts from a paleographic perspective offers invaluable insights into the transmission, development, and preservation of the text. These manuscripts, ranging from small fragments like P52 to complete codices like Codex Sinaiticus, serve as essential witnesses to the early stages of the New Testament and provide a deeper understanding of the textual history and the evolution of the Christian canon. Furthermore, the analysis of scribal practices, handwriting styles, and the physical features of these manuscripts enables scholars to date them and establish relationships, ultimately enhancing our understanding of the rich and complex history of the New Testament.

The Intersection of Paleography, Codicology, and Papyrology: A Multidisciplinary Approach

The study of ancient manuscripts is a complex and multidimensional field, requiring the collaboration and integration of various disciplines to gain a comprehensive understanding of these invaluable historical resources. Three key disciplines that intersect in the study of ancient manuscripts are paleography, codicology, and papyrology. Each of these fields contributes its unique expertise and methodologies, allowing for a holistic analysis of the manuscripts, their contents, and the historical context in which they were produced.

1. **Paleography**: Paleography is the study of ancient and historical handwriting, focusing on the analysis of scripts, letterforms, and writing styles. Paleographers examine the physical features of a manuscript, such as the type of script, the arrangement of text on the page, and the use of abbreviations or punctuation. Through these analyses, paleographers can establish the date and provenance of a manuscript, as well as determine the scribal habits and tendencies of its scribe. In addition, paleography plays a crucial role in the reconstruction of the text, as the identification of specific handwriting styles can help in establishing relationships between manuscripts and understanding the transmission of the text.

2. **Codicology**: Codicology is the study of the physical structure and material aspects of a manuscript, such as its binding, format, and layout. Codicologists analyze the materials used in the production of a manuscript, including the type of writing surface (e.g., parchment, papyrus, or paper), the ink, and the techniques employed in its creation. These analyses can provide insights into the historical context of a manuscript, its function within the community, and the socio-economic status of its patron or owner. Moreover, codicology contributes to our understanding of the development and evolution of the book as a physical object, including its transition from scroll to codex format and the various binding techniques used over time.

3. **Papyrology**: Papyrology is the study of ancient texts written on papyrus; a writing material made from the pith of the papyrus plant. Papyrologists focus on deciphering and interpreting papyri, which often contain literary, documentary, or administrative texts from the ancient world. Papyri are valuable sources of information on various aspects of ancient life, such as religion, law, administration, and daily life. Papyrology, as a discipline, shares some similarities with paleography and codicology, as it also involves the analysis of handwriting, textual content, and the physical properties of the writing material.

The intersection of paleography, codicology, and papyrology in the study of ancient manuscripts allows for a multidisciplinary approach that combines the expertise and methodologies of each field. This collaborative approach enables scholars to gain a more comprehensive understanding of the manuscripts, their historical context, and their significance within the communities that produced and used them. By examining the physical properties, handwriting styles, and content of the manuscripts, researchers can uncover valuable information about the transmission of texts, the development of the book as a physical object, and the socio-cultural context in which these manuscripts were created and used. Ultimately, the integration of paleography, codicology, and papyrology enriches our understanding of the rich and complex history of ancient manuscripts and the people who created them.

Paleographic Advances and Discoveries: New Techniques and Technologies

In recent years, paleographic research has benefited from significant advances and discoveries, driven by the development of new techniques and technologies. These innovations have not only enhanced our ability to analyze and understand ancient manuscripts, but also opened up new avenues for research and collaboration in the field of paleography.

1. **Digital Paleography**: One of the most significant advancements in paleography has been the widespread adoption of digital tools and methods. High-resolution digital imaging allows for the creation of detailed, accurate reproductions of manuscripts, which can be easily accessed, shared, and analyzed by researchers around the world. Digital images can be enhanced, manipulated, or layered to reveal hidden or faint text, enabling paleographers to decipher previously unreadable passages or identify corrections and alterations made by scribes. Digital paleography also allows for the creation of interactive databases and repositories, which

can be used to compare manuscripts, identify common features, and establish relationships between texts.

2. **Multispectral Imaging**: Multispectral imaging is a non-invasive imaging technique that captures images of a manuscript at different wavelengths of light. This method can reveal text that is invisible to the naked eye, such as text that has faded or been erased, or ink that has reacted with the writing surface over time. Multispectral imaging has been instrumental in the discovery of previously unknown texts or the recovery of lost information from damaged or deteriorated manuscripts.

3. **Machine Learning and Artificial Intelligence**: Machine learning and artificial intelligence (AI) have also emerged as valuable tools in paleographic research. By training algorithms to recognize specific handwriting styles, letterforms, or other features, researchers can automate the analysis of large collections of manuscripts, expediting the process of dating and cataloging texts. AI-driven tools can also help identify scribal habits and tendencies, revealing unique characteristics of individual scribes and potentially uncovering previously unknown connections between manuscripts.

4. **Collaborative Research Platforms**: The development of online collaborative platforms has facilitated communication and cooperation between researchers across disciplines and geographical boundaries. These platforms allow paleographers to share their findings, contribute to ongoing research projects, and access resources such as databases, digital repositories, and scholarly publications. In turn, this increased connectivity has led to the formation of international research networks and collaborations, driving the growth of interdisciplinary projects and fostering innovation in the field.

5. **3D Imaging and Virtual Reality**: 3D imaging and virtual reality technologies have the potential to revolutionize the way we study and experience ancient manuscripts. By creating three-dimensional, interactive models of manuscripts,

researchers can examine the physical structure, layout, and material properties of a text in ways that were previously impossible. Virtual reality platforms can also be used to recreate historical environments or simulate the experience of reading a manuscript in its original context, providing valuable insights into the cultural and social significance of these texts.

These advances in paleographic research have not only improved our understanding of ancient manuscripts but have also expanded the possibilities for future discoveries and innovations in the field. As new techniques and technologies continue to emerge, they will undoubtedly reshape the landscape of paleography, offering exciting opportunities for scholars to uncover the hidden secrets of our written past.

The Future of Paleography in New Testament Studies: Challenges and Prospects

The future of paleography in New Testament studies is filled with both challenges and prospects. As scholars continue to uncover, analyze, and interpret ancient manuscripts, the field of paleography will play an increasingly vital role in our understanding of the historical and textual context of the New Testament. Despite the many advances in recent years, the field is not without its obstacles. In this discussion, we will explore some of the key challenges and opportunities that lie ahead for paleography in New Testament studies.

1. **Access to Manuscripts**: One of the primary challenges faced by paleographers is gaining access to manuscripts, many of which are scattered across libraries, archives, and private collections around the world. In some cases, political instability, legal restrictions, or institutional barriers may prevent scholars from studying these valuable resources. The digitization of manuscripts has made it easier to share and access high-quality images of texts, but the process of digitization itself can be time-consuming and costly, particularly for fragile or damaged manuscripts. As a result,

there is a need for continued investment in digitization projects and initiatives to improve access to these crucial resources.

2. **Interdisciplinary Collaboration**: As our understanding of ancient manuscripts evolves, so too does the need for interdisciplinary collaboration. Paleographers must work closely with experts in related fields, such as codicology, papyrology, linguistics, archaeology, and computer science, to develop innovative research methods and draw upon diverse perspectives. Building strong networks and fostering collaboration between scholars from various disciplines will be crucial to advancing our knowledge of the New Testament and its textual history.

3. **Training and Education**: The specialized nature of paleography means that there is a need for ongoing training and education for scholars entering the field. As new techniques and technologies are developed, researchers must continually update their skills and knowledge to stay at the forefront of their discipline. This may involve creating and participating in workshops, conferences, and online courses, as well as promoting the study of paleography at the undergraduate and graduate levels.

4. **Technological Innovation**: The future of paleography in New Testament studies will be shaped by the continued development and adoption of new technologies. Machine learning, artificial intelligence, and advanced imaging techniques have already made significant contributions to the field, but there is still much room for growth and innovation. Researchers must continue to explore the potential of these tools and develop new methods for analyzing and interpreting ancient texts.

5. **Preservation and Conservation**: The physical preservation and conservation of ancient manuscripts is an ongoing challenge for paleographers and institutions alike. As many manuscripts are fragile and susceptible to deterioration, it is essential to invest in conservation efforts to ensure their long-

term survival. This may involve the development of new preservation techniques or the creation of climate-controlled environments for storing and displaying manuscripts.

In conclusion, the future of paleography in New Testament studies holds many exciting prospects, but also poses significant challenges. By addressing these challenges and capitalizing on new opportunities, researchers can continue to deepen our understanding of the New Testament and its historical context. As paleography continues to evolve and adapt to new technologies and methodologies, it will remain a vital and dynamic field within the broader landscape of biblical studies.

CHAPTER 3 The Sources of the New Testament Text

MS 193 The Crosby-Schøyen Codex, Egypt, 3rd c.
The oldest MS of Jonah and 1st Peter, and the oldest book in private ownership

The Formation of the New Testament Canon

The term "Bible" is widely used to refer to the sacred Scriptures and thus, it is interesting to explore its origin and meaning. The word "Bible" is derived from the Greek word bi·bli′a, which translates to "little books." This originates from the Greek word bi′blos, referring to the inner part of the papyrus plant, which was used to produce a writing material in ancient times. Various written works on this type of material were eventually known as bi·bli′a, and this term was used to describe writings, scrolls, books, documents, or scriptures, or even a library collection of small books.

Interestingly, the word "Bible" is generally not found in the text of English or other-language translations of the Holy Scriptures. However, by the second century BCE, the collection of inspired Hebrew Scriptures books was referred to as ta bi·bli′a in Greek. At

93

Daniel 9:2, the prophet wrote, "I myself, Daniel, discerned by the books..."; here, the Septuagint has bi′blois, the dative plural form of bi′blos. In 2 Timothy 4:13, Paul wrote, "When you come, bring...the scrolls [Greek, bi·bli′a]." The Greek words bi·bli′on and bi′blos appear more than 40 times in the Christian Greek Scriptures, typically translated as "scroll(s)" or "book(s)." Later, bi·bli′a was used as a singular word in Latin, and from there, the word "Bible" entered the English language.

It is crucial to note that the Bible is, in the fullest sense, God's Word and His inspired revelation to humanity. Although various individuals contributed to the inspired writing and translation of the original texts into today's written languages, the Bible is still regarded as the divine word. This is evident in the inspired writers' use of phrases such as "expression of Jehovah's mouth" (Deut. 8:3), "sayings of Jehovah" (Josh. 24:27), "commandments of Jehovah" (Ezra 7:11), "law of Jehovah" (Ps. 19:7), "word of Jehovah" (Isa. 38:4), "utterance of Jehovah" (Matt. 4:4), and "Jehovah's word" (1 Thess. 4:15).

The Bible, as it is known today, is a compilation of ancient divinely inspired documents written over a span of 16 centuries. Altogether, this collection of documents forms what Jerome aptly described in Latin as the Bibliotheca Divina, or the Divine Library. This library has a catalog, or an official list of publications, limited to those books that pertain to the library's scope and specialization. All unauthorized books are excluded. Jehovah God is the Great Librarian who establishes the standard for determining which writings should be included. Consequently, the Bible has a fixed catalog containing 66 books, all of which are products of God's guiding Holy Spirit.

The term "Bible canon" often refers to the collection or list of books recognized as genuine and inspired Scripture. Originally, a reed (Hebrew, qa·neh′) served as a measuring rod if a piece of wood was unavailable. The Apostle Paul used the Greek word ka·non′ to refer to both a "rule of conduct" and the "territory" measured out as his assignment (Gal. 6:16, footnote; 2 Cor. 10:13). Canonical books are thus those that are true, inspired, and worthy of being used as a benchmark in determining the right faith, doctrine, and conduct.

Utilizing books that are not "straight" as a plumb line would result in a "building" that is not true, ultimately failing the test of the Master Surveyor.

Determining Canonicity

Establishing Canonicity: What are the divine indications that determine the canonicity of the 66 books of the Bible? Firstly, the documents must address God's affairs on earth, guiding people towards his worship and fostering a deep respect for his name, work, and purposes. They must provide evidence of inspiration, indicating that they are products of the Holy Spirit (2 Pet. 1:21). These writings should not appeal to superstition or idolatry but rather encourage love and service to God. Additionally, none of the individual writings should conflict with the overall internal harmony; instead, each book must support the singular authorship of God by maintaining unity with the others. Furthermore, the writings should demonstrate accuracy down to the smallest details. Besides these fundamental criteria, there are other specific indications of inspiration, and therefore canonicity, depending on the content of each book.

The canonicity of the 27 New Testament books is determined by several factors that demonstrate their authenticity, inspiration, and authority:

1. **Apostolic Authority**: New Testament books must have a connection to an apostle or someone closely associated with an apostle. This connection ensures that the writings have a direct link to the teachings of Jesus Christ and are grounded in eyewitness accounts.

2. **Consistency in Doctrine**: The content of the books should align with the teachings of Jesus and the apostles. The books should present a coherent message and complement the other canonical books without contradictions or inconsistencies.

3. **Widespread Acceptance**: The early Christian community's acceptance of a book as authoritative played a significant role in determining its canonicity. The early church councils and

leaders considered the extent to which a book was being read, cited, and utilized in the worship and teaching of various Christian communities.

4. **Spiritual Impact**: The books should have a transformative effect on the lives of believers, providing guidance, edification, and encouragement in their faith. The Holy Spirit's influence on the writings and their ability to inspire and nurture spiritual growth is a key indicator of canonicity.

5. **Internal Evidence**: The writings should provide evidence of divine inspiration, displaying a unique depth of wisdom, insight, and prophetic understanding that could only come from God. This may include the fulfillment of prophecies, historical accuracy, or the profundity of the teachings.

In summary, the canonicity of the 27 New Testament books is determined by their apostolic authority, consistency in doctrine, widespread acceptance, spiritual impact, and internal evidence of divine inspiration. The early Christian community and its leaders carefully considered these factors in recognizing and affirming the New Testament canon.

Contrary to the claim made by the Roman Catholic Church that it was responsible for deciding which books should be included in the Bible canon, with reference to the Council of Carthage in 397 C.E., the reality is that the canon, encompassing the list of books constituting the Greek New Testament, had already been established by that time. Importantly, the canon was not determined by the decree of any council, but rather by the guidance of God's Holy Spirit—the same Spirit that inspired the composition of those books in the first place. The testimonies of later non-inspired catalogers carry value only as acknowledgments of the Bible canon, which had already been authorized by God's Spirit.

The Evidence of Early Catalogs

The Bible canon, specifically the Greek New Testament, had several fourth-century catalogs predating the Council of Carthage that are consistent with our current canon, with some excluding only Revelation. By the end of the second century, there was universal acceptance of the four Gospels, Acts, and 12 of Paul's letters, with only a few smaller writings being doubted in certain areas. This may be due to their limited initial circulation, which caused a delay in their acceptance as canonical.

One of the most intriguing early catalogs is the Muratorian Fragment, discovered by L. A. Muratori in the Ambrosian Library in Milan, Italy, and published in 1740. Though incomplete, it references Luke as the third Gospel, implying that it first mentioned Matthew and Mark. Dating back to the latter part of the second century C.E., the Latin fragment provides valuable insight into the early understanding of the New Testament canon. The following partial translation demonstrates its significance:

[...] The Muratorian Fragment serves as an early indicator of the canonical status of various New Testament books. It highlights the Gospels, the Acts of the Apostles, and Paul's epistles, as well as mentioning Jude's epistle and two of John's epistles. It also acknowledges the apocalypses of John and Peter, though some individuals did not want the latter read in church. This historical document reflects the evolving understanding of the New Testament canon, informed by divine inspiration and the acknowledgment of the Christian community.

According to the Muratorian Fragment, the New Testament canon is mainly composed of four Gospels, the Acts, thirteen epistles of Paul, the Apocalypse of John, and possibly three of John's epistles, along with Jude's epistle. It is worth noting that the fragment only mentions two epistles of John, likely the second and third, as the writer refers to himself as "the elder." Since the author of the Muratorian Fragment had already discussed the first epistle of John in connection with the Fourth Gospel, they felt it unnecessary to mention it again.

The absence of Peter's first epistle in the Muratorian Fragment may be due to the loss of a few words or a line where I Peter and the Apocalypse of John were named as accepted. This suggests that the canon, as perceived by the Muratorian Fragment, most likely included

I Peter. However, it is important to note that opposition to another of Peter's writings had not yet been entirely resolved.

In conclusion, the Muratorian Fragment provides a crucial perspective on the New Testament canon's composition during the late second century. The canon, as understood by the author of this historical document, comprises the four Gospels, the Acts, Paul's thirteen epistles, John's Apocalypse, and possibly three of John's epistles, Jude's epistle, and I Peter, while the debate surrounding additional Peter's writings persisted.

Origen, around 230 CE, acknowledged the books of Hebrews and James as inspired Scriptures, even though they are absent from the Muratorian Fragment. Although he mentioned that some individuals doubted their canonicity, this demonstrates that the majority of the Greek Scriptures were widely accepted, with only a few minor epistles facing skepticism. Later, Athanasius, Jerome, and Augustine supported the conclusions of earlier lists by defining the canon as the same 27 books that are presently recognized.

The majority of the catalogs present specific lists, indicating which books were accepted as canonical. The lists of Irenaeus, Clement of Alexandria, Tertullian, and Origen are derived from the quotations they made, revealing their perceptions of the referenced writings. These are further supplemented by the records of the early historian Eusebius. However, the absence of certain canonical writings from these writers' works does not imply that they are not canonical; it is possible that they simply did not refer to them in their writings due to personal choice or the topics discussed. One might wonder why there are no exact lists earlier than the Muratorian Fragment.

It was not until the emergence of critics like Marcion in the mid-second century CE that a debate arose concerning the books that Christians should accept. Marcion formed his own canon to align with his doctrines, using only select letters from the Apostle Paul and an edited version of the Gospel of Luke. The proliferation of apocryphal literature throughout the world at that time, along with Marcion's actions, prompted catalogers to specify which books they accepted as canonical.

Apocryphal Writings

Internal evidence substantiates the distinct separation made between the divinely inspired Christian writings and those that were considered spurious or uninspired. The Apocryphal works are markedly inferior in quality, often displaying elements of whimsy and immaturity. These writings are frequently characterized by inaccuracies and inconsistencies, further distinguishing them from their canonical counterparts.

Note the following statements by scholars on these noncanonical books:

"There is no question of any one's having excluded them from the New Testament: they have done that for themselves."— M. R. James, *The Apocryphal New Testament,* pages xi, xii.

"We have only to compare our New Testament books as a whole with other literature of the kind to realize how wide is the gulf which separates them from it. The uncanonical gospels, it is often said, are in reality the best evidence for the canonical."—G. Milligan, *The New Testament Documents,* page 228.

"It cannot be said of a single writing preserved to us from the early period of the Church outside the New Testament that it could properly be added to-day to the Canon."—K. Aland, *The Problem of the New Testament Canon,* page 24.

The individual writers of the Greek New Testament provide compelling evidence for the inspiration of these writings through several factors:

1. **Diversity of backgrounds**: The New Testament authors came from diverse backgrounds, including fishermen (Peter and John), a tax collector (Matthew), a physician (Luke), and a Pharisee (Paul). Despite these differences, their writings harmoniously convey a consistent message.

2. **Eyewitness accounts**: Many of the New Testament authors were eyewitnesses to the events they documented, providing first-hand accounts of the life, teachings, and miracles of Jesus

Christ. Their experiences lend credibility and authenticity to their writings.

3. **Fulfillment of prophecies**: The New Testament writings contain numerous instances where Old Testament prophecies are fulfilled, demonstrating the continuity between the Hebrew Scriptures and the Christian Greek Scriptures and reinforcing the divine inspiration of both.

4. **Transformation of the authors**: The profound transformation experienced by the writers, particularly Paul and Peter, serves as evidence of the divine influence on their lives. Their personal experiences and subsequent changes in their beliefs and actions support the notion that they were guided by a higher power.

5. **Miracles and supernatural events**: The New Testament writings document numerous miracles and supernatural events, such as the resurrection of Jesus and the outpouring of the Holy Spirit at Pentecost. These occurrences, which defy natural explanation, attest to divine intervention and support the claim of inspiration.

6. **Impact and endurance**: The impact of the Greek New Testament writings on individuals and societies throughout history is a testament to their profound influence. The fact that these texts have endured for centuries and continue to be studied, revered, and applied in the lives of countless individuals speaks to their extraordinary and inspired nature.

In summary, the diverse backgrounds of the authors, their eyewitness accounts, fulfillment of prophecies, personal transformation, documentation of miraculous events, and the enduring impact of their writings all contribute to the argument for the divine inspiration of the Greek New Testament.

Autographs: The Original Texts of the New Testament

The autographs, or original texts, of the New Testament are the initial manuscripts that were written by the biblical authors or their scribes. These texts are of utmost importance to biblical scholars and theologians because they are the closest we can come to the original words and ideas of the New Testament writers. Although none of the autographs have survived to the present day, an examination of the available manuscript evidence and the process of textual transmission provides insight into the nature and content of these original texts.

The New Testament consists of 27 books, which were composed between the late first and early second centuries CE. These texts were written by various authors, including the apostles, their associates, and other early Christian leaders. The books include four Gospels, which recount the life and teachings of Jesus Christ, the Acts of the Apostles, which narrates the early history of the Christian church, 21 epistles, which are letters addressing specific communities or individuals, and the book of Revelation, a prophetic work containing visions of the end times.

The autographs of the New Testament were likely written on papyrus, a plant-based writing material that was common in the ancient Mediterranean world. Papyrus was relatively inexpensive and readily available, making it a popular choice for the dissemination of early Christian writings. The texts were written in Koine Greek, a widely spoken form of the Greek language that facilitated communication across the diverse regions of the Roman Empire.

As the original texts of the New Testament were copied and recopied over time, variations inevitably emerged in the manuscripts. Scribes might accidentally omit or change words or phrases, or they might intentionally alter the text to clarify or harmonize passages. These variations have resulted in thousands of textual differences among the surviving New Testament manuscripts, which currently number over 5,800+ in Greek alone.

Despite the presence of these variations, the vast majority of them are minor and do not significantly impact the meaning of the text. Through the process of textual criticism, scholars have been able to reconstruct the likely wording of the autographs with a high degree of accuracy. Textual criticism involves comparing and evaluating the manuscript evidence, taking into account factors such as the age, geographical distribution, and textual family of each manuscript. By examining the patterns of agreement and disagreement among the manuscripts, scholars can make informed judgments about the original text of the New Testament.

The task of reconstructing the autographs is further aided by the early translations of the New Testament into other languages, such as Latin, Syriac, and Coptic. These translations, known as versions, often preserve readings that are not found in the Greek manuscripts and can help to clarify ambiguous passages. Additionally, quotations from the New Testament in the writings of early Christian authors, known as church fathers, provide valuable evidence for the text's original form and content.

Two significant discoveries relevant to the New Testament textual criticism are the Chester Beatty Papyri and the Bodmer Papyri.

The Chester Beatty Papyri, discovered in the 1930s, are a collection of ancient Greek papyrus manuscripts that include portions of both the Old and New Testaments. These papyri are of immense value to scholars because they are some of the earliest surviving copies of the New Testament texts. The collection includes:

1. **Papyrus 45 (P45)**: Contains portions of the four Gospels and the Acts of the Apostles, dating from 175-225 CE.

2. **Papyrus 46 (P46)**: Contains most of the Pauline epistles and is dated to around 110-150 CE. This manuscript is particularly significant as it is one of the oldest extant copies of Paul's letters.

3. **Papyrus 47 (P47)**: Contains a portion of the Book of Revelation and dates to 200-250 CE.

The Bodmer Papyri, discovered in the 1950s, are another important collection of early Christian texts, which include portions of both the Old and New Testaments in Greek and Coptic. Among the most significant New Testament manuscripts in this collection are:

1. **Papyrus 66 (P66)**: An almost complete copy of the Gospel of John, dating to around 110-150 CE. This manuscript is especially valuable because of its early date and the relatively well-preserved condition of the text.

2. **Papyrus 72 (P72)**: Contains the earliest known copies of the Epistles of Jude and 1-2 Peter, as well as some non-canonical Christian texts. It dates to 200-250 CE.

3. **Papyrus 75 (P75)**: Contains portions of the Gospels of Luke and John and dates to 175-225 CE. This papyrus is crucial for establishing the text of these two Gospels in the early Christian period.

Both the Chester Beatty Papyri and the Bodmer Papyri have significantly contributed to our understanding of the textual history of the New Testament. By providing early witnesses to the biblical texts, these collections have helped scholars reconstruct the original wording of the New Testament autographs and confirm the reliability of the transmission process over time.

In addition to the manuscript evidence, the study of the autographs of the New Testament can be informed by an examination of the historical, cultural, and literary context in which the texts were composed. By understanding the social and religious milieu of the first-century Mediterranean world, scholars can gain a deeper appreciation of the meaning and significance of the New Testament writings. This contextual approach to the study of the autographs can help to illuminate the historical Jesus and the early Christian communities that developed in the decades following his death and resurrection.

One essential aspect of this historical and cultural context is the diversity of early Christianity. As the New Testament texts were written by various authors addressing different audiences and responding to different concerns, it is crucial to understand the unique perspectives and theological emphases of each writer. This diversity is evident in the range of literary genres found in the New Testament, such as historical narrative (Gospels, Acts), letters (Pauline and General Epistles), and apocalyptic literature (Revelation). By recognizing the distinctive features of each genre and the particularities of each author's style and theology, scholars can more accurately reconstruct the original intentions and meanings of the New Testament autographs.

Furthermore, the study of the autographs can be enriched by considering the broader Greco-Roman and Jewish contexts in which the New Testament texts were composed. By exploring the philosophical, religious, and cultural influences that shaped the worldviews of the New Testament authors, scholars can better understand the intellectual currents and social dynamics that informed the early Christian movement. This approach can also shed light on the ways in which the New Testament texts engaged with, critiqued, or appropriated various elements of their contemporary environment.

Finally, the analysis of the autographs must take into account the process of canonization that led to the formation of the New Testament as a unified collection of authoritative texts. This process involved complex negotiations among early Christian communities regarding which writings should be considered inspired and authoritative. By examining the criteria that guided these decisions, such as apostolic authorship, antiquity, orthodoxy, and widespread acceptance, scholars can gain insight into how the diverse writings of the New Testament came to be recognized as a coherent and authoritative corpus.

In conclusion, the study of the autographs of the New Testament is a multifaceted endeavor that requires a thorough examination of the manuscript evidence, as well as a deep engagement with the historical, cultural, and literary context of the texts. By considering these various dimensions, scholars can work toward reconstructing the original wording and meaning of the New Testament writings, thereby enhancing our understanding of the foundations of the Christian faith and the development of the early Christian movement.

Early Manuscripts: Papyri, Uncials, and Minuscules

Papyri

The papyri New Testament manuscripts are a vital category of early Christian writings that provide valuable insights into the textual history of the New Testament. Papyri are made from the papyrus plant, which was a common writing material in the ancient Mediterranean world. These manuscripts are some of the oldest surviving copies of the New Testament texts, and they play a crucial role in textual criticism and the reconstruction of the original wording of the biblical texts.

1. **Discovery and preservation**: Papyrus manuscripts were first discovered in Egypt in the late 19th and early 20th centuries. The dry and arid climate of Egypt has allowed many papyri to survive for thousands of years. Since their discovery, numerous papyri fragments have been found in various locations, such as Oxyrhynchus, Nag Hammadi, and the Dead Sea region. These

manuscripts are now housed in various museums, libraries, and private collections worldwide.

2. **Significance**: The papyri manuscripts are significant for several reasons. Firstly, they provide early and, in some cases, the earliest evidence for the New Testament text, often dating back to the 2nd-4th centuries CE. This early dating allows scholars to study the textual history of the New Testament closer to its original composition. Secondly, the papyri offer insights into the diverse textual traditions and variations that existed among early Christian communities. Finally, the papyri can help scholars reconstruct the original wording of the biblical texts by comparing different manuscript readings and evaluating their likelihood of being closer to the autographs.

3. **Notable papyri collections**:

a) **Chester Beatty Papyri**: The Chester Beatty Papyri, discovered in the 1930s, are a collection of twelve early Greek papyrus manuscripts. They include portions of the Old and New Testaments and are considered some of the most important biblical papyri. Among them, P45, P46, and P47 are particularly significant for New Testament studies. P45 contains portions of the four Gospels and Acts, P46 contains most of Paul's Epistles, and P47 contains a portion of the Book of Revelation. These papyri date from the 2nd to the 4th centuries CE.

b) **Bodmer Papyri**: The Bodmer Papyri, discovered in the 1950s, are a collection of twenty-two papyrus manuscripts, including both biblical and non-biblical texts. Among them, P66, P72, and P75 are especially important for New Testament research. P66 is a near-complete copy of the Gospel of John, dating to around 110-15 CE. P72 contains the earliest known copies of the Epistles of Jude and 1-2 Peter and dates to 200-250 CE. P75, from the late 2nd or early 3rd century CE (175-225), contains portions of the Gospels of Luke and John.

4. **Textual criticism and the papyri**: Textual criticism is the scholarly discipline that seeks to establish the original wording of a text by comparing and evaluating different manuscript

readings. The papyri manuscripts are essential for this task, as they provide some of the earliest and most reliable evidence for the New Testament text. By analyzing the textual variants in the papyri, scholars can better understand the transmission and development of the biblical text over time. Moreover, the study of the papyri can reveal insights into the scribal practices, linguistic features, and cultural contexts of the early Christian communities that produced and used these manuscripts.

In conclusion, the papyri New Testament manuscripts are invaluable resources for understanding the textual history of the New Testament. They provide early and, in some cases, the earliest evidence for the biblical text and offer crucial insights into the diverse textual traditions and variations that existed among early Christian communities. By examining these manuscripts, scholars can reconstruct the original wording of the biblical texts and gain a deeper appreciation of the historical, cultural, and linguistic contexts in which they were composed. The ongoing study of the papyri manuscripts continues to shed light on the rich and complex textual history of the New Testament, enhancing our understanding of the development and transmission of these foundational Christian texts.

Uncials

The Uncials are a significant category of New Testament manuscripts that play a vital role in our understanding of the textual history of the New Testament. The term "Uncial" refers to a distinct style of writing that was employed in the early Christian world, characterized by large, rounded, and somewhat separated capital letters. Uncial manuscripts were generally written on parchment or vellum and produced between the 3rd and 9th centuries CE.

Several factors make the study of Uncial manuscripts particularly important for New Testament textual criticism. First, these manuscripts are among the oldest and most reliable witnesses to the biblical text, often predating the later minuscule manuscripts by several centuries. This early dating allows scholars to trace the development of the text and identify changes or variations that may have occurred in later copies.

Second, Uncial manuscripts often contain large portions of the New Testament, sometimes even complete books or collections of books. This comprehensive coverage of the biblical text enables scholars to examine the consistency and coherence of the text within a single manuscript tradition.

There are several key Uncial manuscripts that are especially significant for the study of the New Testament:

1. **Codex Sinaiticus (4th century CE)**: Discovered at the Saint Catherine Monastery on Mount Sinai, this manuscript contains the complete New Testament, as well as parts of the Old Testament. It is considered one of the most important biblical manuscripts due to its antiquity, accuracy, and completeness.

2. **Codex Vaticanus (4th century CE)**: Housed in the Vatican Library, Codex Vaticanus contains nearly the entire Bible, missing only parts of the Old Testament and a few sections of the New Testament. It is highly valued for its early date and accuracy.

3. **Codex Alexandrinus (5th century CE)**: Named after its place of origin in Alexandria, Egypt, this manuscript contains almost the entire Bible, with only a few passages missing. It is particularly significant for its inclusion of the Epistles of

Clement, an early Christian writing not found in other major Uncial manuscripts.

4. **Codex Ephraemi Rescriptus (5th century CE)**: A palimpsest, this manuscript contains portions of the Old and New Testaments written over an earlier, erased text. Despite the difficulties of reading the underlying text, it remains an important witness to the early biblical text.

5. **Codex Bezae (5th or 6th century CE)**: This bilingual manuscript contains the Gospels and Acts in both Greek and Latin. It is noteworthy for its numerous textual variants and unique readings, offering insights into the diversity of early Christian textual traditions.

In conclusion, the Uncial manuscripts are essential resources for understanding the development and transmission of the New Testament text. These ancient witnesses provide critical evidence for reconstructing the original wording of the biblical texts and offer valuable insights into the historical, cultural, and linguistic contexts in which they were composed. The study of Uncial manuscripts continues to enrich our understanding of the New Testament and its textual history, underscoring the importance of these precious documents for biblical scholarship.

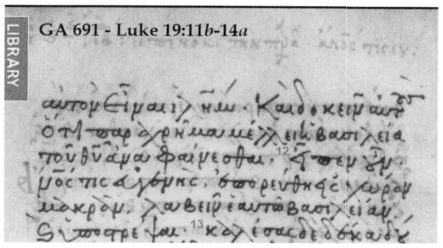

GA 691 - Luke 19:11*b*-14*a*

Minuscules

The Minuscule manuscripts are a crucial category of New Testament manuscripts, playing a vital role in understanding the textual history of the New Testament. Minuscules are distinguished by their small, cursive script, which was developed in the 9th century CE and subsequently became the dominant form of writing for Greek texts. These manuscripts are written on parchment or paper and typically date from the 9th century to the 16th century CE.

There are several reasons why Minuscule manuscripts are essential for the study of the New Testament text:

1. **Quantity**: Minuscule manuscripts are the most abundant category of New Testament manuscripts, with over 2,900 known copies. This large number provides scholars with a wealth of textual evidence for analyzing and comparing the biblical text across different times and geographical locations.

2. **Preservation**: Due to their relatively late dating, many Minuscule manuscripts have survived in better condition than their earlier counterparts, the Uncials and Papyri. This allows scholars to study more complete and legible texts, providing a clearer picture of the textual history and development of the New Testament.

3. **Textual Variants**: The sheer number of Minuscule manuscripts, combined with their diverse origins, has led to the discovery of numerous textual variants. By comparing these variations, scholars can better understand the transmission of the text and work to reconstruct the most likely original reading.

4. **Continuous Text**: Unlike earlier manuscripts, which often employed abbreviations and symbols, Minuscule manuscripts generally contain a continuous text, making them easier to read and analyze.

Some notable Minuscule manuscripts of the New Testament include:

1. **Minuscule 2427 (13th century CE)**: Also known as the "Freer Logion," this manuscript contains a unique variant in the Gospel of Mark, which has generated significant scholarly interest and debate.

2. **Minuscule 33 (9th century CE)**: Often referred to as the "Queen of the Minuscules," this manuscript is highly regarded for its textual accuracy and extensive marginal notes, which provide insights into the manuscript's history and use.

3. **Minuscule 565 (9th century CE)**: This manuscript is notable for its beautiful, artistic script and unique textual readings, which are of great interest to scholars studying the textual history of the New Testament.

4. **Family 13 (11th-15th centuries CE)**: A group of Minuscule manuscripts that share distinctive textual features, providing evidence of a common textual tradition and offering insights into the transmission and development of the New Testament text.

5. **Minuscule 1 (12th century CE)**: Also known as the "Basel Minuscule," this manuscript is valued for its careful and accurate copying, as well as its extensive marginal notes and commentary.

In summary, the Minuscule manuscripts are invaluable resources for the study of the New Testament textual history. The vast number of these manuscripts provides scholars with an unparalleled wealth of evidence for analyzing and reconstructing the biblical text. By examining the unique features, textual variants, and historical contexts of these manuscripts, scholars can gain a deeper understanding of the development and transmission of the New Testament, contributing to a more accurate and nuanced picture of the biblical text.

Important Biblical Codices: Vaticanus, Sinaiticus, Alexandrinus, and Bezae

Codex Vaticanus

Codex Vaticanus (also known as Vaticanus B or Codex B) is one of the oldest and most important extant Greek manuscripts of the Bible, dating back to the 4th century CE. It holds immense significance in the field of biblical studies and textual criticism, as it provides critical information for understanding the development and transmission of the biblical text. The codex is housed in the Vatican Library, where it has been since at least the 15th century.

1. **Description and Contents**: Codex Vaticanus is a large parchment codex, consisting of 759 leaves and measuring approximately 27 x 27 cm. It is written in Greek uncial script, which features large, distinct, and rounded letters, with three columns per page. The manuscript originally contained the entire Old Testament, including the Septuagint (the Greek translation of the Hebrew Bible), as well as the New Testament and some early Christian writings, such as the Epistle of Barnabas and portions of the Shepherd of Hermas. However, parts of the manuscript have been lost or damaged over time, and some books are incomplete.

2. **Textual Features**: Codex Vaticanus is considered one of the best witnesses to the Alexandrian text-type, which is characterized by its relative accuracy, brevity, and polished

style compared to other text-types. It is particularly valuable for its early and reliable representation of the Septuagint, and it is a key source for reconstructing the original text of the New Testament. The manuscript exhibits numerous corrections and revisions made by different scribes over the centuries, providing insight into the textual history and the scribal practices of the time.

3. **Discovery and Study**: Although Codex Vaticanus has been in the Vatican Library for centuries, its significance was not widely recognized until the 19th century. The renowned German scholar Constantin von Tischendorf was granted access to the codex in the mid-19th century and published its text, bringing its importance to the attention of biblical scholars worldwide. Since then, Codex Vaticanus has become a cornerstone for modern critical editions of the Greek Bible, such as the Nestle-Aland Novum Testamentum Graece and the United Bible Societies' Greek New Testament.

4. **Relationship to Other Manuscripts**: Codex Vaticanus, along with Codex Sinaiticus and Codex Alexandrinus, is part of the group of the three earliest and most significant biblical manuscripts. Codex Sinaiticus, also a 4th-century manuscript, is especially important for its complete New Testament text, while Codex Alexandrinus, from the 5th century, contains the entire Bible with some additional early Christian writings. Together, these three manuscripts provide essential information for the study of the early text of the Bible and the history of its transmission.

In conclusion, Codex Vaticanus is a critically important Greek manuscript of the Bible that has significantly contributed to our understanding of the biblical text's early history and transmission. As one of the oldest extant witnesses to the Alexandrian text-type, it has played a crucial role in shaping modern critical editions of the Greek Bible and remains an invaluable resource for biblical scholars and textual critics.

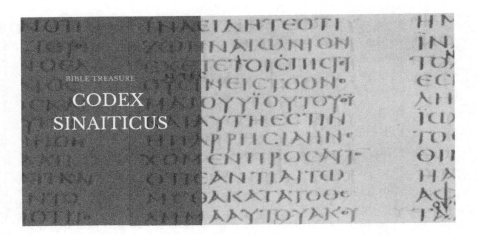

Codex Sinaiticus

Codex Sinaiticus, also known as א or Aleph, is one of the most significant and oldest extant manuscripts of the Greek Bible, dating to the mid-4th century CE. It is an invaluable source for biblical scholars and textual critics, as it provides critical information on the early transmission and development of the biblical text. The codex is currently preserved in various institutions, with the majority of the manuscript held at the British Library in London.

1. **Description and Contents**: Codex Sinaiticus is a parchment codex comprising 400 leaves, each measuring approximately 38 x 34.5 cm. It is written in Greek uncial script, characterized by large, distinct, and rounded letters, with four columns per page. The manuscript originally contained the entire Old Testament, including the Septuagint (the Greek translation of the Hebrew Bible), as well as the complete New Testament, and some early Christian writings, such as the Epistle of Barnabas and the Shepherd of Hermas. Over time, some portions of the manuscript have been lost or damaged, resulting in gaps within certain books.

2. **Textual Features**: Codex Sinaiticus is considered an important witness to the Alexandrian text-type, which is characterized by its relative accuracy, brevity, and polished

style compared to other text-types. It is particularly valuable for its early and reliable representation of the Septuagint, and it is a key source for reconstructing the original text of the New Testament. The manuscript displays numerous corrections and revisions made by different scribes over the centuries, providing insight into the textual history and scribal practices of the time.

3. **Discovery and Study**: The story of Codex Sinaiticus's discovery is intriguing. It was found by the German scholar Constantin von Tischendorf during his visits to Saint Catherine's Monastery on Mount Sinai in the 19th century. In 1844, Tischendorf discovered 43 leaves of the codex and later returned in 1859 to find the majority of the remaining manuscript. The codex was subsequently presented to Tsar Alexander II of Russia, who sponsored its publication. In 1933, the Soviet government sold the manuscript to the British Library, where it is now held.

The publication and study of Codex Sinaiticus have significantly impacted the field of biblical studies, particularly textual criticism. The manuscript has been extensively analyzed, and its text has served as a basis for modern critical editions of the Greek Bible, such as the Nestle-Aland Novum Testamentum Graece and the United Bible Societies' Greek New Testament.

4. **Relationship to Other Manuscripts**: Codex Sinaiticus, along with Codex Vaticanus and Codex Alexandrinus, is part of the group of the three earliest and most significant biblical manuscripts. Codex Vaticanus, also a 4th-century manuscript, is especially important for its representation of the Septuagint, while Codex Alexandrinus, from the 5th century, contains the entire Bible with some additional early Christian writings. Together, these three manuscripts provide essential information for the study of the early text of the Bible and the history of its transmission.

In conclusion, Codex Sinaiticus is an indispensable Greek manuscript of the Bible that has considerably contributed to our understanding of the early history and transmission of the biblical text. As one of the oldest and most complete extant witnesses to the Alexandrian text-type, it has played a crucial role in shaping modern critical editions of the Greek Bible and remains an invaluable resource for biblical scholars and textual critics.

Codex Alexandrinus

Codex Alexandrinus, designated as "A" or "02," is a highly significant and relatively complete manuscript of the Greek Bible, dating to the early 5th century CE. It is an essential resource for biblical scholars and textual critics, providing crucial insights into the early transmission and development of the biblical text. The codex is currently housed in the British Library in London.

1. **Description and Contents**: Codex Alexandrinus is a parchment codex containing 773 leaves, each measuring approximately 32 x 26 cm. It is written in Greek uncial script, characterized by large, distinct, and rounded letters, with two columns per page. The manuscript originally contained the complete Old Testament, including the Septuagint (the Greek translation of the Hebrew Bible), as well as the New Testament, and several early Christian writings, such as the First and Second Epistles of Clement. Over time, some

portions of the manuscript have been lost or damaged, resulting in gaps within certain books.

2. **Textual Features**: Codex Alexandrinus is considered an important witness to the Byzantine text-type, characterized by its tendency for expansion and harmonization of parallel passages. However, in some sections, especially the Gospels, the text exhibits mixed characteristics with Alexandrian and Western readings. The manuscript is particularly valuable for its early and relatively complete representation of the Septuagint, and it is an important source for reconstructing the original text of the New Testament.

3. **History and Study**: The exact origins of Codex Alexandrinus remain uncertain, but it is believed to have been produced in Alexandria, Egypt, or its surrounding region. The manuscript was brought to Constantinople in the early 17th century and later presented to King Charles I of England by the Orthodox Patriarch Cyril Lucar in 1627. After the British Museum was established in 1753, the codex was transferred to its manuscript collection, and it is now held in the British Library.

The publication and study of Codex Alexandrinus have significantly impacted the field of biblical studies, particularly textual criticism. The manuscript has been extensively analyzed, and its text has been considered in the preparation of modern critical editions of the Greek Bible, such as the Nestle-Aland Novum Testamentum Graece and the United Bible Societies' Greek New Testament.

4. **Relationship to Other Manuscripts**: Codex Alexandrinus, together with Codex Vaticanus and Codex Sinaiticus, forms the group of the three earliest and most significant biblical manuscripts. Codex Vaticanus, a 4th-century manuscript, is especially important for its representation of the Septuagint, while Codex Sinaiticus, also from the 4th century, contains the entire Bible and some additional early Christian writings. These three manuscripts provide essential information for the study of the early text of the Bible and the history of its transmission.

In conclusion, Codex Alexandrinus is a vital Greek manuscript of the Bible that has contributed greatly to our understanding of the early history and transmission of the biblical text. As one of the oldest and relatively complete extant witnesses to the Byzantine text-type with mixed characteristics, it plays a critical role in shaping modern critical editions of the Greek Bible and remains an invaluable resource for biblical scholars and textual critics.

Codex Bezae

Codex Bezae, also known as Codex Cantabrigiensis or designated as "D" or "05," is a distinctive and significant ancient manuscript of the Greek New Testament and the Old Latin version. The manuscript, dating to the 5th century CE, contains the Gospels and Acts of the Apostles in both Greek and Latin, with the two languages presented side by side in parallel columns. Codex Bezae is housed at the Cambridge University Library in England.

1. **Description and Contents**: Codex Bezae is a parchment codex containing 406 extant leaves, each measuring approximately 26 x 21.5 cm. It is written in Greek uncial script and Latin script, with one column per page for each language. The manuscript originally contained the complete text of the four Gospels and Acts of the Apostles, as well as the General

Epistle of James and the Third Epistle of John. However, portions of the text have been lost over time, and the surviving leaves are incomplete.

2. **Textual Features**: Codex Bezae is known for its unique textual characteristics, representing the Western text-type, which is marked by extensive additions, omissions, and variations from the standard text. The manuscript is particularly famous for its unusual readings, including some that are not found in any other extant manuscript. The text is often characterized as "free" or "wild," reflecting the scribe's apparent willingness to alter the text, either intentionally or unintentionally. This makes Codex Bezae a crucial resource for understanding the diversity of early Christian textual traditions.

3. **History and Study**: The origin and provenance of Codex Bezae are uncertain, although it is generally believed to have been produced in either southern France or western North Africa. The manuscript was acquired by the French humanist and biblical scholar Theodore Beza in the 16th century, and he later donated it to the University of Cambridge in 1581. Since then, it has been the subject of extensive study and analysis by scholars seeking to understand its unique textual features and the broader history of the New Testament text.

4. **Relationship to Other Manuscripts**: Codex Bezae is one of several important early witnesses to the Western text-type, which includes other Greek, Latin, and Syriac manuscripts. Among these, Codex Bezae is considered one of the most significant due to its bilingual nature and the extent of its textual variations. Other notable manuscripts representing the Western text-type include Codex Washingtonianus, Codex Claromontanus, and the Old Latin versions of the New Testament.

5. **Impact on Biblical Scholarship**: The study of Codex Bezae has had a considerable impact on the field of biblical scholarship, particularly in the area of textual criticism. Its unique textual features have led scholars to reconsider

assumptions about the transmission and development of the New Testament text and to explore the complex relationships between various textual traditions. The manuscript has also been influential in the development of theories about the role of scribes and the processes of textual change in the early Christian period.

In conclusion, Codex Bezae is an invaluable manuscript that offers a unique perspective on the textual history of the New Testament. Its distinctive textual features, bilingual nature, and historical significance make it an essential resource for understanding the development and diversity of early Christian textual traditions, as well as the broader history of the New Testament text.

Textual Families: Alexandrian, Western, Byzantine, and Caesarean

Alexandrian Text-Type

The Alexandrian text type, one of the primary text types of the Greek New Testament, is of significant importance for biblical scholars and textual critics in their efforts to understand and reconstruct the original text of the New Testament. This text type is named after Alexandria, Egypt, which was a major center of learning and manuscript production during the early Christian period. The Alexandrian text type is characterized by several distinctive features, making it a valuable resource for textual analysis and comparison.

1. **Age**: The Alexandrian text type is considered to be one of the oldest and most reliable text types, with its origins tracing back to the early 2nd century CE. Some of the earliest and most important biblical manuscripts, such as Codex Vaticanus (B) and Codex Sinaiticus (א), belong to the Alexandrian text type, and their early dating provides valuable insights into the early transmission of the New Testament text.

2. **Geographical Distribution**: Although named after Alexandria, the Alexandrian text type was not limited to Egypt.

Manuscripts belonging to this text type have been discovered across a broad geographical area, including regions such as Asia Minor, Palestine, and North Africa. This widespread distribution suggests that the Alexandrian text type was highly regarded and widely used during the early Christian period.

3. **Textual Characteristics**: The Alexandrian text type is known for its shorter, more concise readings when compared to other text types, such as the Byzantine text type. It is often considered to be more accurate and closer to the original text, as it tends to avoid additions, harmonizations, and other scribal alterations found in other text types. This focus on accuracy and preservation of the original text has led many scholars to view the Alexandrian text type as the most reliable and authoritative text type of the New Testament.

4. **Manuscript Evidence**: Some of the most important early biblical manuscripts belong to the Alexandrian text type, providing crucial evidence for the study and reconstruction of the New Testament text. These manuscripts include:

- **Papyrus 75 (P75, 2nd/3rd century CE)**: Contains the Gospels of Luke and John and is considered one of the most reliable early witnesses to the New Testament text.

- **Codex Vaticanus (B, 4th century CE)**: One of the earliest and most complete copies of the Greek Bible, containing both the Old and New Testaments. It is considered one of the most important witnesses to the Alexandrian text type.

- **Codex Sinaiticus ([א], 4th century CE)**: Another early and nearly complete copy of the Greek Bible, discovered at the Monastery of St. Catherine on Mount Sinai. It is an essential witness to the Alexandrian text type and provides valuable insights into early textual variants and scribal practices.

In conclusion, the Alexandrian text type is an invaluable resource for understanding the textual history of the New Testament. Its early origins, widespread distribution, and textual accuracy make it a critical text type for scholars in their efforts to reconstruct the original text of the New Testament. The study of the Alexandrian text type, along with other text types such as the Byzantine, Western, and Caesarean, contributes to a deeper and more nuanced understanding of the development and transmission of the biblical text throughout history.

Western Text-Type

The Western text type is one of the primary text types of the Greek New Testament, and it plays a crucial role in the study of the textual history and transmission of the New Testament. The Western text type is characterized by several distinctive features, making it an important resource for textual analysis and comparison.

1. **Age and Origin**: The Western text type is believed to have originated in the early 2nd century CE. Although the exact geographical origin of this text type is uncertain, it is generally associated with the Western regions of the Roman Empire, including North Africa, Italy, and Gaul. The Western text type may have developed as an independent textual tradition, or it may have branched off from an earlier common ancestor shared with other text types.

2. **Textual Characteristics**: The Western text type is known for its longer, more expansive readings when compared to other text types, such as the Alexandrian text type. It often contains additions, paraphrases, and harmonizations not found in other text types, which might reflect the scribes' attempts to clarify or expand upon the biblical text. While these characteristics can make the Western text type less reliable in terms of preserving the original text, they offer valuable insights into the interpretive tendencies and theological concerns of the early Christian communities that produced and used these manuscripts.

3. **Manuscript Evidence**: Some important early biblical manuscripts belong to the Western text type, providing critical evidence for the study and reconstruction of the New Testament text. These manuscripts include:

- **Codex Bezae (D, 5th century CE)**: A bilingual Greek-Latin manuscript containing the Gospels and Acts, with a small portion of 3 John. It is one of the primary witnesses to the Western text type and displays a unique and idiosyncratic textual tradition.

- **Papyrus 45 (P45, 3rd century CE)**: Contains portions of the Gospels and Acts, and it exhibits some Western readings, although its textual affiliation is complex and not exclusively Western. In Matthew, Luke and John, it is between Alexandrian and Western manuscripts. In the book of Acts is shows great affinity with the great uncials: ℵ, A, B. C.

- **Old Latin (2nd century CE onwards) and Old Syriac (3rd century CE onwards) versions**: These early translations of the Greek New Testament into Latin and Syriac, respectively, often reflect Western textual readings and provide additional evidence for the Western text type.

4. **Patristic Evidence**: Early Church Fathers such as Tertullian, Cyprian, and Augustine, who wrote in Latin and were based in the Western regions of the Roman Empire, often quote the New Testament in ways that reflect Western textual readings. Their writings provide important indirect evidence for the Western text type and its circulation and usage within the early Christian communities.

In conclusion, the Western text type is a vital resource for understanding the textual history of the New Testament. Its distinctive textual characteristics, early origins, and diverse manuscript evidence provide a unique perspective on the development and transmission of the biblical text throughout history. The study of the Western text type, along with other text types such as the Alexandrian, Byzantine, and Caesarean, contributes to a richer and more nuanced understanding of the complex textual history of the New Testament.

Byzantine Text-Type

The Byzantine text type, also known as the Majority text or Traditional text, is one of the major text types of the Greek New Testament. It is named after the Byzantine Empire, where it became the dominant form of the Greek New Testament text from the 4th century CE onwards. The Byzantine text type is notable for its extensive manuscript evidence and its influence on the development of the Textus Receptus, which served as the basis for early English translations such as the King James Version.

1. **Origin and Development**: The Byzantine Text, also known as the Majority Text, was not the result of a single revision but rather a gradual process that spanned several centuries. The earliest Byzantine manuscripts date from the 4th century, but the Byzantine Text as a whole did not emerge until the 5th or 6th century. With the rise of the Byzantine Empire this text type gained prominence and became the standard form of the Greek New Testament in the Eastern Orthodox Church. The Byzantine text type continued to be copied and transmitted throughout the Middle Ages and into the early modern period.

2. **Textual Characteristics**: Bruce M. Metzger writes, "It is characterized chiefly by lucidity and completeness. The framers of this text sought to smooth away any harshness of language, to combine two or more divergent readings into one expanded reading (called conflation), and to harmonize divergent parallel passages. This conflated text, produced perhaps at Antioch in Syria, was taken to Constantinople, whence it was distributed widely throughout the Byzantine Empire."[1] This led to a more uniform and consistent textual tradition, but also raises concerns about the accuracy of the Byzantine text type in preserving the original wording of the New Testament.

---

[1] Bruce Manning Metzger, United Bible Societies, *A Textual Commentary on the Greek New Testament, Second Edition a Companion Volume to the United Bible Societies' Greek New Testament (4th Rev. Ed.)* (London; New York: United Bible Societies, 1994), xxi.

3. **Manuscript Evidence**: The majority of the surviving Greek New Testament manuscripts belong to the Byzantine text type, making it the most extensively attested text type. These manuscripts range from the 4th century CE to the invention of the printing press in the 15th century CE. Some of the most notable Byzantine manuscripts include:

   - **Codex Alexandrinus (A, 5th century CE)**: Although it contains some non-Byzantine readings, particularly in the Gospels, it is generally classified as a Byzantine text type witness for the rest of the New Testament.

   - **Codex Ephraemi Rescriptus (C, 5th century CE)**: A palimpsest manuscript with a primarily Byzantine text in the later portions of the New Testament.

   - **Minuscule manuscripts**: The vast majority of the minuscule Greek New Testament manuscripts (9th century CE onwards) belong to the Byzantine text type, providing extensive evidence for this textual tradition.

4. The Textus Receptus and English Translations: The Byzantine text type played a significant role in the development of the Textus Receptus, the Greek text compiled by Erasmus in the 16th century CE, which served as the basis for early English translations such as the King James Version. Although later scholarship and the discovery of earlier Alexandrian manuscripts have led to a reevaluation of the relative value of the Byzantine text type, its influence on the history of Bible translation and its vast manuscript evidence make it an essential resource for understanding the textual history of the New Testament.

In conclusion, the Byzantine text type is a critical element in the study of the textual history of the New Testament. Its widespread manuscript attestation, distinct textual characteristics, and historical influence on Bible translations provide a valuable perspective on the development and transmission of the New Testament text. The study of the Byzantine text type, alongside other text types such as the

Alexandrian, Western, and Caesarean, contributes to a more comprehensive understanding of the complex textual history of the New Testament.

Caesarean Text- Type

The Caesarean text-type is a proposed classification of some Greek New Testament manuscripts, named after the city of Caesarea in Palestine where it was thought to have originated. It is considered to be one of the less well-defined text-types, and its existence as a distinct and coherent group of manuscripts is debated among textual scholars. Nonetheless, it has attracted attention due to its possible early origin and the unique readings found in some of its associated manuscripts.

1. **Origin and Development**: The Caesarean text-type is thought to have emerged in the early Christian period, possibly as early as the 2nd or 3rd century CE. It is named after Caesarea in Palestine, where the early church father Origen lived and worked, and where the library of Pamphilus contained many biblical manuscripts. Scholars originally proposed that this text-type might have been the result of Origen's editorial work, although more recent research has cast doubt on this theory.

2. **Textual Characteristics**: The Caesarean text-type is characterized by a combination of readings found in both the Alexandrian and Western text-types, along with unique readings not found elsewhere. It is considered to be shorter and more concise than the Byzantine text-type but less polished than the Alexandrian text-type. The Caesarean text-type is thought to be most clearly represented in the Gospels, particularly in Matthew and Mark, with less evidence for its existence in the other New Testament books.

3. **Manuscript Evidence**: The manuscript evidence for the Caesarean text-type is limited, and its classification is based primarily on shared readings among a small group of

126

manuscripts. Some of the notable manuscripts associated with the Caesarean text-type include:

- **Codex Koridethi (Θ, 9th century CE)**: An important witness to the Caesarean text-type in the Gospels, particularly in Matthew and Mark.

- **Minuscule 565 (9th century CE)**: A manuscript containing the Gospels with Caesarean readings, especially in Mark.

- **Minuscule 1 (12th century CE)**: Also known as "Basiliensis," this manuscript contains the Gospels and has been associated with the Caesarean text-type, primarily in Mark.

- **The Gospel of Mark in the manuscript family 1**, f1 (comprising minuscules 1, 118, 131, and 209), is also considered to represent the Caesarean text-type.

4. **Scholarly Debate**: The existence of the Caesarean text-type as a distinct and coherent group of manuscripts is a matter of debate among textual scholars. Some argue that the shared readings among the associated manuscripts can be better explained by coincidental agreement or by contamination from other text-types. Others maintain that the Caesarean text-type represents a genuine early tradition of the New Testament text that warrants further investigation.

In conclusion, the Caesarean text-type is a proposed and debated classification of Greek New Testament manuscripts that potentially offers insights into the early textual history of the New Testament. While the evidence for its existence is limited and its status as a distinct text-type is contested, the unique readings found in some of its associated manuscripts continue to be of interest to textual scholars.

Ancient Translations: Old Latin, Syriac, Coptic, and Others

The Syriac Versions

The Syriac Versions refer to a series of translations of the Bible into the Syriac language, which was spoken in Syria during the second half of the second century. The need for a Syriac translation of the Scriptures arose due to the fact that most of the population in Syria was familiar with Syriac and not Greek, which was the language of the original texts.

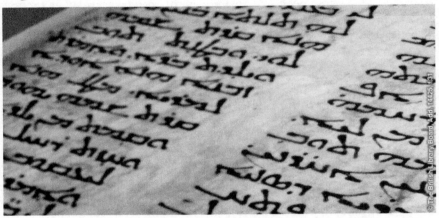

The center of Syriac-speaking Christianity was Edessa, a town in southeast Turkey that became the most important bishopric in Syria. The church there was destroyed in 201 during a flood but may be the oldest known Christian edifice. Many large and well-built villages developed up to the desert edge, and the gospel had a great number of devoted followers throughout all that region.

Parts of the New Testament began to circulate in Syria in what is called the Old Syriac version at the close of the second or beginning of the third century. Only two manuscripts of this version, both containing text from the Gospels, have survived. These are known as the Curetonian and the Sinaitic Syriac manuscripts, written in the fifth and fourth centuries, respectively.

Tatian, a native of Assyria who had become a Christian in Rome between 150 and 165, compiled an edition of the four Gospels in one continuous narrative. This work was known as the Diatessaron (Greek for "through the Four"), and it was used by Christian congregations throughout the Middle East for several centuries.

The form of the Syriac Bible that came to prevail in Eastern churches has, since the ninth century, been called the Peshitta, meaning "simple" or "common." Its origins are shrouded in uncertainty, but it is known that the Peshitta Old Testament was likely the work of Jews. There appear to be tenuous links with the Targums in the Pentateuch, at least. Those who suppose Christian, or Jewish Christian, origin usually locate the translation in Edessa. On the assumption of Jewish origin, however, one may think either of Edessa or of Adiabene, the Jewish kingdom east of the Tigris.

The Peshitta version is the authoritative biblical text of Syriac-speaking churches, including the Syrian Orthodox, Church of the East (or Chaldean Christians), Syrian Catholics, Malabar (or St. Thomas) Christians, and the Syro-Malankarese Church. It contains only twenty-two books since the Syrian church does not (and does not) accept as canonical the four lesser General Epistles (2 Peter, 2 and 3 John, and Jude) and the Book of Revelation.

Following the completion of the Peshitta in the fourth or fifth century, two other Syriac versions of the New Testament were made. At the beginning of the sixth century, Philoxenus, the Jacobite bishop of Mabbug (Hierapolis) in eastern Syria, commissioned Polycarp to revise the Peshitta version on the basis of Greek manuscripts. Now, seemingly for the first time in Syriac, to the twenty-two books included in the Peshitta New Testament, the other five books were added. This work was completed in 508.

In the year 616, the Philoxenian version of the New Testament was drastically revised throughout by Thomas of Harkel. He made use of readings derived from Greek manuscripts in the library of the Enaton near Alexandria. The chief characteristic of the Harclean version is its slavish adaptation to the Greek, to such an extent that here and there even clarity is sacrificed.

Finally, there is another Syriac version, more properly designated the Christian Palestinian Aramaic version. Its language is the Aramaic dialect used in Palestine during the early Christian centuries, and its script resembles somewhat the Estrangela Syriac script. This version is also known as the Old Syriac Version or the Palaestina Syriaca. It was used by the Syriac-speaking Christians in Palestine and Egypt during the sixth, seventh, and following centuries.

The significance of these Syriac versions can be appreciated from the fact that they became the basis, at least in part, of translations in other languages. The early Armenian rendering of the Gospels, made in the fifth century, shows influence from the Old Syriac text, while the Old Testament generally follows the Hexaplaric recension of the Septuagint. The Georgian Bible, completed by the end of the sixth century, had an Armenian-Syriac foundation. The Peshitta Syriac version was also the basis of the Sogdian and some of the Arabic versions.

In conclusion, the Syriac versions played a significant role in the transmission of the Scriptures, particularly in the Eastern Christian world. They were produced by scholars and church leaders who had a deep knowledge of both the Scriptures and the Syriac language. While they were not without their flaws and inconsistencies, they served as important witnesses to the text of the Bible and helped to spread the Christian faith to Syriac-speaking peoples throughout the centuries.

The Latin Versions

The Latin versions of the Bible, and specifically Jerome's Latin Vulgate, had an immense impact on Western culture. This influence extends beyond religious matters and played a role in the development of Latin into the Romance languages. Jerome's terminology, including words such as salvation, regeneration, justification, and sacrament, has been adopted by both Roman Catholics and Protestants.

The origins of the Latin versions are unclear, but it is likely that the Old Latin versions of the Scriptures were in circulation in North Africa by the end of the second century CE. There was no uniform rendering, and some books were translated multiple times by various translators. The Old Testament was based on a pre-Hexaplaric form of the Greek Septuagint.

The Old Latin versions were often painfully literal and lacked polish. There were differences in the quotations of the same passages, indicating that the translations were not uniform. However, the Old Latin was a living creation that constantly grew, and its roots can be found in the practice of double reading of Holy Scripture during divine services, first in the Greek text and then in the vernacular tongue.

The diversity among the Old Latin witnesses led to the development of three types or families of texts: the African, European, and Italian. Augustine lamented the confusing diversity among Latin manuscripts of the New Testament by the close of the fourth century.

In 383, Pope Damasus urged Jerome, the most learned Christian scholar of his day, to produce a uniform and dependable text of the Latin Scriptures. Jerome's first inclination was to decline the invitation, but he eventually agreed to revise a text of the Bible in use at Rome. The shocking diversity among the Old Latin manuscripts prompted Jerome to take on the task.

Jerome was born in Dalmatia near the Adriatic coast and received a first-class education in grammar and rhetoric at Rome. He became familiar with Latin classics and became a follower of Ciceronian traditions. However, he did not learn Greek until he went to Antioch in his late twenties. He learned Hebrew much later, first during his five years of ascetic seclusion in the Syrian desert of Chalcis and afterwards in Bethlehem.

Jerome revised the Old Latin text only when necessary, retaining familiar phraseology in other cases. His revision of the Latin Bible provoked criticism and anger, but opposition subsided over time. For nearly a thousand years, the Vulgate was used as the recognized text of Scripture throughout western Europe. It was the basis of pre-Reformation vernacular Scriptures and the first printed Bibles in various languages.

The Coptic Versions

The Coptic language developed as the latest phase of the ancient Egyptian language, which was originally written in hieroglyphs, hieratic, and demotic scripts. Egyptian Christians began using Greek letters, including seven signs from a more cursive variety of Egyptian demotic, to express their native language. This form of Egyptian, known as Coptic, eventually incorporated a large number of Greek words related to Christian doctrine, life, and worship.

Coptic literature is mostly religious and consists of translations from Greek, including versions of the Bible, apocrypha of the Old and New Testaments, legends of the apostles, and the lives and martyrdoms of saints. The topographical conditions of the Nile valley contributed to the growth and differentiation of similar but distinct dialects in Coptic, which differ in phonetics, vocabulary, and syntax. The major Coptic dialects in which significant portions of the Scriptures are extant include Sahidic, Bohairic, Achmimic, sub-Achmimic, Middle Egyptian, and Fayyumic.

Translations into various Coptic dialects were first made in the third or fourth century CE and were subsequently revised. Sahidic is the oldest and most important dialect, and a considerable number of extant portions of manuscripts can be used to reconstruct the major part of the Old Testament, including a fairly complete Pentateuch. Versions of the Psalms exist in many manuscripts, but the most important is one from the sixth century CE that is complete and contains Psalm 151.

Most scholars agree that the rendering of the Old Testament was made from copies of the Greek Septuagint since it is unlikely that there had been any appreciable amount of Judaistic proselytizing that would have called for a translation of the Hebrew Scriptures into Coptic.

In the early twentieth century, archaeologists discovered a large collection of manuscripts, almost all of them written in Sahidic, near the southern border of the province of the Fayyum. The collection, which comprises fifty-six biblical as well as patristic and hagiographical works, was acquired by the Pierpont Morgan Library in New York and has been published in a magnificent facsimile edition of sixty-three volumes. Other famous collections that include Sahidic manuscripts of the Bible are the Chester Beatty collection in Dublin and the Martin Bodmer collection in Cologny-Geneva.

Bohairic is the latest of the several Coptic versions and shows the influence of Sahidic. Nevertheless, this version must form the basis of any study of the Coptic texts. It is the only version that is completely preserved, and its text is attested throughout by several manuscripts. The dialect ultimately became the accepted Bible in Egypt, and it survived as the ecclesiastical and liturgical language of the Coptic Church even after Arabic had been adopted as the speech of everyday life.

One of the earliest manuscripts written in the sub-Achmimic dialect is an almost complete copy of the Gospel according to John, now in the library of the British and Foreign Bible Society kept at Cambridge University. It is clear that six numbered pages or three leaves of text are missing at the beginning and end of the codex. The handwriting bears a strong resemblance to that of the mid-fourth-century copy of the Greek Bible known as Codex Vaticanus, with allowances being made for the fact that one is on papyrus and the other on parchment.

Along with the influence of the Greek Septuagint, the Coptic versions of the Old Testament frequently show a relationship with the Old Latin versions. For example, the Achmimic version sometimes agrees with the Old Latin against all others, and very rarely does it coincide with the peculiarities of the Bohairic. This is not surprising since the Old Latin version is considered to have been of paramount importance for the African Church. The textual similarities suggest that the Old Latin version was known and used by the Coptic-speaking Christians of Egypt, particularly in the regions where the Achmimic dialect was spoken.

Old Latin version was regarded as having been of preeminent importance for the African Church, which included Egypt. Additionally, there are cases where the Coptic versions of the Old Testament agree with the Septuagint against the Masoretic text, which is the authoritative Hebrew text of the Jewish Bible. This suggests that the Coptic translators may have had access to Greek manuscripts of the Old Testament that differed from the Masoretic text.

In summary, the Coptic versions of the Bible are important translations of the scriptures into the latest phase of the ancient Egyptian language, Coptic. They are almost exclusively religious and include translations from Greek, as well as apocryphal texts of the Old and New Testaments, legends of the apostles, lives and martyrdoms of the saints, and more. The topographical conditions of the Nile valley fostered the growth of similar but distinct Coptic dialects, including Sahidic, Bohairic, Achmimic, sub-Achmimic, Middle Egyptian, and Fayyumic. Sahidic is the oldest and in some respects the most important of these dialects, while Bohairic is the only version that is completely preserved and whose text is attested throughout by several manuscripts.

The Coptic versions of the Old Testament show relationships with the Greek Septuagint and the Old Latin versions. There are cases where the Coptic versions of the Old Testament agree with the Septuagint against the authoritative Hebrew text, which suggests that the Coptic translators may have had access to Greek manuscripts of the Old Testament that differed from the Masoretic text. Overall, the Coptic versions of the Bible provide important insights into the history of Christianity in Egypt and the development of the Coptic language.

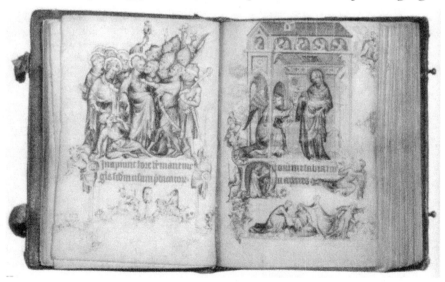

The Gothic Version

The Gothic Version of the Bible is a translation of the Scriptures into the Visigothic language by the Gothic bishop Ulfilas during the fourth century. Ulfilas, who was born in 311, was the son of a Gothic father and a Cappadocian captive. He spent much of his life as a young man at Constantinople, where he was converted to Christianity. In about 341, he was consecrated bishop by the Arian bishop Eusebius of Nicomedia. Shortly afterwards, he returned to the Visigoths and spent the rest of his life as an ardent missionary bishop and temporal leader. His greatest accomplishment was twofold: the creation of an alphabet, composed primarily of Greek and Latin characters, but including elements of Gothic runes, and the translation of the Scriptures into his native tongue, (Visi)Gothic. The Gothic Version embraced the whole Bible except the books of Samuel and Kings, which he omitted as likely to inflame the military temper of the Gothic race with their records of war and conquests.

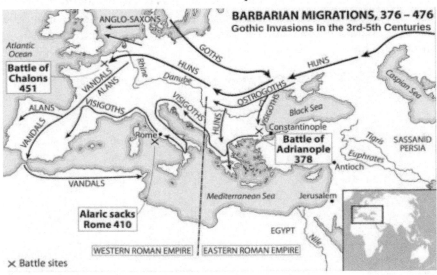

The Goths were an Eastern Germanic people who first entered history in the third century of the Christian era, when they were settled north of the Black Sea. They soon split into two divisions, taking their names from the areas in which they settled. In the fourth century, the Visigoths or West Goths moved farther west under the pressure of the advancing Huns, while the Ostrogoths settled in Pannonia, roughly modern Hungary, which they received as allies of the Eastern Roman Empire. Prompted by Constantinople, they entered Italy in 458, defeated and slew (493) the barbarian Italian king Odoacer, and set up the Ostrogothic kingdom of Italy, with Ravenna as their capital.

During the sixth century, their kingdom was overthrown, and the Ostrogoths gradually lost their identity.

During the fourth century, the Visigoths, who had preceded their Gothic kinsmen into Eastern Europe, peacefully infiltrated Moesia and Dacia, modern Bulgaria and Romania. Here they encountered Christianity, partly as a result of the missionary work of Ulfilas and his translation of the Bible into Gothic. Late in the same century, they began their rampaging migration across southern Europe, eventually conquering Italy and sacking Rome under Alaric in 410. Alaric died soon after, and under Ataulf, the Visigoths left Italy (412) and went into South Gaul and Spain. Their capital was established in Spain, and the Visigoths quietly assimilated the developing Spanish culture and language.

It is remarkable that, although nearly one-third of Europe was at that time under the rule of the Goths, next to nothing remains of the Gothic language, which today is extinct. Of the Old Testament, all that has survived are some words from Genesis 5:3–30 and Psalm 52:2–3 and portions of Nehemiah 5–7. As for the New Testament, we have a little less than half of the text of the Gospels and some portions of all the Pauline Epistles (only 2 Corinthians is complete). No portion of Acts, the Epistle to the Hebrews, the General Epistles, or the Apocalypse has survived. With the exception of the famous Codex Argenteus, which will be described in a moment, all the other Gothic texts are palimpsest. That is, after the Gothic language had become extinct, people needing parchment would erase or scrape off the writing (palimpsest means "scraped again") and reuse the parchment for some other text—often with remnants of earlier, imperfectly erased writing still visible.

Codex Argenteus was used extensively in the study of the Gothic language and culture, as well as in the textual criticism of the New Testament. Its importance lies not only in its rarity, but also in the fact that it is the only nearly complete manuscript of the Gothic Bible, and thus it provides a unique glimpse into the language and culture of the Goths. Additionally, its style and decoration reveal the artistic and cultural preferences of the Ostrogothic court at the time it was produced.

137

Manuscript scholars consider the Codex Argenteus to be a precious and unique witness to the Gothic language and culture. The manuscript has been a subject of intense study, and its text has been carefully analyzed and compared to other versions of the Bible. The Codex Argenteus has also been a source of inspiration for artists, poets, and scholars who have been fascinated by its beauty and historical significance.

In conclusion, the Gothic version of the Bible is an important testimony to the history of the Goths and their encounter with Christianity. Ulfilas, the Gothic bishop and missionary, played a crucial role in the translation of the Bible into the Gothic language, which was then used by the Visigoths in their religious practices. Despite the extinction of the Gothic language, the surviving fragments of the Gothic Bible, particularly the Codex Argenteus, have been a valuable source of information for scholars interested in the history of early Christianity and the Germanic tribes of Europe.

The Armenian Version

The Armenian Version of the Bible is an important translation that enriched and consolidated Armenian culture. Armenia, the first kingdom to accept Christianity as its official religion, was founded by Gregory the Illuminator, an Armenian of royal lineage who received Christian training at Caesarea in Cappadocia. He returned to his native land in order to undertake missionary work and among his converts was Tiridates I, king of Armenia, who commanded all his subjects to adopt Christianity by royal edict. In his program of evangelism, Gregory was assisted by co-workers from various backgrounds, including Armenians trained in Hellenistic culture as well as Armenians under Syrian influence. During this period, books and documents existed only in Greek and Syriac, and their translation was left to oral interpretation. Consequently, it was through such cultural bridges that the Armenians received both Greek and Syriac Christianity, as well as the literature of both these peoples.

The earliest attempt to construct an Armenian alphabet was made by Bishop Daniel, who was probably Syrian and took the Aramaic alphabet as a pattern. However, the alphabet was found to be unsuitable for representing the sounds of the Armenian language. The foundation of Armenian literature, including the translation of the Bible, dates from the early part of the fifth century, and the chief promoters of this cultural development were the catholicos of the Armenian Church, Sahak, a descendant of Gregory the Illuminator, and Sahak's friend and helper, Mesrop, who had exchanged a military career for the life of a monk, missionary, and teacher. With the help of a Greek hermit and calligrapher, Rufanos of Samosata, about 406 CE, Mesrop succeeded in producing an Armenian alphabet of thirty-six letters, twenty letters coming directly from Greek, twelve others being formed according to a Greek model, and four being taken from Syriac.

After creating the Armenian alphabet, Mesrop gathered about him a band of keen scholars. Sending some of them to Edessa, Constantinople, and even Rome in search of manuscripts of the Scriptures and of ecclesiastical and secular writers, he inaugurated a program of translation that enriched and consolidated Armenian culture. The first book of the Bible that Mesrop translated was the Book of Proverbs, which was followed by the New Testament. With the help of Sahak and perhaps other translators, the rest of the Old Testament was finished about 410–14.

The Armenian version of the Bible is unique in that it includes certain books that elsewhere came to be regarded as apocryphal, such as the History of Joseph and Asenath, the Testaments of the Twelve Patriarchs, the Epistle of the Corinthians to Paul, and a Third Epistle of Paul to the Corinthians. Many other uncanonical writings of the Old Testament are preserved in Armenian manuscripts, including The Book of Adam, The History of Moses, The Deaths of the Prophets, Concerning King Solomon, A Short History of the Prophet Elias, Concerning the Prophet Jeremiah, The Vision of Enoch the Just, and The Third Book of Esdras.

More manuscripts of the Armenian version are extant today than those of any other ancient version, with the exception of the Latin Vulgate. The earliest dated manuscript is from the ninth century; it is a copy of the four Gospels written in 887 CE. Among noteworthy features of the Armenian version of the Bible is the inclusion of certain books that elsewhere came to be regarded as apocryphal. The Old Testament included the History of Joseph and Asenath and the Testaments of the Twelve Patriarchs, and the New Testament included the Epistle of the Corinthians to Paul and a Third Epistle of Paul to the Corinthians.

The Armenian version of the Bible stands out for its unique features, including the inclusion of certain apocryphal books and the presence of lengthy colophons in many manuscripts. The Armenian Church has historically held a prominent place in Christianity due to its early adoption of the religion, and the translation of the Bible into Armenian by Mesrop and Sahak was a significant milestone in the development of Armenian culture.

Today, the Armenian Bible continues to play an important role in the Armenian Church and culture. The Armenian Apostolic Church, which traces its roots back to the conversion of Armenia to Christianity in the fourth century, recognizes the Armenian version of the Bible as its official text. In addition, the Armenian Bible has been the subject of scholarly research and study, providing insights into the history and development of both the Armenian Church and the Bible as a whole.

Overall, the Armenian version of the Bible stands as a testament to the rich and diverse history of Christianity, reflecting the influences of Greek and Syrian Christianity on the Armenian Church, as well as the unique cultural heritage of the Armenian people.

National Center of Manuscripts

The Georgian Version

The Georgian version of the Bible is an ancient translation of the Scriptures into the Georgian language, a unique and distinct language that is unrelated to any of the major language families. The country of Georgia, located between the Black Sea and the Caspian Sea, was known in antiquity as Iberia. According to tradition, the introduction of Christianity to Georgia began with the missionary work of a

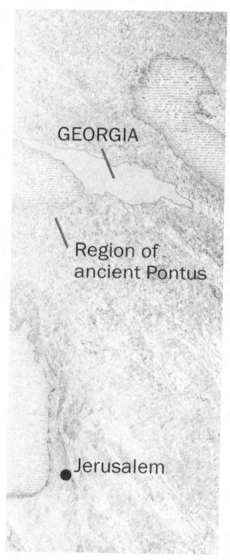

GEORGIA

Region of
ancient Pontus

● Jerusalem

Christian slave woman named Nino during the reign of Emperor Constantine in the 4th century. However, it is not clear when a written version of the Scriptures was first made available to the Georgian people.

Before a translation could be made in written form, the Georgians needed an alphabet of their own. According to Armenian traditions, after St. Mesrop had drawn up an alphabet for his fellow countrymen, he became concerned about the lack of an alphabet among the neighboring Georgian people. After he had invented an alphabet that represented the sounds that occur in that language, King Bakur of Georgia arranged that it should be taught to boys of the lower social classes at various districts and provinces.

At least the Gospels and some other parts of the New Testament were made available in written form for Georgian Christians by about the middle of the fifth century. The Georgian version of the Bible has undergone several revisions, and it is debated whether the translation was made from Greek, Armenian, or Syriac. The oldest manuscripts that are dated in a colophon are of the ninth and tenth centuries, though earlier fragments exist.

One feature of Georgian paleography that bears in some measure upon questions of the dating of manuscripts is the style of the script. The Georgians have employed three alphabets: the ecclesiastical majuscule, in general use until the tenth century and sporadically thereafter in manuscripts; the ecclesiastical minuscule, regularly used in theological manuscripts of the eleventh to the nineteenth century; and the "warrior" or "knightly" hand, the ancestor of the modern Georgian script.

A new stage in the history of the spiritual, literary, and cultural life of Georgia began at the close of the tenth century. Noteworthy in this development was St. Euthymius, a scholarly abbot of the Georgian monastery on Mount Athos. In addition to translating various Greek liturgical and homiletical works, St. Euthymius turned his attention to revising and completing the Georgian New Testament. He was the first to translate the Book of Revelation, which for centuries was not regarded as canonical by the Georgian Church. His work must have been completed sometime before 978 CE, which is the date of the earliest known Georgian manuscript of the Apocalypse.

In addition to the New Testament, the Georgian version of the Bible also includes translations of the Old Testament, some of which are apocryphal. The Book of Enoch, Jubilees, and the Testaments of the Twelve Patriarchs are among the apocryphal works that have been translated into Georgian. The Georgian version of the Bible has played a significant role in the development of Georgian literature and culture, and it continues to be an important spiritual and cultural resource for the Georgian people today.

The Ethiopic Version

The Ethiopic Version is the translation of the Bible into the Ge'ez language, which is the ancient language of Ethiopia. The history of the introduction of Christianity into Ethiopia is unclear and disputed among different accounts. According to Acts 8:26-39, Philip converted an Ethiopian chamberlain to the queen of Ethiopia, and this event is often associated with the introduction of Christianity into Ethiopia. Rufinus's Ecclesiastical History provides the first literary evidence for the presence of Christianity in Ethiopia. The account reports that Frumentius and Ædesius preached the gospel in Aksum, the capital of Ethiopia, during the time of Constantine the Great. After the royal family converted to Christianity, Frumentius went to Alexandria and obtained missionary co-workers from Bishop Athanasius. He was then consecrated as bishop and became the head of the Ethiopian Church.

The arrival of Christianity in Ethiopia during the fourth century is confirmed by inscriptional and numismatic evidence. However, it is unclear how quickly the new faith spread among the populace. There is no indication that the conversion of the king was followed by any royal decree for the enforcement of the faith upon his people. Little specific information about the church in Ethiopia during the next century and a half has come down to us. In the early sixth century, a Christian traveler named Cosmas Indicopleustes visited Ethiopia and reported that he found it thoroughly Christianized. The growth of Christianity in Ethiopia seems to have come partly because of support given by Christian rulers and partly from encouragement provided by the immigration of Christian believers from other lands. These immigrants were mainly Monophysites who were persecuted by Byzantine rulers after being condemned at the Council of Chalcedon in 451. They found refuge in Ethiopia, which, because of its remote geographical location, remained unaffected by religious controversies raging elsewhere.

Among the immigrants who helped to evangelize the remaining pagan areas in the northern part of the Aksumite kingdom were monks, nuns, priests, and hermits from Egypt and Syria. Nine celebrated monks founded monasteries, developed the liturgy, and made translations of sacred books into the native language. These monks were known for their vigorous missionary activity and reputation for piety in Ethiopia, and they have been accorded the status of sainthood.

It is unclear when the Bible, or at least the New Testament, was translated into Ethiopic. The timeline ranges from the apostolic age to a time after the fourteenth century. However, it is probable that the Ethiopic version was made during the fifth and/or sixth century, in connection with the missionary activity of the Nine Saints. There are several thousand Ethiopic manuscripts in European and American collections, but most of these manuscripts are relatively late, dating from the sixteenth to the nineteenth century. The earliest biblical manuscripts come from the fourteenth century. One of the most remarkable Ethiopic manuscripts is the Pierpont Morgan MS. 828 of the four Gospels, 1400-1401 CE, with twenty-six full-page miniatures, eight ornamented canon tables, and four ornamented incipit folios.

In conclusion, the Ethiopic Version of the Bible is the translation of the Bible into the Ge'ez language. The introduction of Christianity into Ethiopia is difficult to ascertain, and there are conflicting traditions in the early church that assign the evangelization of Ethiopia to different apostles. The translation of the Bible into Ethiopic is estimated to have been made during the fifth and/or sixth century, in connection with the missionary activity of the Nine Saints. The growth of Christianity in Ethiopia came partly from support given by Christian rulers and partly from encouragement provided by the immigration of Christian believers from other lands, mainly Monophysites who were persecuted by Byzantine rulers.

The Arabic Versions

The term Arabia in ancient times referred to the region west of Mesopotamia, east and south of Syria and Judea, extending to the Isthmus of Suez. It was divided into three regions by the geographer

Ptolemy: Arabia Felix (the Happy or Fertile), Arabia Petraea (the Stony), and Arabia Deserta (the Desert). The origin of the gospel in this region and how it was brought there remains unclear due to scattered and inconclusive data.

During the first half of the third century, Origen was invited to Arabia at least twice to participate in doctrinal discussions due to certain heretical tendencies on the part of contemporary leaders, namely Beryllus and Heraclides. There were also attempts to introduce Christianity among the nomad tribes, and Christian missions may have penetrated the southern part of the Arabian peninsula from Ethiopia.

The identity of the person who made the first translation of the Scriptures into Arabic is unknown, as different traditions have assigned the honor to different people. However, the earliest translations are believed to date back to the eighth century. According to Ignazio Guidi's analysis of over seventy-five Arabic manuscripts, the Arabic versions of the Gospels fall into six basic groups: those made directly from the Greek, those made directly from or corrected from the Syriac Peshitta, those made directly from or corrected from the Coptic (usually the Bohairic dialect), those made from Latin, manuscripts of two distinct eclectic recensions produced by the Alexandrian Patriarchate during the thirteenth century, and miscellaneous manuscripts, some of which are characterized by being cast in the form of rhymed prose made classic by the Koran. Additionally, more than one Arabic version has been corrected from others derived from a different basic text.

From the Middle Ages to the nineteenth century, various ecclesiastical groups made other Arabic translations of the Bible, and these translations were in various forms of Arabic. Translations were made for Melchites, Maronites, Nestorians, Jacobites, and Copts. The different forms of Arabic used for these translations included classical Arabic, the vernacular language used in Algeria, Chad, Egypt, Morocco, Palestine, Sudan, Tunisia, as well as the vernacular of Malta.

147

The Sogdian Version

Sogdian is a language belonging to the Indo-European family of languages, specifically the Middle Iranian subgroup. It was widely spoken in an area that included Samarkand and parts of Central Asia during the latter part of the first millennium CE. In the early 20th century, numerous Sogdian documents were discovered in northwest China at Turfan, including Christian texts. Among these texts were fragments of the Gospels of Matthew, Luke, and John, as well as a few verses from 1 Corinthians and Galatians.

Experts believe that these Christian documents date back to the 9th to 11th century and were written in a script that resembles the Estrangela Syriac script, which was used by Syriac-speaking Christians. The Sogdian translation was likely created during the Nestorian mission in Central Asia in the 7th century.

The Old Church Slavonic Version

The Old Church Slavonic Version of the Bible has its roots in the ninth century Moravian mission, which had a significant impact on the cultural development of Slavic nations. The mission was undertaken by two brothers, Methodius and Constantine, who were originally from Greece. Upon arrival in Moravia, they began instructing pupils in the Slavic dialect spoken in the region. Constantine translated several liturgical books into Slavonic and trained Moravians for the clergy. The brothers encountered controversy when they introduced the Byzantine rite, sung in the language of the Slavs, into a land over which the bishops of Passau and Salzburg claimed spiritual sovereignty. Despite opposition, popes Hadrian II and John VIII eventually approved the use of the Slavonic vernacular in divine services. However, the Scripture lessons were to be presented first in Latin and then in the Slavonic translation.

After several years of missionary work in Moravia, the two brothers set out for Rome. Constantine fell ill while in Rome and took monastic vows and assumed the name Cyril before passing away fifty days later. Upon his death, Methodius became archbishop of Sirmium in Pannonia, which included Moravia. This put him in conflict with the Bavarian hierarchy, resulting in his imprisonment for two and a half years. Following his election as pope in 872, John VIII secured Methodius's release and reinstated the Slavonic liturgy in Moravia.

Upon Methodius's death in 885, the German clergy renewed their efforts to forbid the use of the Slavonic liturgy in Moravia. The disciples of Methodius were brutally expelled from the country, and Slavonic Christianity was carried by refugees to other Slavic lands.

Before leaving for Moravia, Cyril invented an alphabet for the writing of Slavonic and began translating the gospel message. The extant Old Church Slavonic manuscripts present two distinct alphabets, the Glagolitic and the Cyrillic, which have caused difficulties for modern philologists. Scholars now agree that Cyril invented the Glagolitic alphabet. The Cyrillic alphabet, which is considerably less individualistic than the Glagolitic, may have been devised by St. Kliment, a pupil of Cyril and Methodius and an active missionary in Bulgaria. After some amount of local variation, the Cyrillic alphabet was codified in 893 at a Bulgarian council held at Preslav, making it official for both ecclesiastical and secular use.

The oldest extant manuscripts in the Glagolitic alphabet date from the late tenth or early eleventh century. The earliest known manuscript of the Old Church Slavonic translation of the Bible is the Ostromir Gospels, which is written in Cyrillic and dates from the eleventh century. The Old Church Slavonic Version of the Bible was widely used in Slavic countries and was a key factor in the development of Slavic literature and culture.

The Nubian Version

Nubia was a region located between Egypt and Ethiopia, consisting of three independent kingdoms in the early centuries of the Christian era. It is not known when Christianity first reached the Nubian people, but it is believed that Christian influences began to penetrate the region when the church was established in Upper Egypt during the third and fourth centuries. During the fourth century, several Christians were driven from Egypt by the persecutions ordered by Emperor Diocletian and may have sought refuge in Nubia.

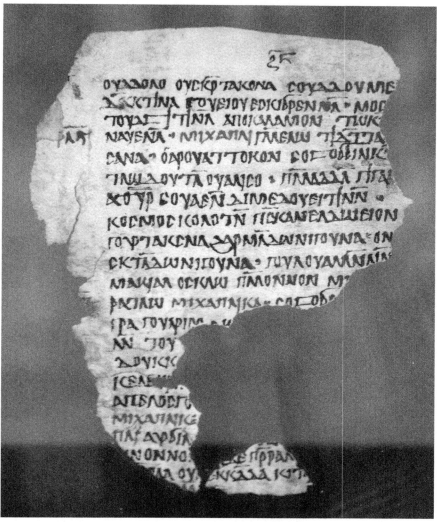

Formally designated missionaries arrived in Nubia in the middle of the sixth century, belonging to rival factions - the Monophysite and the orthodox Melchite. The number of churches in Nubia multiplied in the succeeding centuries, providing the chief cohesive element in

151

Nubian society for about five centuries. However, by the end of the fourteenth century, the weakened Nubian Church was ready to expire after being cut off from the rest of the Christian world by Arab invaders pressing southward from Muslim Egypt. The growing power of the Arabs hemmed in the Nubian Christians on the north, east, and west, and eventually, the whole population embraced Islam.

When the Scriptures were translated into Nubian is not known, but it is probable that soon after the introduction of Christianity on a wide scale in the sixth century, a vernacular version would have been called for by the new converts. Evidence for the Nubian version of the Scriptures came to light only in the twentieth century. In 1906, Dr. Carl Schmidt purchased a quire of sixteen mutilated pages from a parchment codex acquired in Upper Egypt. This contained a portion of a lectionary for Christmastide, corresponding to December 20 to 26. For each day, a section of the Scripture is supplied from the Apostolos (Romans, Galatians, Philippians, and Hebrews) and the Gospel (Matthew and John).

The lectionary is written in an alphabet that is essentially Coptic, reinforced by several additional letters needed to represent sounds peculiar to the Nubian language. The sequence and the choice of the lessons in the Nubian lectionary for Christmastide find no parallel in the Greek and Coptic lectionaries hitherto examined, except for the two passages appointed for December 25, which coincide with those of Greek menologia (i.e., monthly readings on the lives of the saints).

Several other biblical fragments in Nubian came to the attention of scholars toward the end of the twentieth century. These include the Nubian text of verses from the Gospel according to John and the Book of Revelation.

The Use of Lectionaries in the Transmission of the Text

Lectionaries are collections of selected biblical passages arranged for public reading in Christian worship services. They played a crucial role in the transmission of the New Testament text throughout the centuries. The lectionary system ensured that specific portions of Scripture were read at particular times during the liturgical year, such as on Sundays, feast days, and other special occasions. By examining the use of lectionaries in the transmission of the text, we can gain insights into the practices of early Christian communities and the ways in which they engaged with the biblical text.

1. **Composition and Structure**: Lectionaries are organized into two main types: Gospel lectionaries (known as "Evangelistaria") and Epistle lectionaries (known as "Apostoloi" or "Praxapostoloi"). These collections typically present the biblical text in a continuous, non-verse format and are often introduced by a brief description of the liturgical occasion for which the reading is intended. The readings are referred to as "pericopes," which are self-contained units designed to be read aloud in a single service.

2. **Dating and Manuscripts**: The earliest surviving lectionary manuscripts date back to the 6th century CE, but the practice of using lectionaries in Christian worship likely dates to much earlier periods. There are over 2,000 known Greek lectionary manuscripts, which makes them an important source of evidence for the textual history of the New Testament. Lectionary manuscripts are often written in minuscule script and are classified as a distinct group within New Testament textual criticism.

3. **Textual Transmission**: The use of lectionaries in the transmission of the New Testament text is significant for several reasons. Firstly, they demonstrate how early Christian communities engaged with Scripture in their worship practices. The choice of readings and their arrangement within the lectionary can reveal aspects of the community's theological and liturgical priorities. Secondly, the widespread use of lectionaries contributed to the stabilization of the New Testament text by promoting the consistent reading of particular passages across different regions and time periods. This helped to maintain a certain level of textual uniformity and continuity within the broader Christian tradition.

4. **Variants and Textual Criticism**: Lectionary manuscripts can also provide valuable evidence for textual variants and the development of the New Testament text. Although they often reflect the Byzantine text-type, which is characterized by a high degree of uniformity, lectionaries can occasionally preserve older or unique readings. This makes them an important resource for textual critics seeking to reconstruct the earliest possible form of the New Testament text. Additionally, the lectionary system's influence on the transmission of the text can be observed in some non-lectionary manuscripts, where traces of the pericope divisions and other lectionary-related features can be found.

5. **The Role of Lectionaries in Modern Scholarship**: The study of lectionaries has become increasingly important in modern biblical scholarship, as scholars recognize their significance for understanding the history of the New Testament text and the practices of early Christian communities. This has led to efforts to catalog, analyze, and digitize lectionary manuscripts, making them more accessible to researchers worldwide. The use of lectionaries in the transmission of the text continues to be a fascinating area of study that sheds light on the rich and complex history of the New Testament and its reception by Christian communities throughout the centuries.

In conclusion, the use of lectionaries in the transmission of the New Testament text played a vital role in shaping the way early Christian communities engaged with Scripture in their worship practices. The widespread use of lectionaries contributed to the stabilization and continuity of the biblical text, while also providing valuable evidence for textual variants and the development of the New Testament text. The study of lectionaries remains an essential endeavor.

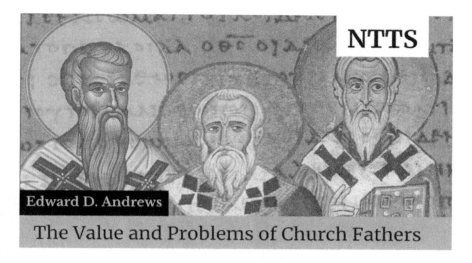

Edward D. Andrews

The Value and Problems of Church Fathers

The Role of Church Fathers in Textual Transmission

The Church Fathers, influential theologians and leaders of the early Christian Church, played a crucial role in the transmission of the New Testament text. Their writings, which include commentaries, sermons, letters, and other works, provide essential evidence for understanding the development and dissemination of the biblical text in the first few centuries of Christianity. In 1500 words, we will explore the various ways in which the Church Fathers contributed to the textual transmission of the New Testament and the significance of their writings in the field of textual criticism.

1. **Preservation of Biblical Quotations**: One of the most important ways in which the Church Fathers contributed to the transmission of the New Testament text is through their extensive quotations of Scripture in their writings. These quotations often predate the oldest surviving biblical manuscripts and can provide valuable evidence for the text's early form. By comparing the quotations in the writings of the Church Fathers with the text of later manuscripts, scholars can identify textual variants and gain insights into the development of the biblical text over time.

2. **Interpretation and Exegesis**: The Church Fathers were instrumental in shaping the interpretation and exegesis of the New Testament. Their commentaries and other exegetical writings reflect their engagement with the biblical text, which often involved wrestling with textual issues and variants. Through their interpretive efforts, the Church Fathers helped to establish the norms and standards for biblical interpretation in the early Christian Church. Their works remain valuable resources for modern scholars seeking to understand the historical and cultural contexts in which the New Testament was read and interpreted.

3. **Development of the Canon**: The Church Fathers played a critical role in the process of canon formation, which involved discerning which texts should be considered part of the authoritative Christian Scriptures. Through their writings, they provided valuable testimony regarding the acceptance and use of various New Testament texts in different Christian communities. The opinions of influential figures such as Athanasius, Augustine, and Jerome helped to shape the consensus on the New Testament canon, which eventually solidified into the 27-book collection that is recognized today.

4. **Defense of Orthodoxy and the Text**: The Church Fathers often engaged in polemical disputes with various heretical groups and rival interpretations of Christianity. In these debates, the accuracy and integrity of the biblical text were frequently at stake. By defending the orthodox interpretation of the New Testament, the Church Fathers contributed to the preservation and transmission of a relatively stable and consistent text. Their arguments and defenses against heretical claims often relied on the authoritative status of the biblical text, which reinforced the importance of textual fidelity within the early Christian Church.

5. **Textual Scholarship and Criticism**: Some Church Fathers, such as Origen and Jerome, were actively involved in textual scholarship and criticism. Origen's Hexapla, a monumental work that presented the Old Testament in six parallel columns

with different textual versions, including the Septuagint and various Greek translations, was an early example of comparative textual analysis. Jerome, who produced the Latin Vulgate translation of the Bible, also engaged in textual criticism by comparing various Greek and Hebrew manuscripts to produce a more accurate and reliable translation. These efforts by the Church Fathers laid the groundwork for the discipline of textual criticism and contributed to the development of a more stable and accurate biblical text.

6. **Dissemination and Copying of the Text**: The Church Fathers played a key role in the dissemination and copying of the New Testament text. As leaders of influential Christian communities, they were responsible for overseeing the production and distribution of biblical manuscripts. The high regard in which their writings were held often meant that their preferred text or manuscript tradition would be more widely disseminated and copied, thus shaping the textual transmission of the New Testament.

7. **Use of Textual Evidence in Modern Scholarship**: The writings of the Church Fathers continue to be an essential resource for modern biblical scholars and textual critics. By analyzing the biblical quotations and references found in their works, scholars can reconstruct the text of the New Testament as it was known in the early centuries of Christianity. Furthermore, the Church Fathers' commentaries and exegetical writings provide important insights into the historical and cultural contexts that shaped the interpretation and transmission of the biblical text.

8. **Challenges and Limitations**: While the Church Fathers' writings are invaluable for textual criticism and the study of the early Christian Church, they also present certain challenges and limitations. For one, their biblical quotations are not always precise or consistent, as they sometimes paraphrase or adapt the text for their purposes. Additionally, the transmission and preservation of the Church Fathers' writings have also been

subject to scribal errors and variations, which can complicate the task of identifying the original biblical text they quoted.

9. **Future Directions in Scholarship**: The study of the Church Fathers' role in the textual transmission of the New Testament remains an active and evolving area of research. With the ongoing discovery of new manuscript evidence and the application of advanced digital technologies, scholars are continually refining their understanding of the early Christian text and its development. By deepening our knowledge of the Church Fathers' writings and their impact on the transmission of the New Testament, we can gain a more nuanced and comprehensive appreciation of the rich and complex history of the biblical text.

In conclusion, the Church Fathers played a critical role in the textual transmission of the New Testament. Their extensive biblical quotations, interpretive efforts, involvement in canon formation, defense of orthodoxy, and textual scholarship all contributed to the preservation, dissemination, and development of the biblical text. As influential leaders and thinkers in the early Christian Church, their writings continue to provide valuable evidence and insights for modern textual criticism and biblical scholarship. Despite the challenges and limitations that their writings present, the study of the Church Fathers' role in the textual transmission of the New Testament remains an essential and fascinating area of research that sheds light on the history and development of the Christian Scriptures.

The Church Fathers, who were theologians, scholars, and leaders of the early Christian Church, played a crucial role in the preservation and transmission of the New Testament text. By quoting and referring to biblical passages in their writings, they helped to establish the original words of the Greek New Testament manuscripts. This essay will explore some of the most influential Church Fathers from the 2nd to the 4th centuries and how their quotes contribute to our understanding of the original Greek New Testament.

1. **Ignatius of Antioch (c. 35-107 CE)**: Ignatius was an early Christian bishop and martyr. His letters to various churches

and individuals, written while he was en route to his execution in Rome, provide evidence of the New Testament text in the early 2nd century. Ignatius quotes from the Gospels, Acts, and several Pauline epistles, demonstrating their early circulation and authority within the Christian community.

2. **Polycarp of Smyrna (c. 69-155 CE)**: Polycarp was a disciple of the Apostle John and the bishop of Smyrna. His letter to the Philippians contains numerous quotations from the New Testament, particularly from the Pauline epistles. Polycarp's use of these texts attests to their early composition and widespread acceptance among Christians.

3. **Justin Martyr (c. 100-165 CE)**: Justin was an early Christian apologist and philosopher. In his writings, he extensively quotes from the Gospels, often referring to them as the "Memoirs of the Apostles." Justin's use of the Gospels as authoritative sources for Christian doctrine and practice illustrates their importance in the mid-2nd century.

4. **Irenaeus of Lyons (c. 130-202 CE)**: Irenaeus was a prominent theologian and bishop who combated heresy in the early Church. His major work, "Against Heresies," is an extensive defense of Christian orthodoxy against Gnostic teachings. Irenaeus quotes from nearly all New Testament books, providing valuable evidence for the early canon and the original text of the Greek manuscripts.

5. **Clement of Alexandria (c. 150-215 CE)**: Clement was a theologian and scholar who served as the head of the Catechetical School of Alexandria. In his writings, he cites passages from the Gospels, Acts, Pauline epistles, and several general epistles. Clement's use of these texts demonstrates their widespread acceptance and authority in the late 2nd and early 3rd centuries.

6. **Tertullian (c. 155-240 CE)**: Tertullian was a prolific Christian author and apologist from Carthage. He wrote extensively on various aspects of Christian theology, often quoting from the New Testament to support his arguments. Tertullian's works

provide important evidence for the text and canon of the New Testament in the early 3rd century.

7. **Origen (c. 185-254 CE)**: Origen was a theologian, philosopher, and biblical scholar from Alexandria. He produced an extensive body of writings, including commentaries, homilies, and the monumental "Hexapla," a critical edition of the Old Testament. In his works, Origen quotes from all the New Testament books, providing a wealth of information on the textual history and interpretation of the Greek manuscripts.

8. **Eusebius of Caesarea (c. 260-340 CE)**: Eusebius was a historian, theologian, and bishop who is best known for his work, "Ecclesiastical History." This comprehensive account of early Christianity contains numerous quotations from the New Testament, as well as references to the writings of earlier Church Fathers. Eusebius's extensive use of the New Testament in his historical narrative demonstrates the canonical status and authority of these texts in the early 4th century.

9. **Athanasius of Alexandria (c. 296-373 CE)**: Athanasius was a prominent theologian, bishop, and defender of Nicene orthodoxy. In his annual Festal Letter of 367 CE, he provided a list of the 27 books that make up the New Testament canon, which is the earliest extant list that matches the modern New Testament. Athanasius quoted extensively from the New Testament in his theological writings, contributing to our understanding of the Greek text in the mid-4th century.

10. **Jerome (c. 347-420 CE)**: Jerome was a scholar, translator, and theologian who is best known for his translation of the Bible into Latin, known as the Vulgate. In his numerous commentaries and letters, Jerome cited the New Testament extensively, providing valuable evidence for the textual history of the Greek manuscripts in the late 4th century.

11. **Augustine of Hippo (c. 354-430 CE)**: Augustine was a philosopher, theologian, and bishop who is considered one of

the most influential figures in Western Christianity. In his numerous works, Augustine quoted and alluded to the New Testament extensively, attesting to the authority and widespread use of these texts in the early 5th century.

These Church Fathers played a vital role in the preservation and transmission of the New Testament text. By quoting and referring to the biblical passages in their writings, they not only demonstrated the authority and acceptance of these texts within the early Christian community but also provided crucial evidence for the original words of the Greek New Testament manuscripts. Their writings enable modern scholars to reconstruct the textual history of the New Testament and to better understand the development of early Christian doctrine and practice.

Moreover, the extensive use of the New Testament by the Church Fathers highlights the importance of these texts in shaping the beliefs, values, and identity of the early Christian community. By studying the writings of these influential figures, scholars can gain insight into the process of canon formation and the emergence of the New Testament as a foundational text for Christianity.

In conclusion, the quotations and references to the New Testament by the 2nd to 4th-century Church Fathers serve as invaluable resources for establishing the original words of the Greek New Testament manuscripts. Their writings provide crucial evidence for the early composition, circulation, and acceptance of these texts, shedding light on the textual history and development of the New Testament canon.

CHAPTER 4 The Transmission of Textual Variants into the New Testament Text

Mistakes found in the manuscripts of the Greek New Testament can be categorized as either accidental or intentional. Here are some of the most common errors encountered in these two categories:

Accidental Errors

A. Faulty Word Division

Faulty word division is a type of accidental error that occurs when a scribe mistakenly divides a word or words in the text. This mistake can lead to confusion, misinterpretation, or even alteration of the intended meaning of a passage. In the example provided from 1 Timothy 3:16, the original Greek text reads "ὁμολογοῦμεν ὡς μέγα" ("confessedly great"), but due to a faulty word division, it has been rendered as "ὁμολογουμένως μέγα" ("we acknowledge how great").

The occurrence of this kind of error can be traced back to the fact that in early Greek manuscripts, words were often written without spaces or punctuation marks between them, making it difficult for scribes to accurately divide and copy the text. This writing style is known as scriptio continua. Here are some additional examples of faulty word division:

1. **1 Corinthians 7:35**: The original text reads "εὐπάρεδρον τῷ κυρίῳ" ("devoted to the Lord"), but due to faulty word division, it may be mistakenly rendered as "εὐπαρέδρων τὸν κύριον" ("well-seated with the Lord").

2. **Ephesians 6:12**: The original text reads "ἐν τοῖς ἐπουρανίοις" ("in the heavenly places"), but due to faulty word division, it may be mistakenly rendered as "ἐν τοῖς ἐποῦρανίοις" ("in the above-sky").

3. **Acts 19:4**: The original text reads "Παύλῳ βαπτίσματι" ("with Paul's baptism"), but due to faulty word division, it may be mistakenly rendered as "Παύλου βαπτίσματι" ("with the baptism of Paul").

These examples demonstrate that faulty word division can significantly alter the meaning of a text, making it essential for scholars to carefully analyze manuscripts and consider the context of each passage when attempting to reconstruct the original wording.

B. Homoeoteleuton

Homoeoteleuton is a type of scribal error that occurs when a scribe's eye skips from one letter or word with a similar ending to the same letter or word farther down the page, causing the unintentional omission of the intervening text. This error often arises when two or more lines of the text end with the same word or sequence of letters. Here are some additional examples of homoeoteleuton:

1. **1 John 2:23**: Many manuscripts skip from the first occurrence of "τὸν πατέρα ἔχει" ("has the Father") to the second occurrence, resulting in the omission of the intervening text,

163

which reads: "ὁ ἀρνούμενος τὸν υἱὸν οὐδὲ" ("whoever denies the Son neither").

2. **Romans 8:12**: In some manuscripts, the phrase "οὐ τῇ σαρκὶ" ("not to the flesh") is mistakenly omitted due to homoeoteleuton. The scribe's eye might have skipped from the ending of "οὖν ὀφειλέται" ("so we are debtors") to the identical ending of "οὐ τῇ σαρκὶ" ("not to the flesh"), causing the omission of the latter phrase.

3. **Ephesians 1:7**: In some manuscripts, the words "ἐν αὐτῷ" ("in him") are omitted due to homoeoteleuton. The scribe's eye might have skipped from the first instance of "ἐν αὐτῷ" to the second, causing the unintentional omission of the words "ἔχομεν τὴν ἀπολύτρωσιν" ("we have redemption").

These examples illustrate the potential impact of homoeoteleuton on the textual integrity of the New Testament. It is crucial for textual critics to be aware of this type of error and to carefully compare manuscripts in order to identify and correct such mistakes, ultimately striving to reconstruct the original text as accurately as possible.

C. Haplography

Haplography is a scribal error that occurs when a letter or word is written once when it should have been written twice. This type of error can lead to changes in the meaning of a text, and it is important for textual critics to be aware of these mistakes when examining manuscripts. Here are some additional examples of haplography in the New Testament:

1. **1 Thessalonians 2:7**: In some manuscripts, the phrase "ἐγενήθημεν ἤπιοι" ("we became gentle") appears, while it should have been "ἐγενήθημεν νήπιοι" ("we became infants"). The error likely occurred because the scribe accidentally copied the letter "ν" only once.

2. **1 Corinthians 15:47**: In certain manuscripts, the phrase "ὁ δεύτερος ἄνθρωπος" ("the second man") is mistakenly written

as "ὁ δεύτερος," with the word "ἄνθρωπος" ("man") omitted. This error might have occurred when the scribe's eye skipped from one instance of the letter "ος" to the next, leading to the omission of "ἄνθρωπος."

3. **Galatians 2:9**: In some manuscripts, the name "Ἰωάννης" ("John") is mistakenly written as "Ἰωάνες," with the letter "ν" written once instead of twice. This error could have resulted from the scribe's eye skipping over the second "ν," leading to the incorrect spelling of the name.

These examples demonstrate the impact of haplography on the textual transmission of the New Testament. Textual critics must be diligent in identifying these errors and comparing manuscripts to reconstruct the original text as accurately as possible. By doing so, they can ensure that the meaning and integrity of the New Testament text are preserved for future generations.

D. Dittography

Dittography is a scribal error that occurs when a letter or word is written twice instead of once. These mistakes can alter the meaning of a text, and it is essential for textual critics to be aware of them when examining manuscripts. Here are some additional examples of dittography in the New Testament:

1. **Mark 12:27**: In some manuscripts, the phrase "ὁ θεὸς θεὸς" ("the God, God") appears instead of the correct "θεὸς" ("God"). The error likely occurred because the scribe unintentionally copied the word "θεὸς" twice.

2. **Acts 19:35**: In certain manuscripts, the word "Διοπετής" ("Zeus") appears as "Διοπετής Διοπετής," with the word written twice instead of once. This dittography might have happened when the scribe's eye inadvertently returned to the beginning of the word, leading to its duplication.

3. **Romans 8:1**: In some manuscripts, the phrase "οὐδὲν ἄρα νῦν κατάκριμα" ("there is now no condemnation") is mistakenly

written as "οὐδὲν οὐδὲν ἄρα νῦν κατάκριμα," with the word "οὐδὲν" ("nothing") repeated. This error could have resulted from the scribe's eye moving from the first "οὐδὲν" to the second, causing an unintended repetition.

These examples illustrate the impact of dittography on the textual transmission of the New Testament. Textual critics must be diligent in identifying these errors and comparing manuscripts to reconstruct the original text as accurately as possible. By doing so, they can ensure that the meaning and integrity of the New Testament text are preserved for future generations.

E. Metathesis

Metathesis is a scribal error involving the transposition of letters or words, resulting in a change in the order of the text. This mistake can lead to alterations in meaning and can pose challenges for textual critics who aim to reconstruct the original text. Here are some additional examples of metathesis in the New Testament:

1. **Mark 14:65**: In some manuscripts, the word "ἔλαβον" ("received") appears instead of the correct "ἔβαλον" ("struck"). This error likely occurred because the scribe switched the order of the letters, resulting in a different word with an altered meaning.

2. **1 Corinthians 12:28**: In certain manuscripts, the word "προφητεία" ("prophecy") appears as "προφήτεια," with the letters eta (η) and iota (ι) transposed. This metathesis might have occurred when the scribe inadvertently switched the order of the letters, leading to a different spelling.

3. **2 Timothy 2:14**: In some manuscripts, the phrase "μαχαὶ λογομαχίας" ("battles of words") is mistakenly written as "λογομαχίας μαχαὶ," with the order of the words reversed. This error could have resulted from the scribe's eye moving from the first word to the second, causing an unintended transposition.

These examples demonstrate the impact of metathesis on the textual transmission of the New Testament. Textual critics must be vigilant in identifying these errors and comparing manuscripts to reconstruct the original text as accurately as possible. By doing so, they can ensure that the meaning and integrity of the New Testament text are preserved for future generations.

F. Itacism

Itacism is a type of scribal error that occurs when vowel sounds are confused, leading to the substitution of one vowel for another. This can result in changes to the meaning of words or phrases in the text. Here are some additional examples of itacism in the New Testament:

1. **Romans 5:1**: In some manuscripts, the word "ἔχωμεν" ("let us have") appears instead of the correct "ἔχομεν" ("we have"). This error likely occurred because the scribe confused the vowel sounds omega (ω) and omicron (o), resulting in a different word with an altered meaning.

2. **1 Corinthians 15:47**: In certain manuscripts, the word "ἐπίγειος" ("earthly") appears as "ἐπίγειον," with the final sigma (ς) replaced by a nu (ν). This itacism might have occurred when the scribe inadvertently confused the similar vowel sounds, leading to a different ending.

3. **Ephesians 4:26**: In some manuscripts, the phrase "ὁ ἥλιος μὴ ἐπιδυέτω" ("do not let the sun go down") is mistakenly written as "ὁ ἥλιος μήτι ἐπιδυέτω," with the addition of the particle "μήτι" due to an itacism. This error could have resulted from the scribe's confusion of the vowel sounds eta (η) and iota (ι), causing an unintended addition to the text.

These examples illustrate the impact of itacism on the textual transmission of the New Testament. Textual critics must carefully identify these errors and compare manuscripts to reconstruct the original text as accurately as possible. By doing so, they can ensure that the meaning and integrity of the New Testament text are preserved for future generations.

Intentional Errors

A. Grammatical Improvements

Intentional errors are those made by scribes who intentionally altered the text, often in an attempt to improve grammar, clarify meaning, or harmonize parallel passages. One category of intentional errors involves grammatical improvements, where scribes sought to correct what they perceived as errors in grammar.

1. **Mark 6:29**: In some manuscripts, the word "ἦλθον" appears instead of the correct "ἦλθαν." This change likely occurred when a scribe attempted to improve the grammar by replacing the third-person plural verb form "ἦλθαν" with the singular form "ἦλθον," even though the plural form is appropriate in context.

2. **Matthew 5:22**: In certain manuscripts, the phrase "ὀργιζόμενος τῷ ἀδελφῷ αὐτοῦ" ("angry with his brother") has been changed to "ὀργιζόμενος ἀδελφῷ" ("angry with a brother"), likely as an attempt to correct the perceived grammatical error of the dative with the article. However, the original construction is correct and more precise in meaning.

3. **John 1:18**: Some believe that in some manuscripts, the phrase "μονογενὴς θεός" ("unique God") has been altered to "μονογενὴς υἱός" ("unique Son"). This change may have been made by a scribe who believed that "unique God" was a grammatical or theological error and sought to "correct" it by substituting "unique Son." The original words were μονογενὴς θεός or ο μονογενης θεος "only-begotten God" or "the only-begotten God" (P⁶⁶ P⁷⁵ ℵ B C* L 33 syrʰᵐᵖ 33 copᵇᵒ) A variant reading is ο μονογενης υιος "the only begotten Son" A C³ (Wˢ) Θ Ψ fˡ· Maj syrᶜ).

4. **1 Timothy 3:16**: In a few manuscripts, the phrase "θεὸς ἐφανερώθη ἐν σαρκί" ("God was manifested in the flesh") has been changed to "ὃς ἐφανερώθη ἐν σαρκί" ("who was

manifested in the flesh"). This alteration may have been made to "correct" the perceived grammatical or theological issue with the original phrase, but it results in a less precise statement of the Incarnation.

These examples show that scribes sometimes introduced intentional errors in an attempt to "improve" the grammar of the New Testament text. Textual critics must carefully identify these alterations and compare manuscripts to reconstruct the original text as accurately as possible. By doing so, they can ensure that the meaning and integrity of the New Testament text are preserved for future generations.

B. Liturgical Changes

Intentional errors in the form of liturgical changes occur when scribes modify the text to better suit the liturgical practices of their time or to align the text with familiar liturgical formulas. These alterations can include adding or omitting phrases, harmonizing passages, or inserting familiar liturgical elements.

1. **Matthew 6:13**: In some manuscripts, the doxology ("For thine is the kingdom, and the power, and the glory, forever. Amen.") is added to the end of the Lord's Prayer, while it is omitted in others. This variation likely resulted from scribes incorporating the doxology, which was commonly used in liturgical recitations of the prayer, into the written text.

2. **Luke 24:36**: In certain manuscripts, the phrase "καὶ λέγει αὐτοῖς, Εἰρήνη ὑμῖν" ("and said to them, 'Peace be with you'") is added to Jesus' appearance to the disciples after his resurrection. This insertion may have been influenced by the liturgical use of the phrase as a standard greeting in Christian worship.

3. **1 Corinthians 11:24-25**: In some manuscripts, the words "τοῦτο ποιεῖτε εἰς τὴν ἐμὴν ἀνάμνησιν" ("do this in remembrance of me") are added after both the distribution of the bread and the cup during the Last Supper. This repetition

likely reflects the liturgical practice of reciting these words during the celebration of the Eucharist.

4. **John 5:4**: The description of an angel stirring the water at the pool of Bethesda is found in some manuscripts but is absent in others. The addition of this verse may have been intended to provide a theological explanation for the healing properties of the water, aligning with popular beliefs and liturgical practices of the time.

These examples demonstrate how scribes sometimes introduced liturgical changes to the New Testament text, either intentionally or unintentionally, based on the religious practices and traditions of their communities. Textual scholars must carefully examine these variations to determine their origins and assess their impact on the overall understanding and interpretation of the biblical text.

C. Elimination of Apparent Discrepancies

Intentional errors in the form of eliminating apparent discrepancies occur when scribes modify the text to resolve perceived contradictions or inconsistencies. These alterations can include changing words, phrases, or references to harmonize passages or align them with other biblical texts.

1. **Mark 1:2**: In some manuscripts, the text reads ἐν τοῖς προφήταις ("in the prophets") while in others, it reads ἐν τῷ Ἠσαΐα τῷ προφήτῃ ("in Isaiah the prophet"). This change may have been made to address the fact that the quotation in Mark 1:2-3 is a composite of two Old Testament passages, one from Isaiah and one from Malachi. Changing the reference to "the prophets" would harmonize this apparent discrepancy.

2. **Luke 4:17**: In some manuscripts, the text reads τὸ βιβλίον τοῦ προφήτου Ἠσαΐου ("the book of the prophet Isaiah"), while in others, it reads τὸ βιβλίον τοῦ προφήτου ("the book of the prophet"). The latter reading may have been introduced to avoid the potential confusion that could arise from Jesus

quoting a passage that is not found in Isaiah in the following verses.

3. **Acts 9:7 and Acts 22:9**: In Acts 9:7, the men traveling with Saul are said to hear the voice but see no one, while in Acts 22:9, they are said to see the light but not hear the voice. Some manuscripts of Acts 22:9 have been altered to read "they did not understand the voice" instead of "they did not hear the voice" in order to resolve this apparent contradiction.

4. **Matthew 27:9**: In some manuscripts, the text reads "Then was fulfilled what was spoken by Jeremiah the prophet," while in others, it reads "Then was fulfilled what was spoken by the prophet." The latter reading may have been introduced because the quotation that follows is not found in Jeremiah but is similar to a passage in Zechariah. Changing the reference to "the prophet" would eliminate this discrepancy.

These examples demonstrate how scribes sometimes introduced changes to the New Testament text to resolve perceived discrepancies, either intentionally or unintentionally. Textual scholars must carefully examine these variations to determine their origins and assess their impact on the overall understanding and interpretation of the biblical text.

D. Harmonization of Parallel Passages

Intentional errors in the form of harmonization of parallel passages occur when scribes modify the text to make it consistent with a similar or parallel passage found in another part of the Bible. This type of alteration may involve the addition or omission of words, phrases, or entire verses to make the two passages more closely aligned. These changes can affect our understanding and interpretation of the text.

1. **Matthew 19:17 (cf. Mark 10:18)**: In Matthew 19:17, Jesus responds to the rich young ruler's question with, "Why do you ask me about what is good? There is only One who is good." In the parallel passage in Mark 10:18, Jesus says, "Why do you

call me good? No one is good except God alone." Some manuscripts of Matthew 19:17 have been altered to read, "Why do you call me good?" to harmonize it with the passage in Mark.

2. **Matthew 8:5-13 and Luke 7:1-10**: In the account of the centurion's servant, the centurion himself approaches Jesus in Matthew's version, while in Luke's account, the centurion sends Jewish elders on his behalf. Some manuscripts of Matthew 8:5-13 have been altered to include a reference to the centurion sending representatives to Jesus, bringing the two accounts into closer alignment.

3. **John 21:15-17 and the Synoptic Gospels**: In John's account of Jesus' post-resurrection appearance, Jesus asks Peter three times if he loves him. This triple questioning is unique to John's Gospel, and some manuscripts have altered the Synoptic accounts (Matthew 26:69-75, Mark 14:66-72, and Luke 22:54-62) to include a reference to Jesus questioning Peter three times, to harmonize the Gospels.

4. **Matthew 3:16 and Luke 3:22**: In the account of Jesus' baptism, the Holy Spirit is described as descending upon Jesus "like a dove" in Matthew 3:16, while in Luke 3:22, the Holy Spirit descends "in bodily form like a dove." Some manuscripts of Matthew 3:16 have been altered to include the phrase "in bodily form," harmonizing the descriptions of the Holy Spirit's appearance in the two accounts.

These examples illustrate how scribes sometimes harmonized parallel passages in the New Testament, either intentionally or unintentionally, to make the accounts consistent with one another. Textual critics must carefully examine these variations and weigh their impact on our understanding and interpretation of the biblical text.

E. Conflation

Conflation occurs when scribes merge two or more variant readings into one, often in an attempt to incorporate all the information from different manuscripts. This process may be done intentionally or accidentally, and it can create readings that are not present in any of the original texts. Here are some additional examples:

1. **Mark 1:40-41**: In the account of Jesus healing a leper, there are two main readings for Jesus' emotional response: one that says Jesus was "moved with compassion" (σπλαγχνισθείς) and another that says he was "moved with anger" (ὀργισθείς). Some manuscripts combine the two readings, stating that Jesus was "moved with compassion and anger" (σπλαγχνισθείς καὶ ὀργισθείς), which is a conflation of the two variant readings.

2. **Acts 20:28**: There are three main readings for the phrase referring to the church: "church of God" (ἐκκλησίαν τοῦ θεοῦ), "church of the Lord" (ἐκκλησίαν τοῦ κυρίου), and "church of the Lord and God" (ἐκκλησίαν τοῦ κυρίου καὶ θεοῦ). The last reading is likely a conflation of the first two variants.

3. **1 Corinthians 15:51-52**: In the discussion of the resurrection, there are two primary readings for the timing of the transformation: "at the last trumpet" (ἐν τῇ ἐσχάτῃ σάλπιγγι) and "in a moment, in the twinkling of an eye" (ἐν ἀτόμῳ, ἐν ῥιπῇ ὀφθαλμοῦ). Some manuscripts contain both phrases, "at the last trumpet, in a moment, in the twinkling of an eye" (ἐν τῇ ἐσχάτῃ σάλπιγγι, ἐν ἀτόμῳ, ἐν ῥιπῇ ὀφθαλμοῦ), which is likely a conflation of the two separate readings.

4. **Revelation 1:11**: In this verse, Jesus instructs John to write what he sees in a book and send it to seven churches. The order of the churches differs among manuscripts, with some listing Ephesus, Smyrna, Pergamum, Thyatira, Sardis, Philadelphia, and Laodicea, while others have a different order. A few manuscripts contain a conflation of these orders, listing the churches in multiple sequences.

These examples demonstrate how conflation can result in the blending of different textual variants, creating readings that might not have been part of the original text. Textual scholars must carefully analyze such cases to determine which reading is most likely to be authentic.

F. Doctrinal Changes

Doctrinal changes are alterations to the biblical text that appear to have been made to support or clarify specific theological beliefs. These changes may have been intentional, stemming from a scribe's desire to emphasize or reinforce particular doctrines. Here are some additional examples:

1. **John 1:18**: In this verse, some manuscripts read "the only begotten Son" (μονογενὴς υἱός), while others read "the only begotten God" (μονογενὴς θεός). The latter variant, found in some early manuscripts, may have been introduced to emphasize the divinity of Jesus more explicitly. The original words were μονογενὴς θεός or ο μονογενης θεος "only-begotten God" or "the only-begotten God" (P[66] P[75] ℵ B C* L 33 syr[hmp] 33 cop[bo]) A variant reading is ο μονογενης υιος "the only begotten Son" A C[3] (W[s]) Θ Ψ f[1.] Maj syr[c]).

2. **Romans 8:1**: In some manuscripts, this verse ends with the phrase "who walk not after the flesh, but after the Spirit" (οἱ μὴ κατὰ σάρκα περιπατοῦντες, ἀλλὰ κατὰ πνεῦμα). This addition, not present in the earliest manuscripts, might have been made to clarify the conditions under which there is no condemnation for those in Christ Jesus.

3. **Acts 8:37**: This verse contains a confession of faith by the Ethiopian eunuch, stating, "I believe that Jesus Christ is the Son of God." However, this verse is absent from the earliest and most reliable manuscripts, suggesting that it may have been added later to emphasize the importance of confessing faith in Jesus.

4. **Mark 16:9-20**: The longer ending of Mark's Gospel, which includes accounts of Jesus' post-resurrection appearances and instructions to his disciples, is absent from the earliest and most reliable manuscripts. Some scholars believe that this

passage was added to provide a more satisfactory conclusion to the Gospel, which would otherwise end abruptly at Mark 16:8.

5. **Matthew 28:19**: In this verse, Jesus instructs his disciples to baptize "in the name of the Father, and of the Son, and of the Holy Spirit." Some scholars have argued that this Trinitarian formula may have been added later to emphasize the orthodox doctrine of the Trinity, as the earliest Christian baptisms were performed in the name of Jesus only (as evidenced in Acts).

These examples illustrate how doctrinal changes might have been introduced into the biblical text over time, either to clarify, emphasize, or support specific theological beliefs. Textual scholars must carefully consider the manuscript evidence and historical context to determine the most likely original readings.

The Process of Transmission and the Emergence of Text Types

A. The Role of Scribes and Copyists

Scribes and copyists played a critical role in the transmission of the New Testament text. These individuals were responsible for copying the original manuscripts and their subsequent copies, ensuring that the biblical texts were preserved and disseminated across the early Christian communities. The process of copying was typically done by hand, which made it susceptible to various types of errors and alterations, both intentional and unintentional. Despite these challenges, scribes and copyists were essential in preserving the New Testament text and enabling its study and analysis today.

1. **Training and Skill Level**: The skill level of scribes and copyists varied significantly. Some were highly trained professionals who dedicated their lives to the meticulous copying of texts, while others might have been less skilled or even amateurs, making errors more likely. The quality of a

manuscript copy could depend on the skill and expertise of the scribe responsible for its creation.

2. **Writing Materials and Techniques**: Scribes used various materials and techniques to copy texts. Early manuscripts were written on papyrus, a relatively fragile and perishable material made from the papyrus plant. Later, parchment (animal skin) was used for its durability. Scribes would use ink and a stylus or reed pen to write on these materials. The quality of the writing materials and the scribe's technique could impact the longevity and accuracy of the manuscript copies.

3. **Working Conditions**: The working conditions for scribes and copyists could also impact the quality of their work. They may have worked in scriptoria (special rooms dedicated to the copying of texts) or in less formal settings. Poor lighting, uncomfortable seating, or distractions could result in errors and inconsistencies in the copied text.

4. **Quality Control**: In some cases, scribes' work was subject to review by a corrector or a group of correctors who would compare the copied text to the exemplar (the manuscript being copied) to identify and correct errors. This quality control process could help to minimize the introduction of errors, but it was not always consistently applied or foolproof.

The role of scribes and copyists in the transmission of the New Testament text was essential, as they were responsible for the preservation and dissemination of the biblical texts. Their varying skill levels, working conditions, writing materials, and quality control measures contributed to the emergence of textual variants and the development of different text types. Textual scholars study these factors to better understand the transmission process and to reconstruct the most likely original readings of the New Testament.

B. The Development of Text Types: Alexandrian, Western, Byzantine, and Caesarean

As the New Testament texts were copied and circulated throughout the early Christian world, various textual traditions emerged. These traditions, or text types, were characterized by distinct patterns of readings, which resulted from the copying process, scribal habits, regional influences, and other factors. Four primary text types have been identified by textual scholars: Alexandrian, Western, Byzantine, and Caesarean.

1. **Alexandrian Text Type**: The Alexandrian text type is named after the city of Alexandria in Egypt, where it is believed to have originated. This text type is considered by many scholars to be the most accurate and reliable, as it tends to have fewer alterations and additions than the other text types. The Alexandrian text type is characterized by its concise and precise language, and its relatively strict adherence to the original wording. Some of the oldest and most important manuscripts, such as Codex Vaticanus and Codex Sinaiticus, belong to this text type.

2. **Western Text Type**: The Western text type is thought to have originated in the western regions of the Roman Empire, particularly in North Africa and Italy. This text type is characterized by a more expansive and paraphrastic style, often including additional explanatory material or harmonizations between parallel passages. Some scholars consider the Western text type to be less reliable due to these additions and alterations. Important manuscripts belonging to the Western text type include Codex Bezae and the Old Latin translations.

3. **Byzantine Text Type**: The Byzantine text type, also known as the Majority Text, is named after the Byzantine Empire, where it was the dominant textual tradition. This text type is characterized by a high degree of uniformity and a tendency to harmonize and smooth out apparent discrepancies or difficulties in the text. The Byzantine text type became the

177

basis for the Textus Receptus, which was used in the production of the King James Version and other early translations. The vast majority of later minuscule manuscripts belong to the Byzantine text type.

4. **Caesarean Text Type**: The Caesarean text type is a less well-defined category, with some debate among scholars regarding its existence and characteristics. It is believed to have originated in the region of Caesarea, and its readings are often seen as a mixture of Alexandrian and Western text types. Some scholars suggest that the Caesarean text type represents an earlier stage in the development of the other text types. Key manuscripts associated with the Caesarean text type include the Chester Beatty Papyri and Codex Koridethi.

The development of these text types reflects the diverse ways in which the New Testament texts were copied, transmitted, and preserved throughout the early Christian world. Textual scholars study the characteristics and relationships of these text types to better understand the history of the New Testament text and to reconstruct the most accurate and reliable readings.

Textual Criticism and the Evaluation of Variants

A. Principles of Textual Criticism

Textual criticism is the scholarly discipline that seeks to analyze and evaluate the various readings found in the manuscripts of a given text, with the ultimate goal of reconstructing the most accurate and original form of the text. In the context of the New Testament, textual critics examine the numerous manuscript copies to determine the most likely original readings. To accomplish this task, textual critics employ a set of guiding principles and methodologies that help them make informed decisions when evaluating variant readings. Some of the key principles of textual criticism include:

1. **External Evidence**: This principle involves examining the manuscript evidence itself, such as the age, geographical distribution, and text type of the manuscripts that contain a particular reading. Generally, older manuscripts and those from a diverse range of text types are given greater weight in the evaluation process, as they are more likely to be closer to the original text.

2. **Internal Evidence**: Internal evidence focuses on the content of the variant readings, as well as the context and style of the author. Two main aspects of internal evidence are considered: transcriptional probability and intrinsic probability. Transcriptional probability assesses which reading is more likely to have given rise to the others, often based on known scribal habits and tendencies. Intrinsic probability considers which reading best fits the author's style, vocabulary, and theological perspective, as well as the immediate context of the passage.

3. **Lectio Difficilior Potior ("the more difficult reading is preferable")**: This principle is based on the assumption that scribes were more likely to simplify or harmonize a difficult or obscure reading rather than intentionally create difficulties in the text. Therefore, when faced with two or more variant readings, the more difficult or challenging reading is often considered more likely to be original.

4. **Lectio Brevior Potior ("the shorter reading is preferable")**: This principle assumes that scribes were more likely to expand or add explanatory material to a text, rather than remove content. As a result, when evaluating variant readings, the shorter reading is often given preference, as it is considered more likely to be closer to the original wording.

5. **The Coherence Principle**: This principle takes into account the overall coherence of a reading with the rest of the text, including the author's style, vocabulary, and theological perspective. A reading that is consistent with the author's

known characteristics and the immediate context is considered more likely to be original.

These principles of textual criticism, along with other more specific methodologies, provide a framework for textual critics to evaluate the variant readings found in the New Testament manuscripts. By applying these principles systematically and carefully, scholars can make informed decisions about the most likely original readings, thereby contributing to a more accurate and reliable understanding of the New Testament text.

B. *Major Textual Criticism Projects and Their Influence on Modern Translations*

Throughout history, several significant textual criticism projects have been undertaken to compile, analyze, and evaluate the manuscript evidence for the New Testament. These projects have had a considerable impact on the development of modern Bible translations, as they provide a more accurate and reliable textual basis for translation work. Some of the most influential textual criticism projects include:

1. Novum Testamentum Graece (Nestle-Aland): The Nestle-Aland Greek New Testament is a critical edition of the Greek New Testament that has undergone numerous revisions since its first publication in 1898. This critical edition compiles and evaluates the manuscript evidence to present the most accurate and reliable reconstruction of the original Greek text. The Nestle-Aland text is widely used as the basis for modern translations and is considered one of the most authoritative sources for New Testament scholarship.

2. United Bible Societies' Greek New Testament (UBS): The UBS Greek New Testament is another critical edition of the Greek text, developed in collaboration with the United Bible Societies. This edition shares much in common with the Nestle-Aland text but is specifically designed for use in Bible translation work, featuring an apparatus that prioritizes variant readings based on their relevance for translators. The UBS text

has been influential in shaping many modern Bible translations.

3. The International Greek New Testament Project (IGNTP): The IGNTP is an ongoing collaborative project that aims to produce comprehensive critical editions of the Greek New Testament, focusing on specific books or sections of the text. The project brings together scholars from various institutions and backgrounds to analyze and evaluate the manuscript evidence. The results of the IGNTP's work contribute to a more accurate understanding of the New Testament text and inform the work of modern translators.

4. The Editio Critica Maior (ECM): The ECM is a long-term research project initiated by the Institute for New Testament Textual Research in Münster, Germany. Its goal is to produce a comprehensive, multi-volume critical edition of the Greek New Testament, incorporating the latest manuscript discoveries and advances in textual criticism methodology. The ECM's findings are expected to have a significant impact on future Bible translations and New Testament scholarship.

These major textual criticism projects have played a crucial role in shaping our understanding of the New Testament text and providing a reliable basis for modern Bible translations. By meticulously analyzing and evaluating the manuscript evidence, these projects help to ensure that contemporary translations accurately reflect the original wording and meaning of the New Testament, enabling readers to engage more deeply with the biblical text.

The Complex History of Textual Variants and Their Impact on the New Testament Text

The New Testament, composed in the first century CE, has a long and intricate history of transmission. Over the centuries, scribes and copyists have meticulously replicated the text, resulting in a vast array of manuscripts. However, despite their best efforts, various textual variants have emerged, impacting the way we understand and interpret the New Testament today. This essay will examine the complex history of textual variants and their impact on the New Testament text.

1. The Process of Manuscript Transmission

The New Testament was originally written in Greek on papyrus scrolls, and later on parchment and vellum. The texts were then copied and recopied by scribes, often within scriptoria attached to monasteries or other religious institutions. With each new copy, the potential for errors and variations increased, as scribes made unintentional mistakes or introduced intentional changes. The sheer number of manuscripts produced over time resulted in a vast array of textual variants.

2. Causes of Textual Variants

Textual variants can arise from a multitude of factors, including scribal errors, misreadings, and intentional alterations. Some common causes include:

a) **Accidental Errors**: Scribes occasionally made unintentional errors while copying the text, such as faulty word division, homoeoteleuton (skipping from one similar ending to another), haplography (writing a letter or word once when it should be written twice), and dittography (writing a letter or word twice when it should be written once).

b) **Intentional Changes**: Scribes sometimes introduced intentional alterations, whether to improve grammar, adjust for liturgical purposes, eliminate discrepancies, harmonize parallel passages, conflate readings, or modify the text for doctrinal reasons.

3. The Emergence of Text Types

Over time, distinct families or text types emerged, each characterized by specific patterns of textual variants. The four primary text types are Alexandrian, Western, Byzantine, and Caesarean. The Alexandrian text type is generally considered the most reliable due to its early origin and careful transmission. The Western text type is characterized by paraphrasing and expansions, while the Byzantine text type is more uniform and represents the majority of extant manuscripts. The Caesarean text type is a less clearly defined group, possibly representing a mixture of the Alexandrian and Western text types.

4. Textual Criticism and the Evaluation of Variants

Textual criticism is the scholarly discipline that aims to reconstruct the original text of the New Testament by analyzing and evaluating textual variants. This process involves several principles, such as favoring the more difficult reading, the shorter reading, and the reading that best explains the origin of the other readings. Through careful analysis of the manuscript evidence, textual critics work to establish the most reliable and authentic text, which forms the basis for modern translations.

5. The Impact of Textual Variants on the New Testament Text

Textual variants have both positive and negative consequences for our understanding of the New Testament. On the one hand, they can introduce confusion and uncertainty, as scholars and readers grapple with discrepancies and alternate readings. Some variants have significant implications for the interpretation of specific passages or doctrines, as seen in the debate surrounding the long ending of Mark or the "Heavenly Witnesses" passage in 1 John 5:7-8.

On the other hand, textual variants also enrich our understanding of the New Testament by providing insights into the historical, cultural, and religious context in which the text was transmitted. They reveal the complex process of transmission and the diverse factors that shaped the text over time. Moreover, the study of textual variants has led to significant advances in the field of textual criticism, as scholars refine their methodologies and develop new techniques for evaluating and interpreting the evidence. This ongoing work has resulted in increasingly accurate and reliable editions of the New Testament text, which serve as the foundation for contemporary translations, commentaries, and theological studies.

6. The Enduring Importance of Textual Variants

Despite the challenges posed by textual variants, their study remains crucial for understanding the history and development of the New Testament text. By examining the various readings and their implications, scholars can continue to deepen our knowledge of the text's original meaning, as well as the historical and cultural factors that shaped its transmission. Furthermore, the examination of textual variants fosters an appreciation for the meticulous work of the scribes and copyists who diligently preserved the New Testament writings for future generations.

In conclusion, the complex history of textual variants has had a profound impact on the New Testament text, shaping its development and interpretation over the centuries. Through the careful study of these variants, scholars have gained valuable insights into the transmission process and the factors that influenced the text. As textual criticism continues to evolve and refine its methodologies, our understanding of the New Testament and its message will only grow more precise and nuanced, ensuring its enduring relevance for generations to come.

CHAPTER 5 The Printed New Testament Text

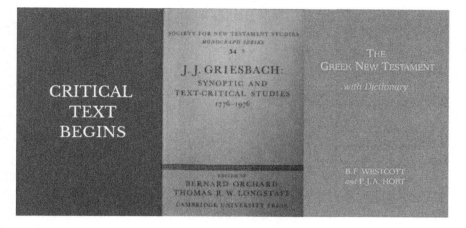

Introduction to the Printed New Testament Era

The printed New Testament era refers to the period in history when the New Testament was reproduced using the newly-invented printing press. This era began in the 15th century, with the advent of Johannes Gutenberg's printing press, and continues to this day with the proliferation of digital versions of the New Testament. The introduction of the printing press revolutionized the way books were produced, making it possible to create large quantities of identical copies quickly and cheaply. Prior to the invention of the printing press, books were produced by hand, which was a laborious and time-consuming process. The ability to print books, including the New Testament, led to a significant increase in their availability and accessibility, especially to the general population.

The printed New Testament era also marks a turning point in the study of the New Testament text. Prior to the printing press, the New Testament was copied by hand, which led to variations and errors in the text. The production of identical copies through the printing press made it possible for scholars to compare different versions of the text more easily, leading to a better understanding of the original text. Additionally, the printed New Testament made it possible to produce critical editions of the text, which included notes and annotations that helped to explain the meaning of the text and the variations in the different versions.

The printed New Testament era also saw the proliferation of translations of the New Testament into many different languages. Prior to the printing press, the New Testament was primarily available in Greek and Latin. However, with the ability to print books quickly and cheaply, it became possible to produce translations of the New Testament into many different languages. This led to a wider dissemination of the text and helped to promote literacy and education, as people were able to read and study the New Testament in their own language.

In summary, the printed New Testament era was a pivotal moment in the history of the New Testament. It allowed for the production of large quantities of identical copies of the text, which increased its availability and accessibility. It also led to the production of critical editions of the text and the proliferation of translations into many different languages. The printed New Testament era has had a profound impact on the study of the New Testament and continues to shape the way we read and understand the text today.

The Invention of the Printing Press and Its Impact on Biblical Texts

The invention of the printing press in the 15th century revolutionized the way books were produced and disseminated throughout Europe. Prior to the printing press, books were produced by hand, making them expensive and accessible only to a limited number of people, primarily those in positions of power and authority. The printing press changed all of that, making it possible to produce books quickly, efficiently, and inexpensively.

The impact of the printing press on biblical texts was profound. Prior to the invention of the printing press, the Bible was primarily accessible only to the clergy and those in positions of power. The production of handwritten Bibles was an expensive and time-consuming process that required a great deal of skill and labor. As a result, there were few copies of the Bible in circulation, and those that did exist were often incomplete or inaccurate.

The printing press changed all of that. With the ability to produce large numbers of books quickly and efficiently, the printing press made it possible to produce complete and accurate copies of the Bible on a large scale. This had a number of important consequences.

First, it made the Bible more accessible to the general public. With the availability of inexpensive printed Bibles, ordinary people could now own their own copies of the Bible and read it for themselves. This was a major departure from the previous era, in which only the clergy and the wealthy had access to the Bible.

Second, it helped to standardize the text of the Bible. Prior to the printing press, the Bible was transmitted through handwritten copies, which were subject to errors and variations. With the ability to produce multiple copies of the same text, the printing press made it possible to establish a standard text of the Bible that could be reproduced with a high degree of accuracy.

Third, it enabled scholars to compare different editions of the Bible and identify errors and discrepancies. With the availability of multiple copies of the same text, scholars could compare different editions of the Bible and identify variations and errors. This led to a renewed interest in textual criticism, the study of the history and transmission of biblical texts.

Finally, it facilitated the spread of new ideas and interpretations of the Bible. With the availability of printed Bibles, new ideas and interpretations could be disseminated more widely and quickly than ever before. This led to a flourishing of religious and intellectual movements throughout Europe, including the Protestant Reformation.

In summary, the invention of the printing press had a profound impact on the production, dissemination, and interpretation of biblical texts. It helped to make the Bible more accessible to the general public, established a standard text of the Bible, facilitated the study of textual criticism, and facilitated the spread of new ideas and interpretations of the Bible.

The First Printed Editions of the New Testament

The Gutenberg Bible

The Gutenberg Bible, also known as the 42-line Bible, is a printed version of the Latin Vulgate translation of the Bible produced by Johannes Gutenberg in Mainz, Germany, around 1455. It is considered one of the most significant works in the history of printing and bookmaking, as it was the first book ever printed with movable type.

Gutenberg's Bible was produced using a revolutionary printing press he invented, which used individual pieces of metal type that could be rearranged and reused to print different texts. Each page of the Bible consisted of two columns of 42 lines each, hence the name "42-line Bible." The typeface used was a Gothic typeface known as Textura, which was commonly used in manuscripts at the time.

The Gutenberg Bible was printed on high-quality paper made from rags, which was expensive and time-consuming to produce. Each page was printed separately, and the ink was applied using a handheld ink roller. The printing process was slow and labor-intensive, with each page taking several minutes to print.

Only around 180 copies of the Gutenberg Bible were printed, with most of them being printed on paper and a few on vellum, a type of parchment made from animal skin. Many of the copies were bound in ornate and expensive covers, with some copies containing hand-painted illuminations.

The Gutenberg Bible had a significant impact on the dissemination of biblical texts, as it made it possible to produce multiple copies of the Bible more quickly and efficiently than ever before. The production of printed Bibles helped to spread literacy and education throughout Europe, as people could now read the Bible for themselves rather than relying on the clergy to interpret it for them.

Today, the Gutenberg Bible is considered a masterpiece of printing and bookmaking, with each copy being highly prized by collectors and institutions around the world.

Erasmus's Textus Receptus

Erasmus's Greek New Testament, also known as the Textus Receptus, was the first printed Greek text of the New Testament. Erasmus's work was a major milestone in the history of the printed Bible and textual criticism. It served as the basis for many subsequent editions of the Greek New Testament, and its influence can still be seen in modern translations of the Bible.

Erasmus's interest in the Greek New Testament began during his studies at the University of Paris in the early 1490s. He recognized the need for a more accurate and reliable edition of the New Testament, as the Latin Vulgate used by the Catholic Church contained errors and discrepancies. To this end, he began collecting Greek manuscripts of the New Testament from across Europe, including Spain, Italy, and Switzerland.

Erasmus's Greek New Testament was first published in 1516, using a relatively small number of manuscripts that he had collected. It was not the first printed Greek New Testament - that honor belongs to the Complutensian Polyglot, which was published in Spain in 1514. However, Erasmus's edition was the first to be widely distributed and used by scholars and theologians throughout Europe.

Erasmus's Greek New Testament was not without its flaws. He had access to relatively few manuscripts, and those that he did have were often incomplete or damaged. As a result, his edition contained many errors, and he was forced to rely heavily on earlier Latin translations of the New Testament. Nevertheless, his work represented a major step forward in the study of the New Testament, and it provided a foundation for subsequent editions.

Erasmus's work was controversial in its time, and he faced criticism from both Catholic and Protestant leaders. Some accused him of promoting heresy by questioning the authority of the Latin Vulgate, while others accused him of promoting humanism and undermining traditional Christianity. Nevertheless, his work was widely influential, and it paved the way for future editions of the Greek New Testament, including those of Theodore Beza and Johann Jakob Griesbach.

In conclusion, Erasmus's Greek New Testament, or the Textus Receptus, was the first printed Greek text of the New Testament. Despite its flaws, it represented a major step forward in the study of the New Testament and served as the foundation for subsequent editions. Its influence can still be seen in modern translations of the Bible, and it remains an important milestone in the history of the printed Bible and textual criticism.

The Complutensian Polyglot

The Complutensian Polyglot is a six-volume work that contains the entire Bible in Hebrew, Greek, and Latin, along with extensive annotations, introductions, and other supplementary material. It was produced under the auspices of Cardinal Francisco Jiménez de Cisneros in the early sixteenth century, and its publication marked a significant milestone in the history of biblical scholarship.

The Complutensian Polyglot was the first printed edition of the entire Bible in its original languages, and it was a monumental achievement in the development of textual criticism. It was produced in the city of Alcalá de Henares, Spain, and took over ten years to complete. The project was commissioned by Cisneros, a prominent churchman and scholar, who hoped that it would serve as a tool for the study of the Bible and as a means of promoting scholarship in the church.

The Polyglot was a collaborative effort that involved many scholars, including the famous Hebrew grammarian and rabbinic scholar, Jacob ben Hayyim. The text was based on a collation of various manuscripts and printed editions of the Hebrew and Greek texts, and it was carefully edited and corrected to produce a highly accurate version of the Bible in its original languages.

The Complutensian Polyglot was printed using the latest printing technology of the time, including movable type and an early form of printing press. The text was printed on high-quality paper, and the pages were beautifully decorated with ornate borders and other decorative elements. The Polyglot was produced in a limited edition of only 600 copies, and it was intended primarily for distribution to scholars and institutions.

The impact of the Complutensian Polyglot on biblical scholarship cannot be overstated. It provided scholars with a reliable and accurate version of the Bible in its original languages, and it helped to promote the study of Hebrew and Greek among scholars and students. The Polyglot was also an important tool for the development of textual criticism, as it provided scholars with a wealth of information about the various manuscripts and printed editions of the Bible that were available at the time.

Despite its significance, the Complutensian Polyglot did not immediately gain widespread acceptance or use. Its publication coincided with the beginning of the Protestant Reformation, which led to a proliferation of competing editions of the Bible in various languages. Nevertheless, the Polyglot remained an important reference work for scholars and theologians throughout the sixteenth and seventeenth centuries, and its impact can still be felt today in the ongoing study of the Bible and its ancient languages.

The Evolution of Textual Criticism and Scholarly Editions

The Critical Editions of the New Testament

The critical editions of the New Testament refer to scholarly editions of the Greek text of the New Testament that aim to provide a reconstructed version of the original text based on the best available manuscript evidence and critical methods of textual analysis. These editions are widely used by scholars, translators, and theologians as the basis for their work on the New Testament.

The critical editions of the New Testament have a long history, dating back to the early modern period when scholars began to study the manuscript evidence and apply critical methods to the textual analysis of the New Testament. Among the early pioneers of critical scholarship were figures such as Desiderius Erasmus, Robert Estienne, and Theodore Beza, who produced important printed editions of the Greek text based on the best available manuscript evidence.

In the 19th and 20th centuries, the critical editions of the New Testament underwent significant development, with the discovery of numerous new manuscripts, advances in textual criticism, and the emergence of new editorial methodologies. One of the most important figures in this period was B. F. Westcott, who, along with F. J. A. Hort, produced a landmark edition of the New Testament in 1881 that became known as the Westcott and Hort text. This edition was based on a careful analysis of the manuscript evidence and incorporated the latest insights from textual criticism, including the idea of text families and the importance of the Alexandrian text-type.

Other significant critical editions of the New Testament include the Nestle-Aland Greek New Testament and the United Bible Societies' Greek New Testament. The Nestle-Aland edition, named after its initial editor Eberhard Nestle and later editor Kurt Aland, has undergone numerous revisions and updates since its first publication in 1898 and is widely used by scholars and translators today. The United Bible Societies' edition, which was first published in 1966, is designed to be more user-friendly than the Nestle-Aland edition, with a simpler and more concise critical apparatus.

In recent years, scholars have continued to produce new critical editions of the New Testament based on the latest manuscript evidence and critical methods. One example is the Editio Critica Maior, a major project that aims to produce a new edition of the Greek New Testament based on a thorough examination of all the available manuscripts and other sources. The project is still ongoing, but its work has already resulted in important new insights into the history and transmission of the New Testament text.

Overall, the critical editions of the New Testament have played a crucial role in the scholarly study and interpretation of the New Testament, providing a reliable and carefully reconstructed version of the original text that serves as the basis for further research and analysis.

The Contributions of Early Textual Critics

The study of the text of the New Testament has a long history, with many scholars throughout the centuries working to identify and preserve the most accurate and authentic readings of the text. These early textual critics, despite not having access to the wealth of manuscripts and resources available to modern scholars, made significant contributions to the field that have endured to this day.

One of the earliest and most significant figures in the history of New Testament textual criticism was Origen of Alexandria (184-253 AD). Origen was a prolific biblical scholar who was particularly interested in the question of the accuracy of the biblical text. In his Hexapla, a massive six-column comparison of various translations and versions of the Hebrew Bible, Origen highlighted differences and discrepancies in the text and provided notes on the variations. While his work was focused primarily on the Hebrew Bible, Origen's attention to detail and his rigorous approach to the study of the text set a precedent for later textual critics.

Another important figure in the history of New Testament textual criticism was Eusebius of Caesarea (260-340 AD), a bishop and historian who wrote extensively on the history of the Christian church. Eusebius was particularly interested in the question of the authenticity of the biblical text, and he compiled a list of canonical books that would later be accepted by the early church. He also made efforts to collect and preserve early manuscripts of the New Testament, recognizing the importance of having accurate and reliable copies of the text.

In the Middle Ages, the work of textual criticism was continued by scholars such as Desiderius Erasmus (1466-1536) and Robert Estienne (1503-1559), both of whom made significant contributions to the field. Erasmus was particularly important, as he produced the first printed Greek New Testament in 1516, known as the Textus Receptus. This edition, based on a handful of manuscripts available to Erasmus, became the standard text for the Reformation and had a lasting impact on the study of the New Testament. Estienne, also known as Stephanus, produced several important editions of the New Testament that incorporated more manuscripts and provided extensive notes on the variations in the text.

In the 18th and 19th centuries, the work of textual criticism took on a new importance as scholars began to use newly-discovered manuscripts and archaeological evidence to refine their understanding of the text. Johann Jakob Wettstein (1693-1754) was one of the earliest and most influential scholars in this new era of textual criticism. Wettstein was particularly interested in the differences between the various text types, and he produced an important edition of the New Testament that incorporated readings from a wide variety of manuscripts.

Another important figure in this era was Johann Jakob Griesbach (1745-1812), a German theologian and biblical scholar who produced a critical edition of the New Testament in which he identified and classified different readings according to their source. Griesbach's work was significant because it laid the groundwork for the later study of textual variants and provided a framework for identifying the most likely original readings of the text.

In the 20th century, the work of textual criticism continued to evolve and expand as scholars gained access to an increasing number of manuscripts and developed new methodologies for analyzing the text. One of the most important scholars of this era was Bruce Metzger (1914-2007), a New Testament scholar who produced numerous editions of the Greek New Testament and provided extensive notes on the variations in the text. Metzger's work was notable for its rigor and attention to detail, and it set a new standard for the study of New Testament textual criticism.

The Development of Modern Textual Criticism

The development of modern textual criticism can be traced back to the 18th century, when scholars began to seriously question the accuracy and reliability of the Textus Receptus, the dominant Greek New Testament text used by the Protestant church. Early textual critics, such as Richard Bentley and Johann Jakob Wettstein, sought to compare and evaluate different manuscripts in order to reconstruct the original text of the New Testament.

However, it was the work of scholars in the 19th and 20th centuries that established the principles and practices of modern textual criticism. The following is a brief overview of some of the key developments in modern textual criticism.

Lachmann and the Science of Textual Criticism

One of the most important figures in the development of modern textual criticism was Karl Lachmann, a German scholar who lived from 1793 to 1851. Lachmann's work represented a major shift in the approach to textual criticism. He rejected the traditional method of comparing different manuscripts and instead focused on the internal evidence of the texts themselves.

Lachmann argued that the original text of the New Testament must have been written in a specific dialect of Greek, and that it would have been transmitted consistently within that dialect. He thus sought to identify the underlying dialect of the New Testament text and to

196

reconstruct the original text based on that knowledge. This approach to textual criticism was a significant departure from previous methods and set the stage for the scientific study of textual criticism that followed.

Tregelles and the Critical Apparatus

Another important figure in the development of modern textual criticism was Samuel Prideaux Tregelles, a British scholar who lived from 1813 to 1875. Tregelles was a proponent of the science of textual criticism and developed the critical apparatus, which provided detailed information about the variants in different manuscripts. This allowed scholars to evaluate the strength of the textual evidence for different readings.

Tregelles also developed a systematic approach to evaluating textual variants, based on the principles of internal evidence, external evidence, and genealogy. These principles are still used by textual critics today.

Westcott and Hort and the Alexandrian Text

Perhaps the most influential figures in the development of modern textual criticism were Brooke Foss Westcott and Fenton John Anthony Hort, two British scholars who lived in the 19th century. Westcott and Hort argued that the Alexandrian text-type, which was represented by a small number of early manuscripts, was the most reliable and accurate representation of the original text.

Westcott and Hort's approach to textual criticism was based on the principles of genealogy and internal evidence. They argued that the Alexandrian text-type was the result of an early and pure transmission of the text, while the Byzantine text-type, which was represented by a large number of later manuscripts, was the result of a gradual corruption of the text.

Westcott and Hort's views were controversial at the time, but their work had a significant impact on the development of modern textual criticism. Their approach to textual criticism, which emphasized the importance of internal evidence and the use of a small number of reliable manuscripts, continues to influence textual critics today.

Conclusion

Modern textual criticism has developed over several centuries and has been shaped by the work of many scholars. From Lachmann's focus on internal evidence to Westcott and Hort's emphasis on the Alexandrian text-type, these scholars have developed principles and practices that continue to guide the work of textual critics today. Through their work, we have gained a greater understanding of the transmission and evolution of the New Testament text and have been able to reconstruct the original text with a greater degree of accuracy than ever before.

Loosing sight of the Goal

Modern New Testament textual criticism has undergone significant developments in the last two centuries, and while it has made tremendous strides in reconstructing the original text of the New Testament, some have criticized it for focusing too much on historical and social issues, rather than the primary goal of reconstructing the original text.

New Testament textual criticism emerged in the late 18th century, and it aimed to reconstruct the original text of the New Testament by comparing and evaluating different manuscripts of the Greek New Testament. Early textual critics such as Johann Jakob Griesbach and Johann Albrecht Bengel contributed significantly to the development of textual criticism by devising various methods of textual analysis and establishing textual rules to guide the evaluation of manuscripts.

During the 19th century, textual criticism continued to advance, and scholars such as Constantin von Tischendorf, who discovered the Codex Sinaiticus, and Westcott and Hort, who produced a groundbreaking critical edition of the Greek New Testament, made significant contributions to the field.

However, in recent decades, some scholars have criticized modern-day textual criticism for deviating from its original purpose of reconstructing the original text of the New Testament. Instead, they argue that it has become more focused on historical and social issues, such as the transmission of texts and the social context in which they were written.

One reason for this shift is the increasing recognition that the process of textual transmission is not straightforward and that texts were often copied and modified to fit the needs of the community in which they were produced. As a result, some scholars have argued that it is important to understand the social context of the texts and the communities in which they were produced to fully appreciate their meaning and significance.

Moreover, the emergence of new technologies and approaches to textual analysis, such as digital humanities and corpus linguistics, has led some scholars to focus on the quantitative analysis of texts rather than the traditional methods of manuscript comparison and evaluation.

While these developments have undoubtedly enriched our understanding of the New Testament and its historical and social context, some critics argue that they have come at the expense of the primary goal of reconstructing the original text. They argue that modern textual criticism has lost sight of the importance of evaluating manuscript evidence and has become too focused on extraneous issues.

However, it is important to note that these two goals are not mutually exclusive. Understanding the social and historical context of a text can provide valuable insights into its meaning and significance, and it can also help scholars to better evaluate manuscript evidence and identify authentic readings.

Furthermore, some scholars have argued that the shift towards a more social and historical approach to textual criticism is not necessarily a departure from the original goals of the discipline but rather a necessary development that reflects the changing landscape of scholarship.

In conclusion, modern-day New Testament textual criticism has undoubtedly undergone significant changes in the last few decades, with some scholars criticizing its focus on historical and social issues at the expense of the primary goal of reconstructing the original text. However, it is important to recognize that these two goals are not mutually exclusive and understanding the social and historical context of a text can provide valuable insights into its meaning and help scholars to better evaluate manuscript evidence.

The Emergence of English Translations

William Tyndale and the First English New Testament

William Tyndale was an English scholar and theologian who lived during the early 16th century. He is best known for his role in translating the Bible into English, specifically the New Testament. Tyndale's translation was the first to be printed in the English language and had a significant impact on the Protestant Reformation.

Tyndale was born in Gloucestershire, England, around 1494. He was educated at Oxford and Cambridge Universities, where he became fluent in several languages, including Greek and Hebrew. In 1523,

Tyndale moved to London to work as a tutor and began working on a translation of the New Testament into English.

At the time, the official language of the church was Latin, and the Bible was only available in Latin or Greek. The common people were not able to read or understand the Bible for themselves, and the clergy often used this to their advantage to maintain their authority. Tyndale believed that every person should have access to the Bible in their own language so that they could understand and interpret it for themselves.

In 1525, Tyndale went to Germany, where he completed his translation of the New Testament into English. He then had it printed in Germany and smuggled copies back into England. The translation was immediately popular, but also controversial. The church and state authorities saw it as a threat to their authority and began to actively suppress it.

Tyndale continued to work on his translation of the Old Testament and published a revised edition of the New Testament in 1534. He also wrote several treatises and polemical works in defense of his beliefs and the translation of the Bible into English.

However, Tyndale's work and influence eventually caught up with him. In 1535, he was arrested and imprisoned for heresy. He was tried and found guilty, and in 1536, he was strangled and burned at the stake. Despite his death, Tyndale's legacy lived on, and his translation of the New Testament became the foundation for later English translations, such as the King James Version.

Tyndale's contribution to the translation of the Bible into English was significant because it helped make the Bible accessible to the common people. It challenged the authority of the church and state, and it was instrumental in spreading the ideas of the Reformation. Furthermore, Tyndale's work laid the foundation for the development of the English language and its literary traditions.

The Geneva Bible and the King James Version

The Geneva Bible and the King James Version are two of the most significant English translations of the Bible. While the Geneva

Bible was the most popular English Bible of the 16th century, the King James Version (KJV) became the standard English Bible for the next few centuries and remains widely used today.

The Geneva Bible was first published in 1560 by English exiles in Geneva during the reign of Queen Elizabeth I. The translation was heavily influenced by the work of William Tyndale and his translation of the New Testament, as well as the work of Miles Coverdale and John Calvin. The Geneva Bible was the first English Bible to include verse numbers, making it easier to reference specific passages. It also included extensive study notes and annotations, making it a popular choice for personal study and devotion.

The Geneva Bible quickly became the most popular English Bible of the 16th century, and it was widely used by both Protestants and Puritans. It was also the Bible used by William Shakespeare and John Bunyan, and it was carried by the Pilgrims on the Mayflower.

However, the Geneva Bible was seen as a threat by the English government, as it contained notes that were critical of the monarchy and supported democratic principles. In response, the government commissioned a new translation of the Bible that would be more favorable to the monarchy and the Church of England.

This new translation, known as the King James Version (KJV), was first published in 1611. It was a collaborative effort by a team of 47 scholars, and it was based on the best Greek and Hebrew manuscripts available at the time. The KJV was notable for its use of elevated language and its poetic style, which made it highly influential in English literature and culture.

The KJV quickly became the standard English Bible and remained so for several centuries. It was widely used by Protestant churches and was the Bible of choice for many famous figures, including John Wesley and Abraham Lincoln.

Despite the popularity of the KJV, the Geneva Bible continued to be used by many Puritans and separatists, particularly in America. It remained in print until the 1640s, and its influence can still be seen in modern translations of the Bible.

In summary, the Geneva Bible and the King James Version are two of the most significant English translations of the Bible. The Geneva Bible was the most popular English Bible of the 16th century, and it was widely used by Protestants and Puritans. The King James Version, on the other hand, was commissioned by the English government as a more favorable translation of the Bible, and it quickly became the standard English Bible for several centuries.

The Proliferation of English Translations in the Modern Era

The proliferation of English translations of the Bible in the modern era can be traced back to the development of printing technology, which made it easier and more affordable to produce and distribute books. As a result, the 16th century saw an explosion of Bible translations in various European languages, including English.

One of the most significant English translations of this period was the King James Version (KJV), which was published in 1611. Commissioned by King James I of England, the KJV was the result of a collaborative effort by a team of scholars and translators who worked from the original Greek and Hebrew texts. The KJV became the standard English Bible for several centuries and has had a lasting impact on the English language and literature.

However, the KJV was not the only English Bible translation of the time. Prior to the KJV, there were several other notable English translations, including the Geneva Bible, which was first published in 1560. The Geneva Bible was translated by a group of Protestant scholars who fled England during the reign of Queen Mary I, and it became popular among Puritans and other dissenters due to its extensive study notes and commentary.

After the KJV, there were several other English translations that emerged in the following centuries. One of the most famous of these is the Revised Version, which was published in the late 19th century and sought to update the language and scholarship of the KJV. The Revised Version was followed by the American Standard Version, which was published in the early 20th century and became popular in the United States.

In the second half of the 20th century, there was a proliferation of English translations of the Bible, including the New International Version, the New American Standard Bible, and the New Revised Standard Version. These translations sought to balance accuracy with readability and were often tailored to specific audiences, such as children or non-native English speakers.

Today, there are dozens of English translations of the Bible available, ranging from literal translations that prioritize accuracy to dynamic translations that prioritize readability and accessibility. In addition to traditional print editions, there are also digital editions and audio editions that make the Bible accessible to a wider audience than ever before.

While the proliferation of English translations has made the Bible more accessible and understandable to many people, it has also led to debates and disagreements over the accuracy and authenticity of certain translations. Textual criticism, which seeks to reconstruct the original text of the Bible, continues to be an important area of study for scholars and theologians, even as new translations continue to be produced.

The Role of Archaeology and Manuscript Discoveries

The Discovery of the Papyri Manuscripts by Grenfell and Hunt

The discovery of the Papyri manuscripts is one of the most significant events in the history of New Testament textual criticism. In the late 19th and early 20th centuries, two British archaeologists, Bernard Grenfell and Arthur Hunt, conducted a series of excavations in Egypt, uncovering thousands of papyri fragments that would later revolutionize the study of the New Testament.

The papyri fragments, written on strips of papyrus, were found in the ancient trash heaps or "mummy cartonnage" in the town of Oxyrhynchus, Egypt. The fragments contained various works, including letters, legal documents, and literary texts, some of which were of significant historical and cultural value.

Among the fragments were several pieces of New Testament manuscripts, including portions of the Gospels, Acts, Pauline Epistles, and even fragments of the book of Revelation. These fragments were dated to the 2nd and 3rd centuries, making them the oldest surviving copies of the New Testament.

The significance of these discoveries cannot be overstated. Prior to the discovery of the Papyri manuscripts, the oldest known manuscripts of the New Testament were from the 4th century. The Papyri fragments, being a century or more older, gave textual critics a window into the state of the text of the New Testament during its early development.

One of the most important Papyri discoveries was the fragment known as P52, or the John Rylands fragment. This tiny fragment, measuring only 3.5 by 2.5 inches, contains portions of John 18:31-33 and 18:37-38. It was dated to the first half of the 2nd century, making it the oldest known copy of the New Testament. This discovery confirmed that the Gospel of John was likely composed in the 1st century, much earlier than some skeptics had previously claimed.

Other significant Papyri fragments include P45, P46, and P66, which contain substantial portions of the Gospels and Pauline Epistles. These fragments have been the subject of intense study and analysis, and have provided valuable insights into the text and transmission of the New Testament during its early stages.

The discovery of the Papyri manuscripts has led to a renewed interest in the study of the New Testament and has paved the way for new developments in the field of textual criticism. Scholars now have a better understanding of the early development of the New Testament text and can more accurately reconstruct the original words of the text. The Papyri manuscripts are a testament to the importance of preserving ancient texts and artifacts and serve as a reminder of the rich cultural and historical heritage that they represent.

The Chester Beatty Papyri and the Bodmer Papyri

The Chester Beatty Papyri and the Bodmer Papyri are two significant collections of ancient manuscripts that have greatly contributed to the field of New Testament textual criticism.

The Chester Beatty Papyri were discovered by Alfred Chester Beatty, a wealthy American collector of manuscripts, in the early 20th century. The collection includes over 100 papyri fragments, dating from the 2nd century to the 4th century AD, and containing portions of the New Testament, as well as other early Christian writings and non-Christian texts. The most notable fragments in the collection are P45, P46, and P47, which together contain almost the entire Pauline corpus. Other important fragments include P66 and P72, both of which contain significant portions of the Gospel of John.

The Chester Beatty Papyri are significant because they represent some of the earliest known copies of the New Testament, predating many of the previously known manuscripts by several centuries. In addition, the fragments contain readings that differ from the majority text, providing valuable evidence for the diversity of early Christian textual traditions.

The Bodmer Papyri, named after their collector, Swiss businessman Martin Bodmer, were discovered in Egypt in the mid-20th century. The collection contains over 80 papyri manuscripts, dating from the 2nd century BC to the 4th century AD, and includes portions of the New Testament, as well as early Christian and non-Christian writings.

The most notable fragments in the Bodmer collection are P66 and P75, both of which contain significant portions of the Gospel of John, and P72, which contains portions of the Pastoral Epistles. Other important fragments include P45, P46, and P47, which are also found in the Chester Beatty collection.

Like the Chester Beatty Papyri, the Bodmer Papyri are significant because they provide some of the earliest known copies of the New Testament, and contain readings that differ from the majority text, providing evidence for the diversity of early Christian textual traditions. In addition, the Bodmer Papyri have helped scholars better understand the development of early Christian theology and the transmission of non-canonical Christian texts.

Together, the Chester Beatty Papyri and the Bodmer Papyri have greatly contributed to our understanding of the early Christian period and the transmission of the New Testament text. They have provided valuable evidence for the diversity of early Christian textual traditions and have helped scholars reconstruct the text of the New Testament with greater accuracy.

Ongoing Manuscript Discoveries and Their Impact on Textual Studies

Manuscript discoveries have played a crucial role in advancing the field of textual studies, particularly in regards to the New Testament. New manuscripts are continually being discovered, and each new discovery provides further evidence for the text's history and development. Here are some examples of ongoing manuscript discoveries and their impact on textual studies:

1. **The Oxyrhynchus Papyri** - The Oxyrhynchus Papyri are a collection of over 500,000 papyrus fragments discovered in Egypt between 1896 and 1907. Many of these fragments contain fragments of classical Greek literature, but a significant number also contain portions of the New Testament. These fragments are important because they provide evidence for the early transmission of the text in Egypt and suggest that different regions may have had their own textual traditions.[2]

---

[2] Bernard Grenfell and Arthur Hunt were British papyrologists who made an extraordinary discovery in the late 19th and early 20th centuries. They excavated a site in Oxyrhynchus, Egypt, which had been an ancient trash dump. There, they uncovered over half a million fragments of papyrus, including literary works, documents, and letters. Among these fragments were many pieces of early Christian writings, including parts of the New Testament.

The discoveries of Grenfell and Hunt were significant for the study of the New Testament because they provided scholars with new and important evidence for the text of the New Testament. Many of the fragments they discovered contained previously unknown or lost portions of the New Testament. For example, in 1896 they found a fragment of the

2. **The Nag Hammadi Library** - The Nag Hammadi Library is a collection of 13 codices containing 52 religious and philosophical texts, including several Gnostic texts. These codices were discovered in Upper Egypt in 1945 and are important because they shed light on early Christian beliefs and practices that were previously unknown.

3. **The Dead Sea Scrolls** - The Dead Sea Scrolls are a collection of Jewish texts that were discovered in the Qumran caves near the Dead Sea between 1947 and 1956. The scrolls include fragments of every book in the Hebrew Bible except for the book of Esther and shed light on the development of Jewish literature during the Second Temple period. Some of the scrolls also contain early copies of biblical books that are important for the study of the Old Testament.

4. **The Bodmer Papyri** - The Bodmer Papyri are a collection of early Christian manuscripts discovered in Egypt in the 1950s and 60s. These manuscripts include the oldest known copy of the Gospel of John (Papyrus 66) and a significant portion of the Gospel of Luke (Papyrus 75). The Bodmer Papyri are important because they provide evidence for the early transmission of the New Testament and suggest that the text was in widespread use even in its early stages.

5. **The Chester Beatty Papyri** - The Chester Beatty Papyri are a collection of early Christian manuscripts that were acquired by Sir Alfred Chester Beatty in the early 20th century. The collection includes portions of every book of the New

---

Gospel of Matthew (known as Papyrus Oxyrhynchus 1) that dated to the late 2nd or early 3rd century, making it one of the earliest known fragments of the New Testament.

The discoveries at Oxyrhynchus also shed light on the early history of Christianity and the transmission of the New Testament text. Many of the papyrus fragments contained copies of letters and documents from early Christian communities, providing insight into their beliefs and practices. The fragments also revealed differences in the way that the New Testament text was copied and transmitted in different regions and at different times.

Overall, the discoveries of Grenfell and Hunt had a significant impact on New Testament textual studies and continue to be studied and analyzed by scholars to this day.

Testament except for Philemon and sheds light on the early transmission of the text.

These ongoing manuscript discoveries continue to shape the field of textual studies and provide valuable insights into the development of the text of the Bible. As new manuscripts are discovered and analyzed, scholars will continue to refine their understanding of the text and its transmission history.

The Influence of Technology on the Study and Transmission of the New Testament Text

Digital Repositories and Online Access to Manuscripts

Digital repositories and online access to manuscripts have revolutionized the study and transmission of the New Testament text in recent years. In the past, scholars and students of the Bible had to travel to different locations around the world to view manuscripts, which could be both time-consuming and costly. However, with the advent of digital technology, many manuscripts have been scanned, digitized, and made available online, allowing scholars and students to access them from anywhere in the world.

One significant benefit of digital repositories is that they have facilitated collaboration and increased access to manuscripts. Scholars and students from around the world can now work together on projects, share information, and collaborate on research. Additionally, online access to manuscripts has led to the discovery of new manuscripts and the verification of existing ones. Scholars can now compare manuscripts from different locations and periods and detect similarities and differences that were previously unknown.

Moreover, digital repositories have facilitated the preservation of manuscripts. Before digitization, many manuscripts were in poor condition, and access to them was limited to a few individuals. However, digital preservation has allowed scholars to create high-quality copies of these manuscripts, which are now available for future generations. Furthermore, the ability to digitize manuscripts has also reduced the risk of damage or loss due to frequent handling or transport.

Finally, digital repositories and online access to manuscripts have made it easier for individuals and organizations to share their collections with others. Institutions such as libraries, museums, and universities can now digitize their collections and make them available online, increasing access to manuscripts that were previously restricted to a select few.

In summary, digital repositories and online access to manuscripts have had a significant impact on the study and transmission of the New Testament text. They have facilitated collaboration, increased access to manuscripts, facilitated preservation, and made it easier to share collections with others. As technology continues to improve, the potential for these digital resources to aid in the study of the New Testament text is vast, and we can expect that they will continue to play a vital role in future research and scholarship.

The Use of Computer-Aided Textual Analysis

Computer-aided textual analysis, also known as computational text analysis, or digital text analysis, is the use of computer software and tools to study and analyze large quantities of textual data. In the context of New Testament textual criticism, these tools have become increasingly useful in analyzing and comparing multiple manuscript versions of the text, identifying patterns and variations in the text, and assessing the overall reliability and authenticity of the text.

One of the most common applications of computer-aided textual analysis in New Testament studies is the creation of a digital critical apparatus. A critical apparatus is a scholarly tool that lists the textual variants found in various manuscript versions of the New Testament. Traditionally, creating a critical apparatus involved manually comparing and evaluating multiple manuscripts, a time-consuming and labor-intensive process. However, with the advent of digital tools, scholars can now input large amounts of textual data into specialized software programs that automatically compare and analyze the manuscripts, producing a comprehensive digital critical apparatus in a fraction of the time.

Another important use of computer-aided textual analysis in New Testament studies is the creation of stemmata, or family trees, that show the relationships between different manuscript versions of the text. Traditionally, creating a stemma involved visually comparing and analyzing the manuscripts, a process that was both time-consuming and prone to error. With digital tools, however, scholars can input large amounts of textual data into specialized software programs that use algorithms to automatically create stemmata based on statistical analyses of the textual variants.

Other applications of computer-aided textual analysis in New Testament studies include the identification of linguistic patterns and the use of machine learning algorithms to classify manuscripts based on their characteristics and textual variants. For example, scholars can use software to identify certain linguistic features that are more common in one manuscript version of the text than in others, providing valuable insights into the history and development of the text.

Overall, the use of computer-aided textual analysis has revolutionized the field of New Testament textual criticism, making it possible to analyze and compare vast quantities of textual data in ways that were previously impossible. While these tools are not without their limitations and challenges, they have opened up new avenues of research and exploration, shedding new light on the history, development, and transmission of the New Testament text.

The Future of New Testament Textual Studies

The future of New Testament textual studies is likely to involve continued advancements in technology and collaboration among scholars from diverse backgrounds. With the increasing availability of digital resources, scholars will have greater access to manuscripts and other sources from around the world, enabling them to more easily compare and analyze variations in the text.

One area of growth is likely to be in computer-aided textual analysis, which can help to identify patterns and relationships in the text that might otherwise be missed. This approach can be used to identify potential errors or inconsistencies in the text, as well as to uncover hidden connections or themes that might have been overlooked.

Another area of potential growth is in interdisciplinary studies, as scholars from different fields work together to explore the historical, social, and cultural contexts in which the New Testament was written and transmitted. This could involve collaboration with historians, archaeologists, linguists, and other experts, with the goal of gaining a deeper understanding of the text and its significance for different communities and cultures.

As the field continues to evolve, there may also be a greater emphasis on inclusivity and diversity, with efforts to incorporate perspectives and voices that have traditionally been marginalized or excluded from the conversation. This could include a greater focus on the contributions of women, people of color, and scholars from non-Western contexts.

Overall, the future of New Testament textual studies is likely to involve a combination of traditional methods and new technologies, as well as greater collaboration and inclusivity among scholars.

CHAPTER 6 The Period of the Critical Text

Desiderius Erasmus—Publishing the First Greek Text

Desiderius Erasmus (1466-1536) was a Dutch humanist scholar and theologian who played a significant role in the Renaissance period. He was known for his works in classical scholarship, biblical studies, and his efforts towards church reform. Among his many accomplishments, one of the most notable was his publication of the first Greek New Testament.

Background and Motivation

During the medieval period, the Latin Vulgate Bible, translated by St. Jerome in the fourth century, was the standard text used by the Western Church. However, the Vulgate contained many errors, and many scholars believed that the original texts of the Bible, written in Hebrew and Greek, held the key to the true meaning of the Scriptures.

213

With the advent of the printing press in the 15th century, the potential for the widespread dissemination of the Bible in its original languages became a real possibility.

Erasmus recognized the importance of the original texts and believed that a knowledge of Greek was necessary for a proper understanding of the Bible. However, few scholars of his time had access to the Greek manuscripts, and those that did, often had to rely on inferior and incomplete copies. Erasmus recognized the need for a critical edition of the Greek New Testament and set out to produce one.

The First Edition (1516) In 1516, Erasmus published the first edition of his Greek New Testament, titled Novum Instrumentum omne. Erasmus used several sources to compile his edition, including several Greek manuscripts, the Latin Vulgate, and a critical edition of the Latin New Testament by Lorenzo Valla. Erasmus also made use of the Complutensian Polyglot, a six-volume edition of the Bible in Greek, Latin, and Hebrew, which was being produced at the time but had not yet been published.

Erasmus's edition was not without its flaws, and he acknowledged that he had relied heavily on his own abilities as a scholar in producing the text. He also admitted that he had not seen some of the manuscripts he used, relying instead on the judgment of others. Nevertheless, his edition was a significant step forward in the study of the New Testament.

Erasmus's edition was unique in several ways. Firstly, it was the first printed edition of the Greek New Testament. Secondly, it was the first Greek New Testament to be produced using a printing press, which allowed for a more accurate and consistent text. Thirdly, it was the first edition to include a Latin translation, which made the text accessible to a wider audience.

Erasmus's edition also included a critical apparatus, which provided variant readings from different sources. This apparatus was a significant innovation and provided scholars with a tool for comparing and evaluating different manuscripts.

Revisions and Later Editions

Erasmus's first edition was not without its critics, and he received a great deal of criticism from scholars who believed that he had not used the best sources available. In response, Erasmus produced several revised editions of his Greek New Testament, each one incorporating new manuscript evidence and refining the text.

Erasmus's third edition, published in 1522, was the most significant. It was the first edition to include a revised text of the Latin Vulgate, which had been produced by his friend and fellow humanist, Cardinal Ximenes. Erasmus's third edition was also the first to include the Comma Johanneum, a disputed passage in 1 John 5:7-8, which had been omitted from his previous editions.

Erasmus's later editions were widely used and highly regarded, with many scholars believing that they represented the most accurate text of the New Testament available. However, they were not without their flaws, and later scholars would produce even more accurate and comprehensive editions.

Legacy

Erasmus's Greek New Testament was a significant milestone in the history of biblical scholarship, and it had a lasting impact on the study of the New Testament. The publication of the Greek text paved the way for further scholarship and study, as well as providing the foundation for future translations of the New Testament.

Erasmus's work also played a significant role in the Protestant Reformation, providing a new source for the reformers' emphasis on the original text of the Bible. The ability to read the New Testament in its original language allowed for a greater understanding of the text and a more critical examination of traditional theological beliefs.

The Greek text was widely used in academic circles and became the basis for many subsequent editions of the New Testament. However, it was not without its critics, who argued that Erasmus's methodology was flawed and that his text contained errors and omissions.

Despite these criticisms, Erasmus's work was instrumental in shaping the study of the New Testament and remains an important part of biblical scholarship today. His contribution to the field of textual criticism paved the way for future scholars to examine and evaluate the many manuscripts that make up the New Testament.

Conclusion

Desiderius Erasmus's publication of the first Greek New Testament was a significant achievement in the history of biblical scholarship. The ability to read the New Testament in its original language allowed for a greater understanding of the text and a more critical examination of traditional theological beliefs.

Erasmus's methodology was innovative, combining the use of various manuscript sources to create a new Greek text. While his work was not without its flaws, it provided the foundation for further study and scholarship in the field of textual criticism.

Today, scholars continue to examine and evaluate the many manuscripts that make up the New Testament, and the study of textual criticism remains an important part of biblical scholarship. Erasmus's contribution to this field remains significant, and his work continues to be a valuable resource for scholars and theologians around the world.

Textus Receptus (Latin for "Received Text")

The Textus Receptus is the name given to a specific Greek New Testament text type that was widely used in the Western church during the Reformation era. The term "Textus Receptus" (meaning "Received Text" in Latin) was coined by the Dutch scholar, Bonaventure Elzevir, in the preface to his 1633 edition of the Greek New Testament.

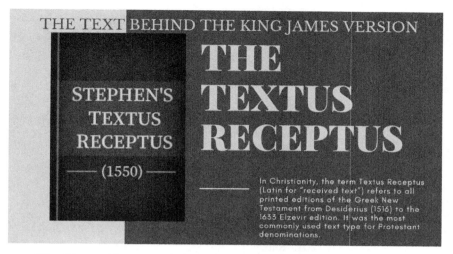

The Textus Receptus is based primarily on the Byzantine text-type of Greek manuscripts, which was the dominant form of the New Testament text in the Eastern Church during the Middle Ages. This text-type is characterized by its relative uniformity and simplicity, with a tendency towards harmonization and smoothing out of difficult readings. It is also known for its inclusion of several longer readings and additional phrases that are not found in other text-types.

The Textus Receptus was compiled by a number of scholars over a period of several centuries. Its origins can be traced back to the work of the Dutch humanist, Desiderius Erasmus, who produced the first printed Greek New Testament in 1516. Erasmus's text was based on a handful of late Byzantine manuscripts, as well as several Latin translations of the New Testament.

Erasmus's text was subsequently revised and expanded by a number of other scholars, including Robert Estienne (also known as Stephanus) in the 16th century, and Theodore Beza in the 17th century. These editions became increasingly influential in the Western church, particularly among Protestant reformers who saw them as more faithful to the original text than the Latin Vulgate, which had been the standard Bible for the Western church for over a millennium.

The Textus Receptus reached the height of its popularity in the 17th century, when it became the standard text used for most translations of the Bible into the vernacular languages of Europe. It was used as the basis for the King James Version of the Bible, which was published in 1611 and became one of the most influential and enduring translations of all time.

However, with the advent of modern textual criticism in the 19th century, the Textus Receptus began to lose its status as the authoritative Greek New Testament text. Scholars began to discover earlier and more diverse Greek manuscripts that did not conform to the Byzantine text-type, leading to the development of alternative critical texts such as the Westcott and Hort text and the Nestle-Aland text.

Today, the Textus Receptus is still used by some conservative Christian groups, particularly in the King James Only movement, which holds that the King James Version of the Bible is the only inspired and authoritative English translation. However, it is generally recognized by most scholars that the Textus Receptus is not the most accurate or reliable Greek New Testament text, and that other critical editions based on more diverse and ancient manuscript evidence provide a better representation of the original text.

Bruce Metzger writes, "The term *Textus Receptus*, as applied to the text of the New Testament, originated in an expression used by Bonaventura and Abraham Elzevir (Elzevier), who were printers in Leiden. The preface to their second edition of the Greek Testament (1633) contains the sentence: *Textum ergo habes, nunc ab omnibus receptum, in quo nihil immutatum aut corruptum damus* ("Therefore you [dear reader] have the text now received by all, in which we give nothing changed or corrupted"). In one sense this proud claim of the Elzevirs on behalf of their edition seemed to be justified, for their edition was, in most respects, not different from the approximately 160 other editions of the printed Greek Testament that had been issued since Erasmus's first published edition of 1516. In a more precise sense, however, the Byzantine form of the Greek text, reproduced in all early printed editions, was disfigured, as was mentioned above, by the accumulation over the centuries of myriads of scribal alterations, many of minor significance but some of considerable consequence. It was the corrupt Byzantine form of text that provided the basis for almost all

218

translations of the New Testament into modern languages down to the nineteenth century. During the eighteenth century scholars assembled a great amount of information from many Greek manuscripts, as well as from versional and patristic witnesses. But, except for three or four editors who timidly corrected some of the more blatant errors of the Textus Receptus, this debased form of the New Testament text was reprinted in edition after edition. It was only in the first part of the nineteenth century (1831) that a German classical scholar, Karl Lachmann, ventured to apply to the New Testament the criteria that he had used in editing texts of the classics. Subsequently other critical editions appeared, including those prepared by Constantin von Tischendorf, whose eighth edition (1869–72) remains a monumental thesaurus of variant readings, and the influential edition prepared by two Cambridge scholars, B. F. Westcott and F. J. A. Hort (1881). It is the latter edition that was taken as the basis for the present United Bible Societies' edition. During the twentieth century, with the discovery of several New Testament manuscripts much older than any that had hitherto been available, it has become possible to produce editions of the New Testament that approximate ever more closely to what is regarded as the wording of the original documents."[3]

Defenders of the Textus Receptus

The Textus Receptus (TR) was the most commonly used Greek text for centuries, and as such, many theologians and scholars became its defenders. They believed that the TR was the inspired and inerrant Word of God, and any deviations from it were considered corruptions or errors. These defenders of the TR were also known as "TR advocates" and believed that the TR was the most reliable and trustworthy Greek text.

One of the most prominent defenders of the TR was the German theologian Johann Bengel (1687-1752), who strongly believed in the reliability of the TR and rejected any other critical editions that

---

[3] Bruce Manning Metzger, United Bible Societies, *A Textual Commentary on the Greek New Testament, Second Edition a Companion Volume to the United Bible Societies' Greek New Testament (4th Rev. Ed.)* (London; New York: United Bible Societies, 1994), xxiii–xxiv.

deviated from it. He believed that the TR had been preserved by God and was the only accurate text of the Bible. Bengel wrote extensively in defense of the TR and criticized scholars who favored other texts, such as the Codex Vaticanus or the Codex Sinaiticus.

Another notable defender of the TR was the British theologian John William Burgon (1813-1888). Burgon was a strong advocate of the King James Version of the Bible, which was based on the TR. He believed that the TR was the only accurate text of the New Testament and rejected any critical editions that did not agree with it. Burgon was critical of the textual criticism methods used by scholars, such as Westcott and Hort, and believed that their approach led to the corruption of the text.

Burgon's defense of the TR was not without controversy. Some scholars believed that his views were based more on sentimentality than on critical scholarship. However, Burgon's work was influential in the defense of the TR and played a significant role in the textual criticism debate.

The defenders of the TR continued to hold strong opinions even as newer critical editions, such as Nestle-Aland, emerged. They believed that these new editions were corrupt and that the TR was the only reliable and trustworthy text. However, as more manuscripts were discovered and analyzed, the TR began to lose its dominance in the field of textual criticism.

In conclusion, defenders of the TR were theologians and scholars who strongly believed in the accuracy and reliability of the Textus Receptus. They rejected other critical editions and believed that the TR was the only inspired and inerrant text of the New Testament. Despite criticism and controversy, their work played a significant role in the history of textual criticism and the development of the modern Bible.

Defenders of the Textus Receptus have put forward several arguments to support the use of this Greek text in the translation and interpretation of the New Testament. Some of the most common arguments include:

1. The Textus Receptus is based on the majority of manuscripts: Advocates of the Textus Receptus often argue that this Greek text is based on the vast majority of existing manuscripts, and therefore represents the most accurate representation of the original text. However, this argument has been challenged by modern textual scholars who argue that the number of manuscripts is not the only factor to consider when evaluating the accuracy of a text. Quality, age, and geographical distribution are all important factors to consider.

2. The Textus Receptus has been used for centuries: Defenders of the Textus Receptus often point to its long history of use as evidence of its accuracy and reliability. However, scholars point out that the widespread use of a text does not necessarily mean it is the most accurate. Historical usage does not automatically validate the accuracy of a text.

3. The Textus Receptus has been divinely preserved: Some defenders of the Textus Receptus argue that this Greek text has been divinely preserved by God and is therefore the most accurate representation of the original text. However, this argument is based on faith rather than evidence and is not widely accepted by mainstream scholars.

Textual scholars such as Daniel Wallace, J. Harold Greenlee, and Bruce Metzger have challenged these arguments and provided evidence to support the use of modern critical editions of the Greek New Testament. For example, they have argued that:

1. The quality, age, and geographical distribution of manuscripts are more important than the number of manuscripts. The earliest and most geographically diverse manuscripts are typically considered to be the most reliable.

2. The long history of use of a text does not necessarily mean it is the most accurate. Textual changes can be introduced over time, and later copies may be less accurate than earlier ones.

3. The idea that a particular text has been divinely preserved is not supported by evidence and is not a valid argument for the accuracy of a particular text.

In addition to these arguments, textual scholars have also pointed out specific instances where the Textus Receptus diverges from the most reliable manuscripts, such as the Codex Sinaiticus and Codex Vaticanus. For example, the Textus Receptus contains the Comma Johanneum, a disputed passage in 1 John 5:7-8, which is not found in the earliest and most reliable manuscripts. Defenders of the Textus Receptus argue that this passage is genuine and has been removed from modern critical editions for theological reasons. However, textual scholars argue that the passage is a later addition and is not supported by the oldest and most reliable manuscripts.

Overall, while defenders of the Textus Receptus may have valid concerns about the accuracy and reliability of modern critical editions, textual scholars argue that the use of modern critical editions based on the most reliable manuscripts is the best approach for interpreting and translating the Greek New Testament.

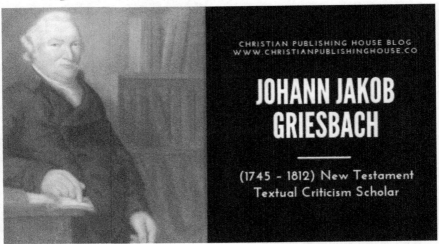

CHRISTIAN PUBLISHING HOUSE BLOG
WWW.CHRISTIANPUBLISHINGHOUSE.CO

JOHANN JAKOB GRIESBACH

(1745 - 1812) New Testament Textual Criticism Scholar

The Textual Theory of Johann Jakob Griesbach

Johann Jakob Griesbach (1745-1812) was a German biblical scholar and a pioneer in the field of New Testament textual criticism. Griesbach's textual theory played a significant role in shaping the discipline during the late 18th and early 19th centuries. His work laid the groundwork for many subsequent developments in textual criticism and helped to establish critical methodologies that are still in use today.

Griesbach's Textual Theory:

1. **Recension Theory**: Griesbach proposed that the New Testament text underwent two major "recensions" (revisions) in the early centuries of its transmission. The first recension was the "Alexandrian," which he believed to be characterized by a polished and refined Greek style. The second recension was the "Western," which he considered to be characterized by a more free and expansive style. According to Griesbach, these recensions were responsible for many of the textual variants found in the New Testament manuscripts.

2. **Hypothesis of Gospel Dependence**: Griesbach is perhaps best known for his theory of gospel dependence, which suggested that the Gospel of Matthew was the first to be written, followed by the Gospel of Luke, and finally the Gospel of Mark. This hypothesis, known as the "Griesbach Hypothesis" or "Two-Gospel Hypothesis," posited that Mark's Gospel was an abridged version of Matthew and Luke, combining elements from both. This view contrasted with the more widely accepted "Two-Source Hypothesis," which argues that both Matthew and Luke independently drew upon Mark's Gospel and a hypothetical "Q" source.

3. **Canon of Internal Evidence**: Griesbach developed several canons or principles for evaluating textual variants based on internal evidence, i.e., the content and context of the readings themselves. Among these principles were:

a. **The more difficult reading is preferable**: Griesbach argued that scribes were more likely to simplify or harmonize a difficult reading rather than introduce difficulties into the text.

b. **The shorter reading is preferable**: Griesbach believed that scribes were more likely to expand or explain the text than to shorten it, making the shorter reading more likely to be original.

c. **The reading that best explains the origin of the others is preferable**: Griesbach suggested that the original reading should be able to account for the development of the other variant readings in the manuscript tradition.

Griesbach's textual theory had a significant impact on the field of textual criticism, and many of his principles and methods continue to influence the discipline. While some aspects of his theory, such as the Griesbach Hypothesis, have been challenged and revised over time, his contributions to the field remain foundational and have laid the groundwork for many subsequent advances in New Testament textual criticism.

The Textual Theory of B. F. Westcott and F. J. A. Hort

Brooke Foss Westcott (1825-1901) and **Fenton John Anthony Hort (1828-1892)** were British biblical scholars who made groundbreaking contributions to the field of New Testament textual criticism. Their joint work, which culminated in the publication of "The New Testament in the Original Greek" (1881), established a new critical text of the Greek New Testament and laid the foundation for modern textual criticism. The Westcott-Hort textual theory is characterized by several key principles and ideas:

1. **The concept of text-types**: Westcott and Hort were among the first to systematically classify New Testament manuscripts into distinct "text-types" based on their shared characteristics. They identified four primary text-types: the Alexandrian, the Western, the Caesarean, and the Byzantine. Westcott and Hort considered the Alexandrian text-type to be the most reliable, and their critical text was primarily based on this text-type.

2. **The superiority of the Alexandrian text-type**: Westcott and Hort believed that the Alexandrian text-type, represented primarily by the Codex Vaticanus (B) and Codex Sinaiticus (ℵ), was the closest to the original text of the New Testament. They argued that this text-type was characterized by a more restrained and accurate scribal tradition, resulting in a text with fewer interpolations, expansions, or harmonizations compared to the other text-types.

3. **The Lucianic Recension**: Westcott and Hort posited that the Byzantine text-type, which forms the basis of the Textus Receptus and the King James Version, was the result of a deliberate and systematic revision of the New Testament text in the 4th century. They attributed this revision to the church father Lucian of Antioch, labeling it the "Lucianic Recension." According to Westcott and Hort, the Byzantine text-type was less reliable due to its tendency toward expansion, harmonization, and conflation of earlier readings.

225

4. **The principle of "intrinsic probability"**: Westcott and Hort emphasized the importance of considering the internal evidence of the text, such as style, vocabulary, and context, when evaluating variant readings. They believed that the reading that best fits the author's style, purpose, and overall context is more likely to be original.

5. **The principle of "transcriptional probability"**: Westcott and Hort also considered the external evidence of the manuscript tradition when assessing variant readings. They developed the concept of "transcriptional probability," which examines the likelihood of a reading arising from scribal habits and tendencies. For example, they argued that the more difficult or shorter reading is often more likely to be original, as scribes tended to simplify or expand the text.

The Westcott-Hort textual theory was groundbreaking in its time and had a significant impact on subsequent scholarship in New Testament textual criticism. While some aspects of their theory have been revised or challenged over the years, their emphasis on the Alexandrian text-type, the systematic classification of manuscripts, and their methodological principles remain foundational to the field.

The Work of Hermann von Soden

Hermann von Soden was a German biblical scholar and textual critic who lived from 1852 to 1914. He was known for his work in compiling and analyzing the various textual traditions of the New Testament and for his development of a classification system for these traditions.

One of von Soden's most significant contributions was his recognition of the existence of multiple text-types within the Greek manuscript tradition of the New Testament. He observed that certain groups of manuscripts exhibited distinctive patterns of variation and agreement, and he classified these groups into different text-types based on their shared characteristics.

Von Soden identified four main text-types, which he labeled I, II, III, and IV. Type I, which he also called the Alexandrian text-type, was characterized by a tendency toward brevity and an emphasis on grammatical correctness. Type II, the Western text-type, was marked by a freer approach to translation and a tendency toward paraphrase and embellishment. Type III, which von Soden called the Byzantine text-type, was the most common type and was characterized by a preference for longer readings and a tendency toward harmonization and simplification. Finally, Type IV, which von Soden called the Caesarean text-type, was a relatively small and specialized group of manuscripts that showed a mixture of Alexandrian and Western readings.

Von Soden's classification system was a significant advancement in the field of textual criticism, as it allowed scholars to better understand the relationships between the various manuscripts and to make more informed decisions about which readings were most likely to be original. However, his system was also criticized for oversimplifying the complex nature of the manuscript tradition and for failing to take into account the nuances and variations within each text-type.

Despite these criticisms, von Soden's work had a significant impact on the development of textual criticism, and his classification system remains influential today. His insights into the existence of multiple text-types and their distinctive characteristics paved the way for further research and analysis, and his methods continue to inform the work of scholars in the field.

Eberhard Nestle's Greek Text

Eberhard Nestle's Greek New Testament is a critical edition of the New Testament in Greek, which has been widely used since its first publication in 1898. Nestle, a German biblical scholar, sought to create a more accessible and affordable Greek New Testament for students and scholars, building upon the work of earlier editors such as Tischendorf and Westcott and Hort.

Nestle's critical text represents a conservative approach to textual criticism, seeking to reconstruct the text of the New Testament as it existed in the earliest extant manuscripts. Nestle employed a system of textual families to classify the various manuscripts, and he gave preference to readings supported by the oldest and most reliable manuscripts.

The first edition of Nestle's Greek New Testament was based on a comparison of three leading critical editions of the time: the Westcott and Hort edition, the Tischendorf edition, and the Weymouth edition. Where the editions agreed, Nestle followed their text; where they disagreed, he typically sided with the reading supported by two of the three editions.

Nestle's Greek New Testament quickly gained popularity and underwent numerous revisions over the years, incorporating new manuscript discoveries and advancements in textual criticism. The eighth edition, published in 1952, was the first to include a critical apparatus, which provided scholars with information about the various textual variants and their sources.

Nestle's work was continued by his son Erwin Nestle, who edited the ninth and tenth editions of the Greek New Testament. Kurt Aland, a renowned New Testament textual critic, joined the editorial team for the eleventh edition and made significant contributions to the development of the Nestle-Aland text, which has since become the standard critical edition of the Greek New Testament.

Today, the Nestle-Aland Greek New Testament is in its 28th edition, and it continues to be widely used by scholars, theologians, and Bible translators for its accuracy and reliability in reconstructing the original text of the New Testament.

Aland's Local-Genealogical Method

Kurt Aland (1979) supports a type of textual criticism called the local-genealogical method. He explains that it is not possible to assume a manuscript stemma for the New Testament, as one would for other Greek texts. Instead, decisions must be made on a case-by-case basis. Although this method has been labeled as eclecticism, Aland disagrees with this characterization.

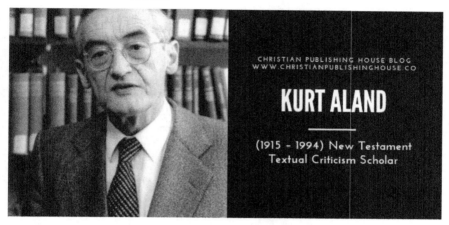

The local-genealogical method involves carefully examining the various readings of a passage and their possible interpretations. Then, based on external and internal criteria, it determines which reading is the original one from which the others are derived. According to Aland, this method is the only one that adequately addresses the unique requirements of the New Testament textual tradition.

The local-genealogical method assumes that any manuscript (or group of manuscripts) could potentially preserve the original text for any given variation unit. However, this approach to textual criticism leads to extensive eclecticism, as editors must decide the most likely authorial intent on a case-by-case basis. This eclecticism is evident when examining the selection process for variant readings within a single verse, such as Mark 6:51.

In Mark 6:51, the phrase "and they were exceedingly, extremely amazed in themselves" is found in the A f Maj manuscripts and was adopted as the text for the NU edition. It is possible that this longer reading was preferred over the shorter text (which omits "extremely"), found in א B (L), based on the assumption that Alexandrian scribes of א, B, and L were pruning excessive modifiers. However, in the next part of the verse, the shorter reading "they were amazed," found in א B L, was adopted by NU, as opposed to the longer reading "they were amazed and marveled," found in A D W f Maj. This illustrates atomistic eclecticism (i.e., eclecticism on a variant-unit basis), where the reading of א B L was first rejected and then later accepted within the same verse.

A more consistent approach would be to consider that א B L present the original text in both instances, and that both longer readings are scribal expansions meant to emphasize the disciples' amazement over the miracle they just witnessed. This interpretation aligns with our understanding of the overall character of these manuscripts.

Inconsistency in the local-genealogical method is not unusual. For example, in Matthew 8:21, the NU edition rejected the witness of א B 33, which reads, "Another of the disciples said to him, 'Lord, let me first return and bury my father'." Instead, NU favored the reading found in C L W Θ 0250, which adds "his" after "disciples." Metzger's comments in TCGNT reveal that most of the committee believed that "his" was deleted by the scribes of א B 33 to clarify that the scribe mentioned in 8:19 was not one of Jesus' disciples. Consequently, the strong documentary testimony of א B 33 was dismissed due to internal considerations.

Interestingly, just four verses later (in 8:25), the testimony of the same manuscripts is accepted for the exclusion of "his disciples" at the beginning of the verse. This example highlights the inconsistency that can arise when editors rely on the local-genealogical method, as it often leads to a preference for internal evidence over documentary evidence.

Another instance of atomistic eclecticism can be observed in the NU text of John 9:4. In the first part of the verse, NU reads "it is necessary for us," following the testimony of P66 P75 א* B D L W 0124. However, in the second part of the verse, NU reads "the one having sent me," following the testimony of אc A B C D 0124 and rejecting the testimony of P66 P75 א* L W, which reads "the one having sent us." Interestingly, in the first part of this verse, the testimony of P66 P75 א B L W is accepted, but in the next part of the same clause, the testimony of P66 P75 א* L W is rejected.

This occurrence exemplifies the outcome of eclecticism, where internal evidence is given more importance than documentary evidence (as referenced in TCGNT). Such inconsistencies highlight the challenges faced by editors when using the local-genealogical method, as it often leads to discrepancies in the selection of readings.

In another instance, Romans 8:11 demonstrates an intriguing case. The NU text accepts the reading "the one having raised Christ from the dead" based on the authority of B D2 F G. The only advantage of the NU reading is its brevity. However, it is worth noting that the NU editors generally held reservations about readings supported by B alongside D F G (refer to TCGNT on Rom 8:11b). Thus, it appears inconsistent for this reading to be accepted based on B D2 F G. This inconsistency is yet another result of the eclectic method employed in textual criticism.

These few examples demonstrate that numerous modern textual critics attempt to incorporate a synthesis of two conflicting theories: one asserting that the best readings are preserved in the most reliable manuscripts, and another suggesting that the best readings are those that fit the text best, regardless of the manuscripts they originate from. In my opinion, the most effective approach involves first determining the most reliable manuscripts (or groups of manuscripts) for each specific book or section (e.g., Paul's Epistles, General Epistles) of the New Testament. Once established, the burden of proof for any textual variation lies in demonstrating that these manuscripts do not contain the original wording.

As always, the critic must initially search for transcriptional causes of error or variation. If transcriptional errors cannot account for the variation, the critic must then consider criteria for internal evidence. However, it requires robust arguments on internal grounds to overturn strong documentary attestation. Naturally, this implies that the critic must be well-acquainted with each manuscript and possess sufficient knowledge about the craftsmanship and tendencies of the scribe who created it.

The Textual Theory of Bruce M. Metzger

With a vast number of individual manuscripts, textual critics often categorize them into text-types to facilitate the evaluation of textual variants. Renowned textual critic Bruce Metzger classified the extant manuscripts into four text-types: Alexandrian, Western, Caesarean, and Byzantine.

1. Alexandrian Manuscripts

Alexandrian manuscripts were produced by scribes trained in the esteemed Alexandrian scriptoral tradition, known for accuracy and craftsmanship. These manuscripts can be divided into early (or proto-Alexandrian) and later Alexandrian, with the earlier ones being less polished and closer to the original writings. The high percentage of textual agreement between P75 and B exemplifies the faithful transmission of the early Alexandrian text.

2. Western Manuscripts

The Western text-type is a loose category, often characterized by scribal expansion, harmonization, and amelioration. It likely developed during the mid-to-late second century in Western Christendom, circulating in North Africa, Italy, Gaul, Egypt, and other Eastern locations. Western text is represented in Old Latin and Syriac manuscripts, as well as in the writings of Marcion, Tatian, Irenaeus, and Tertullian.

3. Caesarean Manuscripts

The Caesarean text-type is a small group of manuscripts thought to have originated from a mixture of Alexandrian and Western readings. These manuscripts are only found in the Gospels, and include P45, W, family 1 (f1), family 13 (f13), Θ, 565, and 700.

4. Byzantine Manuscripts

The Byzantine text-type comprises the largest group of manuscripts, but is generally considered to be the furthest removed from the original text in most sections of the New Testament. The exception is the book of Revelation, where several Byzantine manuscripts preserve a purer form of the text.

Metzger argues that a variant reading supported by a combination of Alexandrian and Western witnesses is usually superior to any other reading. However, he cautions against relying solely on these readings and emphasizes the importance of evaluating all variant readings based on transcriptional and intrinsic probabilities.

In conclusion, Metzger's classification of text-types serves as an essential tool for textual critics evaluating textual variants. Nevertheless, it is crucial to consider the early and diverse documentary support for each reading, ensuring a thorough evaluation of its originality.

The Nestle-Aland Greek New Testament

The Nestle-Aland Greek New Testament: Overview and History

The Nestle-Aland Greek New Testament (NA) is a critical edition of the Greek New Testament, providing scholars, theologians, and Bible translators with the most accurate and up-to-date reconstruction of the original text. Named after its initial editor, Eberhard Nestle, and subsequent editor Kurt Aland, this edition has undergone numerous revisions and updates over the years, making it one of the most respected and authoritative critical editions available.

History of the Nestle-Aland Greek New Testament

1. Early Beginnings

The Nestle-Aland Greek New Testament has its roots in the late 19th century when Eberhard Nestle, a German biblical scholar, recognized the need for a more accessible and affordable Greek New Testament for students and scholars. At the time, the primary critical text available was the Westcott and Hort Greek New Testament, which, despite its academic merits, was expensive and difficult to obtain.

2. First Edition (1898)

Nestle sought to create a text that would combine the best features of the Westcott and Hort edition with those of two other leading editions of the time: the Tischendorf edition and the Weymouth edition. The first edition of the Nestle Greek New Testament, published in 1898, was essentially an eclectic text based on a comparison of these three editions. Where the editions agreed, Nestle followed their text; where they disagreed, he typically sided with the reading supported by two of the three editions.

3. Early Revisions and the Involvement of Kurt Aland

The Nestle Greek New Testament underwent several revisions in the early 20th century, with Eberhard Nestle's son, Erwin Nestle, taking over the editorship after his father's death in 1913. During this period, the text continued to be refined, incorporating new manuscript discoveries and advancements in textual criticism.

In the 1950s, Kurt Aland, a renowned New Testament textual critic, joined the editorial team. Aland contributed significantly to the development of the Nestle-Aland text, bringing new insights and rigor to the critical apparatus and methodology. Under Aland's leadership, the Nestle-Aland Greek New Testament evolved from an eclectic text based on a few leading editions to a more comprehensive and methodologically sound critical edition.

4. The United Bible Societies' Greek New Testament (UBS)

In the 1960s, the United Bible Societies (UBS) initiated a project to produce a new Greek New Testament for use in Bible translation. Kurt Aland was invited to join the editorial committee, which also included other distinguished scholars such as Bruce Metzger, Matthew Black, and Allen Wikgren. The UBS Greek New Testament, first published in 1966, was designed to be more user-friendly than the Nestle-Aland edition, with a simpler and more concise critical apparatus.

While the UBS and Nestle-Aland editions initially had separate editorial committees and distinct purposes, they eventually converged in terms of their underlying text. Starting with the 3rd edition of the UBS Greek New Testament and the 26th edition of the Nestle-Aland Greek New Testament, both editions shared the same base text, with the primary difference being the presentation of the critical apparatus.

5. The 27th and 28th Editions

The 27th edition of the Nestle-Aland Greek New Testament, published in 1993, introduced several significant changes, including the incorporation of new papyri discoveries and a reevaluation of the text in light of the latest research on text-types and manuscript relationships. The critical apparatus was also expanded and refined, providing more information on the textual variants and their supporting evidence.

The most recent edition, the 28th edition of the Nestle-Aland Greek New Testament, was published in 2012. This edition introduced further refinements to the text and critical apparatus, as well as a completely revised textual reconstruction of the Catholic Epistles based on the Editio Critica Maior project. The 28th edition also incorporated the latest manuscript discoveries and research, ensuring that the Nestle-Aland Greek New Testament remains the most up-to-date and authoritative critical edition available.

Significance of the Nestle-Aland Greek New Testament

The Nestle-Aland Greek New Testament has played a crucial role in the field of biblical studies and has been widely used by scholars, theologians, and Bible translators for over a century. Its significance can be seen in several areas:

1. **Textual Criticism**: The Nestle-Aland Greek New Testament serves as a primary resource for textual critics seeking to reconstruct the original text of the New Testament. Its extensive critical apparatus provides valuable information on the thousands of textual variants found in the manuscript tradition, allowing scholars to weigh the evidence and assess the most likely original readings.

2. **Bible Translation**: The Nestle-Aland Greek New Testament is widely used as the basis for modern Bible translations, ensuring that these translations are grounded in the most accurate and reliable reconstruction of the original text. This is especially important for translations intended for use in scholarly and academic settings, where fidelity to the original text is a primary concern.

3. **Biblical Studies**: The Nestle-Aland Greek New Testament is an essential tool for students and scholars engaged in the study of the New Testament. Its accurate and up-to-date text, along with its comprehensive critical apparatus, provides a solid

foundation for in-depth research and analysis of the New Testament's language, theology, and historical context.

4. **Preservation of the New Testament Text**: The ongoing work of the Nestle-Aland editorial team, in partnership with the United Bible Societies and other organizations, helps to ensure that the text of the New Testament is preserved and transmitted accurately for future generations. This includes the continued discovery, cataloging, and analysis of new manuscript evidence, as well as the development of new methodologies and technologies for the study of the New Testament text.

In conclusion, the Nestle-Aland Greek New Testament represents a significant achievement in the field of biblical studies, providing scholars and students with the most accurate and reliable reconstruction of the original New Testament text. Through its long history and numerous revisions, the Nestle-Aland Greek New Testament has become an indispensable resource for those engaged in the study, translation, and interpretation of the New Testament.

CHAPTER 7 The Practice of New Testament Textual Criticism

Major Critical Texts of the New Testament

- **Byz RP**: 2005 Byzantine Greek New Testament, Robinson & Pierpont

- **TR1550**: 1550 Stephanus New Testament

- **Maj**: The Majority Text (thousands of minuscules which display a similar text)

- **Gries**: 1774-1775 Johann Jakob Griesbach Greek New Testament

- **Treg**: 1857-1879 Samuel Prideaux Tregelles Greek New Testament

238

- **Tisch**: 1872 Tischendorf's Greek New Testament

- **WH**: 1881 Westcott-Hort Greek New Testament

- **NA28**: 2012 Nestle-Aland Greek New Testament

- **UBS5**: 2014 Greek New Testament

- **NU**: Both Nestle-Aland and the United Bible Society

- **TGNT**: 2017 The Greek New Testament by Tyndale House

- **GENTI**: 2021 Greek-English New Testament Interlinear[4]

Collecting the manuscript evidence is a laborious process, but it is a little more straightforward than the evaluation process. In the collection process, the goal is to gather as much evidence as possible concerning various readings of a specific text. In the evaluation process, the aim is to determine which reading has the best evidence for being the original reading. The evaluation process is complicated by the fact that not all scholars agree on which evaluation principles are to be used or the relative importance of each of them.[5]

Evaluation Principles

- There can only be one reading, which is the original reading.

- Manuscripts are to be weighed not counted. Certain families of manuscripts are more trustworthy (e.g., Alexandrian over Byzantine, Western, or Caesarean). In addition, certain manuscripts within a family are more faithful than others (e.g., P[66] P[75] 01 03)

- Generally, the reading that is weighty from both internal and external evidence is preferred.[6]

---

[4] https://christianpublishinghouse.co/greek-english-interlinear/

[5] Paul D. Wegner, A Student's Guide to Textual Criticism of the Bible : Its History, Methods & Results (Downers Grove, Ill.: InterVarsity Press, 2006), 239.

[6] However, the Documentary Approach gives great weight to the external evidence of the documents.

- The external evidence of the manuscript witnesses is to be evaluated first; thereafter, will the internal evidence be considered.

- The primary weight of external evidence goes to the original language manuscripts. If the weight is so evenly distributed, it is difficult to make a decision; the versions and Church Fathers may serve to tip the scales.

- Probability is determined based on paleographical details and the habits of scribes.

The Internal Textual Criticism Process

- The reading that the other reading(s) most likely came from is likely the original. This is the fundamental principle of textual criticism.

- The *more difficult* or *awkward* reading is often preferable. The reading at first will seem to be more difficult or awkward to understand, but after further investigation, it will be discovered that a scribe deliberately or mistakenly changed the text to an easier reading.

- The *shorter* reading is generally preferred if the change is *intended*. This is a reflection of scribal tendency, as a scribe is far more likely in his efforts at clarification, willfully to make an addition to a text. Very rarely will a scribe intentionally add to his text by mistake.

- The *longer* reading is generally preferred if the change is *unintended*. This again is a reflection of scribal activity, in that a scribe is far more likely to omit a word or phrase mistakenly, as to intentionally adding.

- The *longer* reading is preferred if there is clear reason(s) internally as to why the scribe omitted a word or phrase, like difficulties (perceived contradictions) or awkwardness. For example, a scribe may willfully remove or alter a verse that is repeating one of the previous verses.

- Within the synoptic gospels especially, a *less identical* reading is preferred as scribes had a tendency to harmonize readings.

- An *author-style* reading is preferred. If a reading matches the style of the author, it is preferred, and the variants that are foreign to that style are questionable.

- An *author-vocabulary* reading is preferred. If a reading matches the vocabulary of the author, it is preferred, and the variants that are foreign to that vocabulary are questionable.

- An *author-doctrine* reading is preferred. If a reading matches the doctrine of the author, it is preferred, and the variants that are foreign to that doctrine are questionable, especially if they are of a later period in Christian history, anachronistic.

- The reading that is deemed *immediately at odds with the context* is preferred if deemed intentional because a scribe is more likely to have smoothed the reading out.

The External Textual Criticism Process

- The *Alexandrian text*-type is generally preferred (especially P^{66} P^{75} 01 03), unless it appears to be a "learned" correction.

- A *represented* reading from more than one geographical area may be preferred to even an Alexandrian text-type reading. The reason is that the odds are increased greatly against a reading being changed from the original in such a wide geographical and family spectrum.

- An *overwhelming* Alexandrian representation (P^{66} P^{75} 01 03), numerous Alexandrian manuscripts of great quality and trustworthiness can overrule a widely *represented* reading from all geographical areas and families.

- The *Byzantine reading* is always questionable until proven otherwise.

- The *most faithful* to a text-type is preferred if they are divided in support.

New Testament textual criticism is the study of the existing manuscripts of the New Testament to establish the most accurate and original text. The field seeks to identify and resolve any discrepancies, variations, or errors that may have occurred during the copying and transmission process throughout history. Scholars employ various approaches to achieve this goal. Two of the main approaches are the Thoroughgoing Eclecticism and the Reasoned Eclecticism.

Different Approaches to New Testament Textual Criticism

1. **Thoroughgoing Eclecticism**: This approach, also known as radical eclecticism, is characterized by evaluating every individual variant reading in the New Testament manuscripts without giving priority to any particular text type, group, or family. This means that each variant is assessed on its own merits, rather than favoring certain manuscripts based on their age, geographical distribution, or other factors. Thoroughgoing eclectics believe that the best way to establish the most original reading is through an in-depth examination of each variant.

This method relies on several key principles:

a. **Internal evidence**: This includes evaluating the reading based on the linguistic style, grammar, and vocabulary of the author, as well as the context within the passage.

b. **Transcriptional probability**: This principle seeks to determine which reading is more likely to have led to the other(s) by examining the potential scribal errors or intentional changes that may have occurred during copying.

c. **Intrinsic probability**: This considers the author's intention, theological views, and the overall coherence of the passage.

Thoroughgoing Eclecticism has its strengths and weaknesses. Its main strength lies in its objective and impartial evaluation of the text, which can help uncover the most accurate reading. However, its weakness is that it can sometimes lead to an overly individualistic and

242

subjective assessment of variants, making it difficult to arrive at a consensus.

2. **Reasoned Eclecticism**: This approach is a more moderate form of eclecticism that combines both internal and external evidence to establish the original text. Reasoned eclectics give more weight to certain text types, families, or groups based on their age, geographical distribution, and overall quality.

In addition to considering the principles of internal evidence, transcriptional probability, and intrinsic probability, Reasoned Eclecticism also takes into account the following factors:

a. **Manuscript evidence**: The age, quality, and geographical distribution of the manuscripts that contain a particular variant are taken into consideration.

b. **Textual relationships**: The affiliations between manuscripts, text types, or families are examined, with preference often given to the Alexandrian text type or the earliest attested readings.

Reasoned Eclecticism aims to strike a balance between relying solely on internal evidence and giving undue preference to certain text types. Its strength lies in its balanced and systematic approach, which can lead to a more reliable reconstruction of the original text. However, critics argue that this method can still be influenced by the subjective preferences of scholars and may overlook significant individual readings in favor of established text types.

3. **Reasoned Conservatism**: Reasoned Conservatism, as advocated by H. A. Sturz in his work "The Byzantine Text-Type & New Testament Textual Criticism," is another approach to New Testament textual criticism. This method is characterized by giving more weight to the Byzantine text-type, also known as the Majority Text, which is the textual family found in the majority of extant Greek New Testament manuscripts.

Sturz's Reasoned Conservatism is based on the following principles:

a. **Byzantine priority**: While Sturz does not argue that the Byzantine text-type should be followed blindly, he contends that it should not be dismissed outright, as is the case with some critics. Sturz believes that the Byzantine text-type has preserved many early readings and that these readings should be considered carefully.

b. **Manuscript evidence**: Sturz emphasizes the importance of evaluating all available manuscript evidence, including those from the Byzantine text-type, before making a decision on the most likely original reading. This approach requires scholars to consider the full range of manuscript evidence without automatically dismissing readings found in the Byzantine text-type.

c. **Internal and external evidence**: Like Reasoned Eclecticism, Reasoned Conservatism also takes into account both internal and external evidence when evaluating variant readings. However, the key difference lies in the weight assigned to the Byzantine text-type.

The strengths of Reasoned Conservatism include its openness to considering the Byzantine text-type as a valuable source of early readings and its comprehensive evaluation of manuscript evidence. This approach can lead to the identification of genuine early readings that might otherwise be overlooked.

However, the main criticism of Reasoned Conservatism is that it might assign too much importance to the Byzantine text-type, which is generally considered to be a later, more secondary text-type. This could potentially result in the selection of later readings instead of the original ones. Despite this, H. A. Sturz's work has contributed to a more balanced and inclusive approach to New Testament textual criticism by advocating for the careful consideration of the Byzantine text-type.

4. **Byzantine Priority**: The Byzantine Priority approach to New Testament textual criticism, as championed by scholars like Maurice A. Robinson, Zane C. Hodges, and Arthur L. Farstad, gives primary importance to the Byzantine text-type, also known as the Majority Text. This textual family is found in the majority of extant Greek New Testament manuscripts and is characterized by a more standardized and harmonized text.

The main principles of Byzantine Priority are:

a. **Majority support:** Advocates of Byzantine Priority argue that the sheer number of manuscripts supporting the Byzantine text-type should not be ignored, as it indicates a strong and consistent transmission history. They contend that the majority of the manuscripts must have been based on an earlier, reliable text.

b. **Byzantine antiquity:** While the majority of Byzantine manuscripts are from the later period, proponents of Byzantine Priority maintain that the text-type itself can be traced back to a much earlier stage in the textual transmission history, potentially even to the autographs (original writings) themselves. Daniel Wallace has shown this to be false, which we have known for many decades.

c. **Consistency and accuracy:** Scholars who support Byzantine Priority emphasize the consistency and accuracy of the Byzantine text-type compared to other text-types. They believe that the process of transmission and copying was more controlled and stable in the Byzantine tradition, leading to a more accurate representation of the original text.

The strengths of Byzantine Priority include the acknowledgment of the significance of the majority of manuscripts and the attention given to the possibility of early and accurate readings within the Byzantine text-type. By focusing on the majority of the manuscripts, this approach can reveal readings that may have been overlooked by other methods.

However, the main criticism of Byzantine Priority is that it often neglects or downplays the importance of other text-types, such as the Alexandrian, which is generally considered to be earlier and closer to the original text. Critics argue that the sheer number of manuscripts does not necessarily imply greater accuracy or reliability and that the Byzantine text-type can sometimes reflect a later, more harmonized version of the text.

Despite these criticisms, the work of Robinson, Hodges, and Farstad has contributed to the ongoing debate in New Testament textual criticism and has encouraged scholars to reevaluate the role of the Byzantine text-type in reconstructing the original text.[7]

5. **Documentary Approach**: The Documentary Approach to New Testament textual criticism, as advocated by scholars like F. J. A. Hort, Ernest C. Colwell, and Philip W. Comfort, focuses on the study of individual manuscripts, text-types, and families, with the goal of reconstructing the original text by examining the genealogical relationships between these documents.

The main principles of the Documentary Approach are:

a. **Textual genealogy**: This approach emphasizes the importance of understanding the relationships between manuscripts, text-types, and families in order to trace the development and transmission of the text. Scholars examine the shared readings, omissions, and variations in the manuscripts to establish the most likely genealogical lineage.

b. **Text-types and families**: The Documentary Approach gives significant weight to the identification and analysis of distinct text-types, such as Alexandrian, Western, and Byzantine, as well as smaller manuscript families. Each text-type or family is evaluated based on its age, geographical distribution, and textual characteristics.

c. **External evidence**: The Documentary Approach relies heavily on external evidence, including the age and quality of the manuscripts, their geographical distribution, and the patristic citations (quotations from early church fathers). This approach tends to prioritize older manuscripts and text-types that are considered to be closer to the original text, such as the Alexandrian text-type.

d. **Critical editing**: Scholars using the Documentary Approach often engage in critical editing, a process in which they compare and analyze the variant readings in the manuscripts and then produce a critical edition of the text that represents their best reconstruction of the original.

---

[7] David Alan Black, New Testament Textual Criticism: A Concise Guide (Grand Rapids, MI.: Baker Books, 1994), 39.

The strengths of the Documentary Approach lie in its systematic and comprehensive examination of the manuscript evidence and its emphasis on the genealogical relationships between the manuscripts. By focusing on text-types and families, this approach can provide valuable insights into the transmission history of the New Testament text.

However, the main criticism of the Documentary Approach is that some fell that it can sometimes prioritize certain text-types or families at the expense of others, potentially overlooking valuable readings in less favored text-types, such as the Byzantine. This just is not the case, as the Documentary Approach does consider all manuscript families. Additionally, the reconstruction of the original text based on genealogical relationships can be complex and subjective, as it often involves making difficult decisions about which readings are more likely to be original.

Despite these challenges, the Documentary Approach has been influential in the field of New Testament textual criticism and has contributed to a better understanding of the textual transmission history and the relationships between the manuscripts.

This author's approach to New Testament Textual Studies is almost identical to Philip W. Comfort. I started my research and studies in NTTC in 1996. Metzger's TEXT OF THE NEW TESTAMENT was the book to read. I respect the textual scholars from the 1700s to the 21st century, some being J. J. Griesbach (1745–1812), Karl Lachmann (1793-1851), to Samuel Tregelles (1813–1875), to Constantin von Tischendorf (1815–1874), to Westcott (1825 – 1901) and Hort (1828 – 1892), to the Nestles and Alands of the Nestle Aland Text.

The Coherence-Based Genealogical Method (CBGM)

The Coherence-Based Genealogical Method (CBGM) is a computational approach to textual criticism, developed by the Institute for New Testament Textual Research (INTF) in Münster, Germany.

The goal of this method is to reconstruct the genealogical relationships among the thousands of existing manuscripts of the New Testament, in order to determine the most likely original text.

The CBGM operates on the principle of "coherence," which refers to the consistency of readings found within a group of related manuscripts. The method involves a series of steps:

1. **Collecting and analyzing manuscript data**: The CBGM starts with the collection and analysis of data from thousands of Greek New Testament manuscripts, including information about their text, date, and geographical origin.

2. **Comparing textual variants**: The CBGM analyzes the differences between the manuscripts, known as textual variants. It then quantifies the relationships between these variants, calculating the degree of agreement between them.

3. **Constructing a local stemma**: For each textual variant, the CBGM constructs a "local stemma," which is a hypothetical family tree that shows the relationships between the manuscripts containing that variant. This process involves comparing the coherence of various possible stemmata and selecting the one that best explains the available data.

4. **Merging local stemmata into a global stemma**: The CBGM then combines the local stemmata into a "global stemma," which is a comprehensive family tree representing the relationships between all the manuscripts under consideration.

5. **Assessing the initial text**: Based on the global stemma, the CBGM identifies the most likely original text of the New Testament, also known as the "initial text." This text is the one that best explains the relationships among the existing manuscripts and the development of the textual tradition.

Critics of the CBGM argue that the method is too complex and relies too heavily on computer algorithms, making it difficult for scholars to understand and evaluate its results. However, proponents of the CBGM argue that it represents a significant advancement in the field of textual criticism, offering a more objective and reliable approach to reconstructing the original text of the New Testament.

Aland's Local-Genealogical Method

Aland's Local-Genealogical Method is a textual criticism approach developed by Kurt Aland, who argued that it is impossible to determine the original New Testament text by using a single manuscript family tree. Instead, he suggested that decisions must be made on a case-by-case basis, considering both external and internal criteria. This method has been criticized for leading to extensive eclecticism, where editors make decisions about the original text on a variant-unit basis, resulting in potential inconsistencies.

The Local-Genealogical Method assumes that any manuscript may have preserved the original text for a specific variant unit. However, this leads to a problem when editors must decide what the authors most likely wrote for each variant unit. This can result in atomistic eclecticism, where editors accept or reject manuscript readings based on internal evidence, leading to potential inconsistencies within single verses.

Several examples of such inconsistencies can be found in the New Testament, such as Mark 6:51, Matthew 8:21, John 9:4, and Romans 8:11. In each case, the selection of variant readings seems to be influenced by eclecticism, often prioritizing internal evidence over strong documentary attestation. This can result in accepting one manuscript's reading in one part of a verse and rejecting the same manuscript's reading in another part of the same verse.

To address this issue, it is suggested that textual critics should first determine the best manuscripts or groups of manuscripts for each specific book or section of the New Testament. Once these are identified, the burden of proof for any textual variation is to show that these manuscripts do not have the original wording. Transcriptional errors should be considered first, followed by internal evidence criteria. However, strong arguments on internal grounds are required to overthrow strong documentary attestation.

In conclusion, Aland's Local-Genealogical Method is an approach to New Testament textual criticism that focuses on making decisions on a variant-unit basis, considering both external and internal criteria. Despite its potential for leading to inconsistencies due to atomistic eclecticism, it remains an important contribution to the field of textual criticism. Critics should be well-versed in each manuscript and scribe's tendencies to make informed decisions about the original text.

Metzger's Evaluation of Variant Readings Based on Text-Types

Given the vast number of individual manuscripts, textual critics face the challenge of understanding the unique characteristics of each manuscript. To address this, many critics, including renowned textual critic Bruce Metzger, classify the manuscripts into text-types, which are then used to evaluate textual variants. Metzger identified four primary text-types: Alexandrian, Western, Caesarean, and Byzantine, each of which warrants further explanation.

1. Alexandrian Manuscripts

Alexandrian manuscripts were produced by scribes trained in the Alexandrian scriptoral tradition, considered the best in Greco-Roman times. These scribes were skilled in creating accurate and well-crafted copies. New Testament manuscripts include early (or proto-Alexandrian) and later Alexandrian manuscripts. Generally, earlier manuscripts are purer, as they are closer to the original writings and exhibit minimal creative interaction with the text.

A notable example of a faithful transmission is the high percentage of textual agreement between P75 and Codex Vaticanus (B), supporting Hort's theory that Codex Vaticanus traces back to an early, pure text. Metzger (1992) lists numerous Alexandrian witnesses, categorized as "Proto-Alexandrian" and "Later Alexandrian."

2. Western Manuscripts

The "Western" text is a loosely defined category, characterized by scribal expansion, harmonization, and amelioration. Proponents of this text-type argue that it likely developed in the mid-to-late second century in Western Christendom. This version of the Gospels, Acts, and Paul's Epistles circulated in North Africa, Italy, and Gaul, as well as Egypt and other Eastern locations. The Western text is represented in Old Latin manuscripts, Syriac manuscripts, and the D-text, and is prevalent in the writings of Marcion, Tatian, Irenaeus, and Tertullian. Metzger (1992) lists several "Western" witnesses.

3. Caesarean Manuscripts

A small group of manuscripts, known as the Caesarean text, emerged when scholars such as Streeter and Lake demonstrated that Origen brought a text from Egypt to Caesarea, which was then transported to Jerusalem. This text, exhibiting a mix of Alexandrian and Western readings, is apparent in several Gospel manuscripts, including 𝔓45, W, family 1 (f1), family 13 (f13), Θ, 565, and 700.

4. Byzantine Manuscripts

The Byzantine manuscripts constitute the largest group and are typically the furthest removed from the original text in most New Testament sections, with the notable exception of the book of Revelation. Several Byzantine manuscripts preserve a purer form of the text in Revelation. Metzger lists numerous Byzantine manuscripts.

According to Metzger (1992), a variant reading supported by a combination of Alexandrian and Western witnesses is generally superior to other readings. However, he also emphasizes the importance of evaluating all variant readings in light of both transcriptional and intrinsic probabilities, and the possibility that the original reading may be preserved in any group of manuscripts, even in rare instances within the Koine or Byzantine text.

It is crucial to consider that diverse testimony among later manuscripts signals the reading's widespread copying in various church sectors, but does not necessarily validate its originality. Early and diverse documentary support is essential in determining the originality of a reading.

In summary, Metzger's approach to evaluating variant readings based on text-types offers valuable insights for textual critics. By categorizing manuscripts into Alexandrian, Western, Caesarean, and Byzantine text-types, critics can better understand the origins, characteristics, and transmission histories of these texts.

However, it is essential to remember that diverse testimony among later manuscripts might not necessarily indicate the originality of a reading. Instead, critics should prioritize early and diverse documentary support when assessing the originality of a reading. This approach allows for a more nuanced and comprehensive understanding of the New Testament manuscripts and their variant readings, contributing to the ongoing quest for the original text of the New Testament.

The Importance of the Documentary Approach

Reasoned eclecticism, or the local-genealogical method, often prioritizes internal evidence over external evidence, which can lead to atomistic eclecticism. In order to recover the original text, it is crucial to prioritize external evidence. Westcott and Hort, in their work on The New Testament in the Original Greek, stressed the importance of documentary evidence over internal evidence.

Colwell similarly emphasized the importance of considering documentary evidence and urged scholars to reconstruct the history of the manuscript tradition. However, many scholars were skeptical about reconstructing a stemma, or a manuscript family tree, for the Greek New Testament. A stemma can help scholars understand the relationships between manuscripts, their origins, and their associations, and it may reveal that some of the earliest manuscripts are the closest to the original text.

One key piece of evidence for the importance of documentary considerations is the second-century papyrus P75. This manuscript, containing the Gospels of Luke and John, has been recognized as a highly accurate copy. Its close textual relationship with Codex Vaticanus demonstrates that it was not the result of a fourth-century recension but a direct copy of an early, accurate manuscript.

Prior to the discovery of P75, scholars believed that second- and third-century papyri displayed a text in flux, characterized by individual independence. They thought that scribes in Alexandria must have used several such manuscripts to produce a good recension, as seen in Codex Vaticanus. However, P75's close affinity with Vaticanus disproved this theory, revealing that Vaticanus was a copy of a manuscript much like P75.

The discovery of P75 also changed Kurt Aland's thinking about the textual history of the New Testament. Aland used to describe second- and third-century manuscripts as exhibiting a text in flux or a mixed text, but after the discovery of P75, he stated that a recension of the text at Alexandria in the fourth century was no longer a valid supposition.

Gordon Fee argued that there was no Alexandrian recension before the time of P75 and that both P75 and Vaticanus represented a relatively pure form of preservation from the original text. This suggested that the original text of Luke and John was virtually preserved in P75.

Despite these findings, some scholars remain unconvinced that the P75/B type of text is superior to another early text called the Western text. This form of text circulated primarily in western regions and was used by early Christian figures such as Marcion, Irenaeus, Tertullian, and Cyprian. However, many scholars recognize that the Western text is not a true text-type, but rather a loose categorization of early non-Alexandrian texts.

Critics argue that the preference for P75 and B is based on subjective appreciation rather than theoretical reconstruction. However, many textual critics who have worked extensively with actual manuscripts maintain that manuscripts like P75 and B represent the best textual purity, as they contain fewer errors, expansions, harmonizations, and interpolations than Western manuscripts.

In conclusion, it is essential to prioritize documentary considerations in textual criticism to better understand the relationships between manuscripts and their origins. P75's discovery has significantly impacted the field, demonstrating the importance of documentary evidence and providing insights into the transmission history of the New Testament. This evidence supports the notion that some of the earliest manuscripts, such as P75 and Codex Vaticanus, may be the closest replications of the original text.

Determining the Original Text

As we've discussed, there are numerous instances in the New Testament where ancient manuscripts, translations, and quotations from early church figures differ. With so many variations, how can we determine the original text of the New Testament? How can we know what the inspired authors actually wrote?

Firstly, it's essential to remember that despite the significant number of variations, most of the manuscript texts agree with each other. Secondly, most of these variations do not impact the overall meaning of the text. Only a few variants present meanings that may be considered false, usually due to scribal errors found in a single manuscript or a small number of them.

Therefore, the purpose of studying these manuscripts is not to determine if the New Testament teaches specific fundamental truths, but rather to decide on minor details and subtle nuances. Some might question the necessity of such studies if no significant truths are at stake. However, the New Testament holds such immense importance that any effort to bring our understanding closer to the original text or to confirm that our current text is as close to the original as possible is undoubtedly worthwhile.

Most individuals, of course, lack the expertise to study the Greek manuscripts and must rely on translations or versions in their native languages. This is entirely appropriate. These readers trust the decisions made by the translators of the versions they are reading. Even so, these readers may sometimes wonder about differences between various translations. So, how do we decide between the differences in the manuscripts to determine which version is most likely the original text?

254

Textual scholars employ various methods and principles to assess the numerous variations and determine the most probable original reading. These methods involve analyzing both internal and external evidence, as well as considering the history and context of the manuscripts. Internal evidence looks at factors such as the writing style of the author, the context of the passage, and the likelihood of scribal errors or intentional changes. External evidence examines the manuscripts themselves, their dates, and the geographical distribution of the readings.

By carefully considering both internal and external evidence, textual critics can make informed decisions about which reading is most likely to be the original. This process is not infallible, and some variations may remain unresolved. However, the extensive study of these manuscripts has led to a high degree of confidence in our current understanding of the New Testament text, ensuring that it remains a reliable source of spiritual guidance and historical insight.

Determining the Original Reading

The formatting below is similar to and borrowed from Philip W. Comfort, New Testament Text and Translation Commentary: Commentary on the Variant Readings of the Ancient New Testament Manuscripts and How They Relate to the Major English Translations (Carol Stream, IL: Tyndale House Publishers, Inc., 2008)

Matthew 5:44 - Analyzing Textual Variants

In Matthew 5:44, there are two primary readings:

1. **WH NU**: "pray for those persecuting you" Supported by: ℵ B f1 itk syrc, cop Origen

2. **Variant/TR**: "bless those who curse you, do good to those who hate you, pray for those who despitefully use you and persecute you" Supported by: D L W Θ f13 33 Maj

The textual evidence favors the shorter reading (WH NU) for three reasons: (1) the Greek manuscripts supporting the shorter reading are from the 4th century, which is one century earlier than those supporting the longer reading (5th century and later); (2) the quotations from early church fathers supporting the shorter reading come from earlier sources; and (3) the additional words in the longer reading (variant/TR) appear to have been borrowed from Luke's account of the Sermon on the Mount (Luke 6:27-28). If the longer reading had originally been in Matthew's gospel, there would be no reasonable explanation for its removal.

Although Jesus did teach that we should bless those who curse us and do good to those who hate us, these specific words were not recorded by Matthew but by Luke. It seems that Jesus gave several similar sermons, using varying language as He saw fit. Consequently, Matthew's "Sermon on the Mount" is not an exact replica of Luke's "Sermon on the Plain." However, some scribes felt compelled to harmonize the two gospels in passages they believed were describing the same event. The Textus Receptus (TR) includes most of these harmonizations, which were then translated into the King James Version (KJV) and the New King James Version (NKJV). Most modern translations do not include this harmonization in Matthew 5:44.

Matthew 6:13 - Analyzing Textual Variants

In Matthew 6:13, there are six primary variants related to the doxology at the end of the Lord's Prayer:

1. **WH NU**: Omit doxology at end of prayer Supported by: א B D Z 0170 f1

2. **Variant 1**: Add αμην ("amen") Supported by: 17 vgcl

3. **Variant 2**: Add "because yours is the power forever." Supported by: itk syrp

4. **Variant 3**: Add "because yours is the power and the glory forever. Amen." Supported by: copsa (Didache omits αμην)

5. **Variant 4**: Add "because yours is the kingdom and the glory forever. Amen." Supported by: syrc

6. **Variant 5/TR**: Add οτι σου εστιν η βασιλεια και η δυναμις και η δοξα εις τους αιωνας. αμην. "because yours is the kingdom

and the power and the glory forever. Amen." Supported by: L W Δ Θ 0233 f13 33 Maj syr

7. **Variant 6**: Add οτι σου εστιν η βασιλεια του πατρος και του υιου και του αγιου πνευματος εις τους αιωνας. αμην. "because yours is the kingdom of the Father and the Son and the Holy Spirit forever. Amen." Supported by: 157 (1253) None

The textual evidence suggests that the original version of the Lord's Prayer concluded with a petition for deliverance from evil. The diversity of variants and their gradual expansion indicate that the doxology was added later. Early scribes adapted terms like "power" and "glory" from verses such as 1 Chr 29:11, Ps 62:3 LXX, Dan 2:37, 1 Pet 4:11, and Jude 25. The Didache, a compilation of early church traditions, contains a longer form of the Lord's Prayer, which may have been in use as early as the end of the 1st century. This form gained popularity due to its inclusion in the Textus Receptus (TR) and the King James Version (KJV).

Modern translations generally exclude the doxology, but it remains ingrained in Christian tradition and is still recited in private and public worship. The doxology is likely included because it offers a glorious and uplifting conclusion to the prayer, which would have motivated early scribes to add it.

Matthew 8:28 - Analyzing Textual Variants

Main Text (WH NU): τὴν χώραν τῶν Γαδαρηνῶν "the country of the Gadarenes" Supported by: (Γαζαρηνων ℵ*) B C Θ syr,p,

Variant 1 (TR): την χωραν των Γεργεσηνων "the country of the Gergesenes" Supported by: 2ℵ L W f1, Maj

Variant 2: την χωραν των Γερασηνων "the country of the Gerasenes" Supported by: 892c syrhmg copsa

In each Synoptic Gospel that records Jesus' visit to the region on the eastern side of the Sea of Galilee (where he healed the demoniac), there is textual variation concerning the region's name. In Matthew 8:28, Mark 5:1, and Luke 8:26, all three readings occur: "Gerasenes,"

Edward D. Andrews

"Gergesenes," and "Gadarenes." The textual variations in the three synoptic gospels reflect the scribes' confusion (Bruce 1979, 144).

Origen (Comm. Jo. 5.41.24), while commenting on John 1:28, discussed this confusion. He objected to Gadara (a reading he saw in a few manuscripts), located about five miles southeast of the Sea of Galilee. He also rejected Gerasa, situated thirty miles southeast of the Sea of Galilee. Origen suggested the name Gergesa based on some local tradition and because its name supposedly meant "dwelling of those that have driven away." Fond of finding etymological significance in names, Origen said the name suited the place because the citizens asked Jesus to leave their territory.

"Gadarenes" has the best testimony in Matthew and adequately suits the context for the story. Josephus (Life 42.9) stated that Gadara had territory and villages on the border of the lake; one of these villages must have been called "Gerasa," the name found in the best manuscripts in Mark 5:1 and Luke 8:26. The first variant, "Gergesenes," likely demonstrates the influence Origen had on later traditions, while the second variant, "Gerasenes," represents scribal harmonization to Mark 5:1 and Luke 8:26.

Mark 9:44, 46 - Analyzing Textual Variants

Main Text (WH NU): omit verses 44 and 46 Supported by: ℵ B C L W Δ Ψ 0274 f1 28 565 itk syrs cop

Variant (TR): add verses 44 and 46 (which are identical to 9:48 in NU) οπου ο σκωληξ αυτων ου τελευτα και το πυρ ου σβεννυται. "where the worm does not die and the fire is not extinguished" Supported by: A D Θ f Maj

Although one could argue that scribes omitted these verses, considering the repetition unnecessary, such deletion is unlikely to occur in manuscripts with as much diversity as those supporting the absence of these verses. On the other hand, verses 44 and 46 were likely added as a sort of prophetic refrain that enhances oral reading. Many textual variants entered the textual stream due to scribes improving the text for oral reading in the church, and this case serves as a classic example. Several modern English versions omit these

258

verses, but they include notes for readers familiar with their place in the KJV tradition. By retaining the verses in the text, the HCSB maintains the KJV tradition.

Luke 22:43-44 - Analyzing Textual Variants

Main Text (TR WH NU): include verses 43-44 "43 And an angel from heaven appeared to him, strengthening him. 44 And being in agony, he prayed more earnestly, and his sweat became like great drops of blood falling down on the ground." Supported by: ℵ*, D L Θ Ψ 0171 0233 f Maj (with asterisks or obeli: Δc Πc 892c 1079 1195 1216 copMSS) most Greek MSS according to Anastasius MSS according to Jerome MSS according to Epiphanius, Hilary Justin Irenaeus Hippolytus Eusebius

Variant 1: place verses after Matt 26:39 Supported by: f13 (13*) and some lectionaries with additions

Variant 2: omit verses Supported by: P69vid P75 ℵ A B N T W itf syrs copsa some Greek MSS according to Anastasius MSS according to Jerome some Greek and Old Latin MSS according to Hilary Marcion Clement Origen

These verses are absent from ancient witnesses across diverse text-types. Other factors suggesting their non-originality include (a) some manuscripts marking them with asterisks or obeli, indicating doubt about their originality, and (b) their placement after Matt 26:39 in family 13 manuscripts and several lectionaries. Despite this, their presence in many manuscripts (some ancient) and their citation by various early Christian writers indicate the account's antiquity.

It is more likely that these verses were added from an early source of extra-canonical traditions concerning Jesus' life and passion, rather than being original but omitted by those who found Jesus' display of human weakness inconsistent with his divine omnipotence. Nevertheless, the passage is retained in double square brackets in some texts due to its antiquity and importance in the textual tradition. Modern translations are divided: some omit the verses (RSV), some include them (NIV, NJB, REB, TEV, TOB, Seg), and others place them within square brackets (FC) or double brackets (NRSV).

259

The absence of Luke 22:43-44 from the manuscript P.Oxy. 2383 (designated as P69) was not acknowledged in the third edition of the United Bible Societies (UBS3), but it is now indicated in the fourth edition (UBS4) in parentheses. The editors of P69 were convinced that the only explanation for the large gap in the manuscript (from Luke 22:41 to Luke 22:45) is that the copyist's source did not include Luke 22:43-44 and the scribe's eye moved from προσηυχετο in 22:41 to προσευχης in 22:45. This was because they calculated that these two words would have been located at the end of lines, four lines apart. The manuscript 0171 should be listed as "vid" (as in UBS4), as it only shows a part of 22:44, but there are no obeli or asterisks, as indicated in UBS4.

The manuscript evidence for this textual variation strongly supports the exclusion of Luke 22:43-44. This is evident from the impressive list of Greek manuscripts (dating from the 2nd to 5th century) that favor its exclusion, including P69, P75, ℵ, B, T, and W. Additionally, manuscripts that mark the passage with obeli or cross it out, such as the first corrector of ℵ, further support its dubious nature. Its transposition to Matt 26 in some manuscripts and lectionaries indicates that it was a free-floating passage that could be inserted into any passion narrative.

On the other hand, the manuscripts that support the inclusion of the verses are fewer and date from the 5th century or later. The earliest witness is 0171vid, which dates to around 300. However, several early church fathers, such as Justin, Irenaeus, Hippolytus, Dionysius, and Eusebius, recognized this portion as part of Luke's gospel.

Examinations of the writings of early church fathers reveal that many of them noted both the presence and absence of the "bloody sweat" passage in the manuscripts they were familiar with. For instance, Epiphanius indicated that the verses were found in some "uncorrected copies" of Luke, suggesting that the Gospel of Luke was being copied in two forms, one with and one without the "bloody sweat" passage, in the early stages of textual transmission.

Metzger, as well as Westcott and Hort, believed that it was more likely that the verses were added from an early source (oral or written) of extra-canonical traditions concerning the life and passion of Jesus, rather than deleted by those who felt the account of Jesus being overcome by human weakness was incompatible with his sharing the divine omnipotence of the Father. Despite considering the passage to be a later addition to the text, a majority of the Committee decided to retain the words in the text but enclose them within double square brackets due to its antiquity and importance in the textual tradition.

As a result, Luke 22:43-44 shares a similar position with the pericope of the adulterous woman (John 7:53-8:11) in the NU text, as both are kept in the text due to their place in tradition, even though they are not part of the original writings. Most Bible translations keep these passages in the text, providing notes about their absence in ancient witnesses, perpetuating their authenticity in the minds of Christians who rely solely on translations. The only exception was the Revised Standard Version (RSV), which excluded both passages. However, due to outside pressure, John 7:53-8:11 was restored to the text after its initial printing, but Luke 22:43-44 was not.

Most Christians believe that the detail about Jesus' passion in Luke 22:43-44, which is often referred to as the "bloody sweat" passage, is authentic and came from Luke as he received it from the eyewitnesses of Jesus (Luke 1:1-4). However, it is often misinterpreted to mean that Jesus was sweating blood, when in fact, the text says that he was sweating so profusely that it appeared like blood dripping from a wound.

John 7:53-8:11 - A More Constructive Comprehensive Explanation

The Pericope Adulterae, found in John 7:53-8:11, is a passage that has been widely debated among scholars due to its presence in some New Testament manuscripts and absence from others. Its origins, placement, and authorship have been questioned, as there is substantial external evidence against its inclusion as part of the original Gospel of John.

1. **Manuscripts that omit the passage**: The passage is absent from many early and diverse manuscripts, including the oldest forms of the Syriac, Sahadic, sub-Achmimic, and older

Bohairic versions. It is also missing from some Armenian manuscripts, Old Georgian versions, the Gothic version, and several Old Latin manuscripts.

2. **Manuscripts that include the passage**: Despite the strong evidence against its inclusion, the passage is present in other manuscripts, such as D, F, G, H, K, M, U, and Γ. It is also found in various positions in different manuscripts, indicating uncertainty about its original placement.

3. **Stylistic and contextual differences**: The style and vocabulary of the passage differ noticeably from the rest of the Fourth Gospel, and its presence interrupts the narrative flow between John 7:52 and 8:12.

4. **Indications of historical truth**: The account has signs of historical truth and seems to be a piece of oral tradition that circulated in parts of the Western church. This oral tradition was eventually incorporated into various manuscripts at different locations.

5. **Copyists' uncertainty**: In many of the manuscripts that contain the passage, it is marked with asterisks or obeli, indicating that the copyists were aware that it was not part of the original text.

6. **Inclusion in double square brackets**: Although the passage is not considered part of the original Fourth Gospel, it is enclosed in double square brackets in certain editions (NA27 and UBS4) due to its antiquity and significance in the Christian tradition.

The pericope of the adulteress (7:53–8:11) is not found in any of the earliest manuscripts of the New Testament, including P66 and P75, which date back to the second to fourth centuries. The other witnesses, such as the fourth-century codices (א A B C T), Diatessaron, the early versions, and most of the early church fathers, also exclude this passage. Its first appearance in a Greek manuscript is in Codex D from around 400, but it was not included in other Greek manuscripts until the ninth century. Although the story may have been circulating in the oral tradition as early as the second century, the pericope's appearance in the written text is an example of how oral tradition can eventually be incorporated into the written text.

Many scholars have pointed out that the vocabulary used in the pericope is not consistent with the rest of John and that its insertion in the text greatly disrupts the narrative flow. The pericope also interrupts the connection between 7:40–52 and 8:12–20. The internal evidence, therefore, suggests that the pericope was not written by John.

Despite the strong evidence against its Johannine authorship, the Pericope Adulterae remains an important passage in the biblical tradition and continues to be studied and commented on by scholars. Its historical and spiritual value makes it a significant part of the Christian faith, even though its origins and placement in the Gospel of John are certain. It must be emphatically stated that 7:53–8:11 was not part of the Gospel of John.

Romans 11:6 - Analyzing Textual Variants

Main Text (WH NU): οὐκέτι γίνεται χάρις "it [grace] would no longer be grace" Supported by: P46 ℵ* A C D F G 1739 cop

Variant 1 (TR): ουκετι γινεται χαρις. ει δε εξ εργων ουκετι εστι χαρις, επει το εργον ουκετι εστιν εργον "it [grace] would no longer be grace. But if it is of works, then it is no longer grace; otherwise work is no longer work." Supported by: (B omits εστι and replaces final εργον with χαρις) 2ℵ Ψ 33 Maj (syr)

The textual variants in Romans 11:6 revolve around whether the passage should include the additional sentence found in the variant/TR. In analyzing the textual evidence, the main text (WH NU) has significant support, including P46, ℵ*, A, C, D, F, G, and 1739.

The variant reading, on the other hand, has a smaller but still considerable group of witnesses, including 2ℵ, Ψ, 33, and the Majority text. Notably, this variant includes an additional sentence: "But if it is of works, then it is no longer grace; otherwise work is no longer work."

There is no compelling reason to account for the omission of the second sentence in the main text if it were originally part of the epistle.

Consequently, the variant is likely an interpolation that may have been created as early as the fourth century. Furthermore, this gloss does not help clarify the passage's message. The main text clearly conveys the nature of grace as being a free gift, not a reward for doing work. The variant's additional sentence, rather than enhancing this meaning, detracts from it with the ambiguous statement, "otherwise work is no longer work."

Considering the strong textual evidence supporting the main text and the lack of clarity added by the variant's additional sentence, the main text's shorter reading is more likely to be the original version of Romans 11:6.

Romans 16:24 - Analyzing Textual Variants

Main Text (WH NU): omit verse Supported by: P46 P61 ℵ (A) B C 1739 it cop

Variant 1 (TR): include verse (same as in 16:20—see note) Supported by: D (F G omit Ιησου Χριστου [Jesus Christ]) Ψ Maj syrh

The textual issue in Romans 16:24 revolves around whether the verse should be included or omitted. The main text (WH NU) omits the verse, and this reading is strongly supported by the earliest manuscripts, including 𝔓46, 𝔓61, ℵ, A, B, C, and 1739.

On the other hand, the variant (TR) includes the verse, which is the same as in 16:20. This reading is supported by a smaller group of witnesses, including D, Ψ, and the Majority text. The Western manuscripts (D, F, G) add the benediction at 16:24 because they do not include 16:25–27. The verse's inclusion in the TR and Majority Text leads to its presence in the KJV and NKJV translations.

The omission of this verse is more plausible, as it is likely that a scribe (or scribes) copied the verse from 16:20, thinking it was appropriate to follow the postscript (see note on 16:20). All modern translations, following superior testimony, do not include the verse. However, these translations provide a textual note concerning this verse due to its presence in traditional English translations.

In summary, considering the strong textual evidence supporting the omission of Romans 16:24 and the fact that it duplicates the content found in 16:20, it is more likely that the original text of Romans did not include this verse.

1 Timothy 3:16 - Analyzing Textual Variants

Main Text (WH NU): ὃς ἐφανερώθη "who was manifested" Supported by: ℵ* A* C* F G 33 Didymus

Variant 1: ὃ εφανερωθη "which was manifested" Supported by: D*

Variant 2/TR: θεος εφανερωθη "God was manifested" Supported by: ℵc Ac C2 D2 Ψ 1739 Maj

The textual problem in 1 Timothy 3:16 generated significant debate in the nineteenth century, as it deals with the doctrine of the incarnation. The issue revolves around whether the original text read "who was manifested," "which was manifested," or "God was manifested."

The main text (WH NU) reads "who was manifested," supported by the earliest manuscripts, including ℵ*, A*, C*, F, G, and 33. The first variant reads "which was manifested," found in manuscript D*. The second variant, "God was manifested," is the reading in the TR and is supported by later corrected manuscripts and the Majority text. This reading is also found in the KJV translation.

It has been suggested that a scribe mistook OC (equivalent to ος) for Θ̄C̄ (the nomen sacrum for θεος) and made the change. However, it is unlikely that multiple scribes would make this error. The more plausible explanation is that scribes intentionally altered the text to emphasize that it was "God" who was manifested in the flesh.

Although some scholars feared that the doctrine of the incarnation would be undermined by the reading "he who was manifest in the flesh," the subject of the verse is still Christ. Most commentators identify "who" (or "he") with Christ, the God-man who revealed his deity through his humanity. Modern English translations, beginning with the ASV and ERV, reflect the superior text, and most provide the variant readings in marginal notes. The debate surrounding this textual issue does not undermine the doctrine of the incarnation but merely highlights the importance of accurately preserving the original text.

1 Peter 5:8 - Analyzing Textual Variants

Main Text (NU): ζητῶν [τινα] καταπιεῖν "seeking someone to devour" Supported by: Maj

Variant 1/TR: ζητων τίνα καταπιειν "seeking whom he may devour" Supported by: L P 1739

Variant 2/WH: ζητων καταπιειν "seeking to devour" Supported by: B Ψ 0206

The textual issue in 1 Peter 5:8 involves the precise wording of the description of the devil's actions, whether he is "seeking someone to devour," "seeking whom he may devour," or simply "seeking to devour." The manuscripts P72, ℵ, and A are not listed above, as the word τινα is unaccented in these manuscripts and could have been interpreted as either a definite or indefinite pronoun by ancient readers. In the majority of later manuscripts, the word was accented to indicate a specific interpretation.

The second variant, "seeking to devour," has the support of two fourth-century manuscripts (B and 0206) and is likely the original reading. This variant probably gave rise to the other variants, each of which adds a substantive after ζητων ("seeking"). With this reading, the focus is on the activity of the devil, who is described as a lion-like figure seeking to devour, rather than the object of his action, which can be assumed. This interpretation emphasizes the relentless and dangerous nature of the devil's pursuits, urging believers to remain vigilant and resist his advances.

Jude 5 - Analyzing Textual Variants

Main Text (WH) NU: πάντα ὅτι [ὁ] κύριος ἅπαξ "[knowing that] the Lord having once for all" Supported by: C* (ℵ Ψ omit ο) syrh Examples of English translations: RSVmg, NRSV, ESVmg, NASB, NIV, TNIV, NEB, REB, NJB, NAB, NLTmg, HCSB

Variant 1: απαξ παντα, οτι Ιησους "[knowing] once for all, that Jesus" Supported by: A, B, 33, Cyril, Jerome, Bede

Variant 2: παντα, οτι Ιησους απαξ "[knowing] everything, that Jesus once" Supported by: 1739, 1881, Origen (according to mg), cop

Variant 3: απαξ παντα, οτι θεος Χριστος "[knowing] once for all, that God [the] Messiah (or, Messiah God)" Supported by: P72 (P* παντας)

Variant 4: απαξ παντα, οτι ο θεος "[knowing] once for all, that God" Supported by: C2, vgMS

Variant 5/TR: απαξ τουτο, οτι ο κυριος "once [you knew] this, that the Lord" Supported by: (K L) Maj

The primary textual issue in Jude 5 concerns the identity of the one who delivered the people out of Egypt. The first two variants present "Jesus" as the deliverer, while the other variants use "Lord," "God," or "God the Messiah." The reading with "Jesus" is found in several important early manuscripts, including A, B, 33, 1739, 1881, and the writings of Origen, Cyril, Jerome, and Bede. 𝔓72 may also indirectly support this reading, as it contains a messianic title, "Christ."

From a textual perspective, it is easier to argue that the reading with "Jesus" is the original one, as scribes were not known for inventing difficult readings. Some scholars have suggested that Jude might have intended "Joshua" instead of "Jesus," but this is unlikely, as Joshua led the Israelites into Canaan, not out of Egypt. Instead, Jude likely viewed Jesus as Yahweh the Savior, present with the Israelites and operative in their deliverance from Egypt. Paul shared a similar view in 1 Corinthians 10:4 and 10:9.

The first English translation to adopt the reading with "Jesus" was NLT, with other recent versions such as TNIV and NET also adopting this reading. Most other English translations have included it in the margin. While the United Bible Societies' Greek New Testament initially contained the reading with "Jesus," a slim majority of editors later voted to change it to "Lord." Despite this change, the reading with "Jesus" should be considered the original and more accurate reading.

Revelation 11:8 - Analyzing Textual Variants

Main Text (WH) NU: ὁ κύριος αὐτῶν ἐσταυρώθη "their Lord was crucified" Supported by: אc, A, C, P, syr

Variant 1/TR: ο κυριος ημων εσταυρωθη "our Lord was crucified" Supported by: 1

Variant 2: ο κυριος εσταυρωθη "the Lord was crucified" Supported by: P47, א*

The textual issue in Revelation 11:8 involves the identity of the Lord in relation to the witnesses or those in Jerusalem. The three textual variants show three different scribal perspectives on this issue.

The WH NU reading indicates that "the Lord" (referring to Jesus) is either the Lord of the two witnesses or the Lord of those in Jerusalem, symbolized by the names "Sodom and Egypt." This reading could be interpreted as Jesus being the Lord of the witnesses or the Lord of Jerusalem.

In contrast, variant 1, found in minuscule 1 and incorporated by Erasmus in the Textus Receptus, changes the text to "our Lord," reflecting a personalization of the text or an attempt to resolve a perceived theological issue. The question raised here is how Jesus could be the Lord of the city that crucified him.

The third variant, supported by the two earliest manuscripts (P47 and א*), is neutral because it lacks a pronoun and simply states that "the Lord was crucified." This reading could either be the original wording or a scribal alteration to remove the ambiguity of the expression "their Lord."

It is worth noting that the scribe of P47 wrote the verb "crucified" as a nomen sacrum with an unusual form: εστρω. While other early scribes (P46, P66, P75) also used the nomen sacrum form for "cross" and "crucify," this is the only instance of its use in Revelation among extant papyri predating 300 C.E.

The preferred method of getting at the original words of the original text is the **documentary method**, which considers internal and external evidence, as well as all manuscripts, yet giving the greater weight to the trusted documents (dates of the manuscripts supporting a reading, the geographical distribution of the manuscripts, and the overall quality both of the individual manuscripts and textual "families."), and so, it is Codex Vaticanus and Codex Sinaiticus that are the deciding factor in going against the NU text.

Worksheet for New Testament Textual Criticism[8]

PASSAGE: _____

Various Readings		
Variant 1	Variant 2	Variant 3
Internal Evidence:	Internal Evidence:	Internal Evidence:
External Evidence:	External Evidence:	External Evidence:
What is the weight of the external evidence?		
What textual principles apply?		
Conclusion:		

---

[8] Paul D. Wegner, *A Student's Guide to Textual Criticism of the Bible: Its History, Methods & Results* (Downers Grove, IL: InterVarsity Press, 2006), 228.

Edward D. Andrews

CHAPTER 8 The Collation and Classification of New Testament Manuscripts

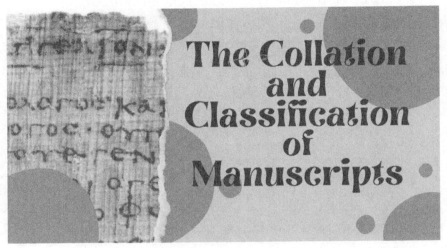

Variant Reading(s): differing versions of a word or phrase found in two or more manuscripts within a variation unit. Variant readings are also called alternate readings. **Variation Unit**: any portion of text that exhibits variations in its reading between two or more different manuscripts. It is important to distinguish variation units from variant readings. Variation units are the places in the text where manuscripts disagree, and each variation unit has at least two variant readings. For example, in **COLOSSIANS 1:2**, we have "God our Father" in the following manuscripts (B D K L Ψ 33 1739 it syr cop) and "God our Father and the Lord Jesus Christ" in (ℵ A C F G I Maj it (syrh**) cop Jerome). **COLOSSIANS 2:2** is a great example of a number of variants in a variation unit. We have the reading found in the critical texts WH NA and UBS "the mystery of God, Christ" in (P46 B), **variant 1** "the mystery of God, which is Christ" (D*), **variant 2** "the mystery of God" (D1 H P 1881), **variant 3** "the mystery of Christ" (81 (1739) itb) **variant 4** "the mystery of God, Father of

270

Christ" (א* A C 048vid) **variant 5** "the mystery of God, even the Father of Christ" (2א Ψ 0208) **variant 6/TR** "the mystery of God and of the Father and of Christ" (D2 Maj syr**). Having so many variants is an indication that the scribes struggled with this text. Comparing the manuscripts with another is called collating.

Simple Textual Variant

Simple Textual Variant

John 3:13 The Greek-English New Testament Interlinear (GENTI) [WH NU]
And no one has ascended into the heaven if not the (one) out of the heaven having descended, the Son of the man.
13 καὶ οὐδεὶς ἀναβέβηκεν εἰς τὸν οὐρανὸν εἰ μὴ ὁ ἐκ τοῦ οὐρανοῦ καταβάς, ὁ υἱὸς τοῦ ἀνθρώπου.
P66 P75 א B L T Ws 083 086 cop Diatessaron

John 3:13 Updated American Standard Version (UASV)
13 And no one has ascended into heaven except the one who descended from heaven, the Son of man.

John 3:13 variant/ Stephanus New Testament (TR1550)
And no one has ascended into the heaven if not the (one) out of the heaven having descended, the Son of the man. who is in the heaven
13 καὶ οὐδεὶς ἀναβέβηκεν εἰς τὸν οὐρανὸν εἰ μὴ ὁ ἐκ τοῦ οὐρανοῦ καταβάς, ὁ υἱὸς τοῦ ἀνθρώπου **ο ωνεντωουρανω**
(A* omit ων) Θ Ψ 050 f1, Maj

John 3:13 New King James Version (NKJV)
13 No one has ascended to heaven but He who came down from heaven, *that is*, the Son of Man **who is in heaven.**

Collation: a base text of the Greek New Testament together with an apparatus of variant readings for any place in the text where the manuscripts selected for the collation disagree. Disagreements can range from a single letter to a phrase, and the latter sometimes includes the order of the words. Diacritical marks are noted as well, but of course, these marks are late additions and are subject to change at the will of the critic. The formal term for places of disagreement is "variation unit" (q.v.). - Don Wilkins

Collating in New Testament Textual Studies is comparing and analyzing one NT manuscript with another. One can only imagine the daunting task of comparing and analyzing every NT manuscript. This is especially true when we consider that the New Testament has 5,898 Greek New Testament manuscripts, 10,000 Latin manuscripts, and an additional 9,300 other manuscripts in such languages as Syriac, Slavic, Gothic, Ethiopic, Coptic, and Armenian. Then, we must consider the Scriptural quotations from the Apostolic Fathers of the late first and early second centuries C.E., as well as the churchmen who were called Apologists and other early Church Fathers near the middle of the second century C.E. through its end, and the Church Fathers of the third to the sixth centuries C.E. If it was not for the scholars who poured through these manuscripts, comparing and analyzing (collating) them, we would have no practical way of putting them to use.

Collating, comparing, and analyzing every manuscript is how we know what variants there are in a given variation unit. **Variant Reading(s)**: differing versions of a word or phrase found in two or more manuscripts within a variation unit. Variant readings are also called alternate readings. **Variation Unit**: any portion of text that exhibits variations in its reading between two or more different manuscripts. It is important to distinguish variation units from variant readings. Variation units are the places in the text where manuscripts disagree, and each variation unit has at least two variant readings. For example, in **Colossians 1:2**, we have [θεοῦ πατρὸς ἡμῶν] "God our Father" in the following manuscripts (B D K L Ψ 33 1739 it syr cop) and [θεου πατρος ημων και κυριου Ιησου Χριστου] "God our Father and the Lord Jesus Christ" in (ℵ A C F G I Maj it (syrh**) cop Jerome). **Matthew 22:30** is a great example of a number of variants in a variation unit. We have the reading found in WH NA and UBS [ὡς ἄγγελοι ἐν τῷ οὐρανῷ εἰσιν] "they are like angels in heaven" in (B D 700), **variant 1** [ως οι αγγελοι εν τω ουρανω εισιν] "they are like angels in heaven" (Θ f), variant 2 [ως αγγελοι θεου εν τω ουρανω εισιν] "the mystery of God" (D1 H P 1881), **variant 2/TR** "they are like angels of God in heaven" (ℵ L f¹³ 33; W Maj add οι before αγγελοι = the angels). Having so many variants is an indication that the scribes struggled with this text. Comparing the manuscripts with another is called collating.

In addition, in textual studies, collation is also comparing the manuscripts with a critical text like 1881 WH, 2012 NA (28th ed.), 2015 UBS (5th ed.), or 2017 THGNT. As you can see from Colossians 2:2, we refer to the first reading within the critical texts WH NU and the others are listed as variants, even the TR. By doing this, we have access to the entire Greek NT and its differences without having to look through all of the manuscripts. In this, the critical text (WH WH NU THGNT) is the standard upon which all of the other manuscripts are compared. Then, the differences are listed in the apparatus of the critical text. If more evidence were to come to light; then. a variant reading in the apparatus could very well be placed in the main text and the reading in the main text becomes a variant reading in the apparatus. Then again, more evidence could be discovered that adds more testimony to the reading in the critical text, reinforcing the decision that has already been made.

The textual scholar of a translation committee, for example, in certain circumstances should be willing to verify the decisions that have been made by the textual scholars of the critical text. For instance, there may be a reading that has long been disputed as to what the manuscript contains because of damage to that manuscript. Aside from this rare occasion, the textual scholars over the centuries and recent decades have compiled a storehouse of information on as they have collated the manuscripts for us. Nevertheless, the textual scholar working on a translation or another critical text could differ in the decision made by the manuscript evidence as well. As we have learned early on the NA text is supposed to be a reasoned eclectic text where the scholars consider internal and external evidence equally. However, the textual scholars of the NA text tend to lean toward internal evidence often. In other words, the textual scholars might refer to the excellent weighty evidence (P66, P75 ℵ B) in the first half of a verse and then ignore that same evidence in the second half of a verse, favoring internal evidence, which shows an inconsistency. This author favors the documentary approach in making textual decisions, which means that I look at both internal and external, giving a little extra weight to the external, which is less subjective. I have thus decided against a number of decisions made by the editors of the NU text. Below is one example.

Matthew 9:26 2019 *Greek-English New Testament Interlinear* (GENTI WH)

<small>And went out the report of [about] her into whole the land that</small>

26 Καὶ ἐξῆλθεν ἡ φήμη **αὐτῆς** εἰς ὅλην τὴν γῆν ἐκείνην.

ΚΑΤΑ ΜΑΤΘΑΙΟΝ 9:26 2012 Nestle-Aland / Stephanus New Testament (TR NU TGNT SBLGNT)

<small>And went out the report this into whole the land that</small>

26 Καὶ ἐξῆλθεν ἡ φήμη **αὕτη** εἰς ὅλην τὴν γῆν ἐκείνην.

Matthew 9:26 Updated American Standard Version (UASV)	Matthew 9:26 English Standard Version (ESV)	Matthew 9:26 New American Standard Bible (NASB)
²⁶ And the **report about her** spread into that whole region.	²⁶ And the **report of this** went through all that district.	²⁶ This news spread throughout all that land.

GENTI εξηλθεν η φημη αυτης "the report of [about] her went out" ℵ C* Θ f¹ 33	Variant 1/TR WH NU TGNT SBLGNT εξηλθεν η φημη αυτη "this report went out" B W f¹³ Maj	Variant 2 εξηλθεν η φημη αυτου "his fame went out" D cop

The likely original wording in Matthew 9:14 is "the report of [about] her went out" (εξηλθεν η φημη αυτης) in good documentary witnesses ℵ C* Θ f¹ 33 and GENTI. We have **a variant**, "this report went out" (εξηλθεν η φημη αυτη) in B W f¹³ Maj and TR WH NU TGNT SBLGNT. There is a second variant, "his fame went out" (εξηλθεν η φημη αυτου) in D cop.

Some Sopherim (scribes) of the Hebrew Old Testament altered the text if they felt it showed irreverence for God or the attention was focused on something else instead of God Himself. In the marginal notes of the Masoretic text, there are notes that read: "This is one of the eighteen emendations of the Sopherim," or comparable words. "The report of [about] her went out" (εξηλθεν η φημη αυτης) was likely altered by the scribes who felt the attention was being given to the girl as opposed to the fact that it was Jesus who raised her from the dead. Therefore, the words "the **report about her**" was likely changed with one letter from αυτης [of her] to αυτη [this] making it "the **report of this**." Others made the change from αυτης [of her] to αυτου [of him], which would be similar to Luke 4:14 (καὶ φήμη ἐξῆλθεν καθ᾽ ὅλης τῆς περιχώρου περὶ αὐτοῦ) "and a report about him went out through all the surrounding country."

Example of a Collation

John 1:16	John 1:16	John 1:16	John 1:16
GENTI WH NU	P⁶⁶ P⁷⁵ ℵ B C* D L 33	TR MAJ BYZ	A C³ Wˢ Θ Ψ f¹⋅
¹⁶ ὅτι ἐκ τοῦ πληρώματος αὐτοῦ ἡμεῖς πάντες ἐλάβομεν, καὶ χάριν ἀντὶ χάριτος·	¹⁶ ὅτι ἐκ τοῦ πληρώματος αὐτοῦ ἡμεῖς πάντες ἐλάβομεν, καὶ χάριν ἀντὶ χάριτος·	¹⁶ Καὶ ἐκ τοῦ πληρώματος αὐτοῦ ἡμεῖς πάντες ἐλάβομεν, καὶ χάριν ἀντὶ χάριτος.	¹⁶ Καὶ ἐκ τοῦ πληρώματος αὐτοῦ ἡμεῖς πάντες ἐλάβομεν, καὶ χάριν ἀντὶ χάριτος.
¹⁶ **For from** his fullness we have all received, and grace upon grace.	¹⁶ **For from** his fullness we have all received, and grace upon grace.	¹⁶ **And of** his fullness have we all received, and grace upon grace.	¹⁶ **And of** his fullness have we all received, and grace upon grace.

On this Philip Comfort writes, "The replacement of καὶ for ὅτι is a scribal adjustment intended to make a more logical connection between 1:15 and 1:16. However, ὅτι in 1:16 connects with 1:14 inasmuch as 1:15 is a parenthetical statement (usually set off by parentheses in English translations). Connecting the end of 1:14 with ὅτι at the beginning of 1:16 gives this reading: "we saw his glory, glory as of the only Son of the Father, full of grace and truth … because (ὅτι) from his fullness we have all received, even grace added to grace." John was saying that he (and the other apostles) knew by experience that the Son of God was full of grace and truth because they had continually been recipients of that full supply."[9]

The originals were perfect in every sense because the authors were moved along by the Holy Spirit. The copyist was not inspired and, in some cases, they were not even Christian but worked at scriptoriums. We had 1,400 years of mostly accidental errors and some intentional errors, and now we have 500 years of restoration. In these latter parts of the last day, it falls on textual scholars to give a restored text that is a mirror-like reflection of the original. We must remember that

---

[9] Philip W. Comfort, *New Testament Text and Translation Commentary: Commentary on the Variant Readings of the Ancient New Testament Manuscripts and How They Relate to the Major English Translations* (Carol Stream, IL: Tyndale House Publishers, Inc., 2008), 254.

Edward D. Andrews

Westcott and Hort brought us so very close in 1881 as their text is 99.5% the same as the 2012 Nestle-Aland Greek New Testament. I believe that between WH and NA, we have a restored text of 99.99 percent. The literal translations today are based on these restored texts of WH and NA. This would not have been possible without collations. Modern technology has made it so much easier to collate. We can see from the Logos Bible Software below just how easy it is to compare the differences.

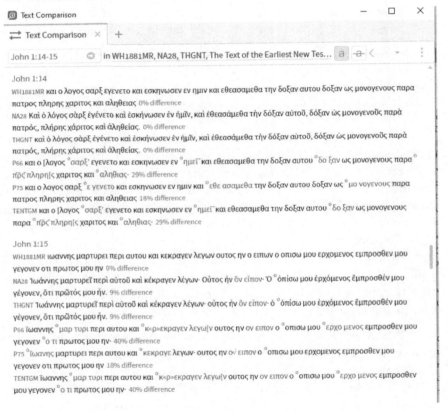

A Brief History of Collation

John Mill (1645-1707) was a fellow at Queen's College, Oxford, who spent some 30 years in textual studies, which ended with his majorly important Greek text that ended up being published a mere two weeks before he died at the age of 62. Mill had a critical introduction to his Greek text, wherein his work recorded over 30,000 discrepancies between some 100 extant New Testament manuscripts. He decided against changing Stephanus's 1550 Textus Receptus Greek text or adding an apparatus in the critical text. So, he left the time-honored corrupt Textus Receptus undamaged. Nevertheless, here is where we find the first real Textus Receptus Only arguments. Mill's Greek New Testament and especially his critical introduction to his Greek text came under attack by Daniel Whitby and Anthony Collins. Whitby's *Examen* claimed that Mill had basically, in essence, began the destruction of the Word of God. Whitby argued that Mill had damaged the authority of God's Word and that his tampering with the text was tampering with the Word of God. These same arguments are still used today by what we call the Textus Receptus Only and the King James Version Only. Bentley came to Mill's defense remarking that actually, Mill was not accountable for the differences between the various manuscript, they were already there, Mill simply pointed them out. John Mill, *Novum Testamentum Graecum, cum lectionibus variantibus MSS* (Oxford 1707). In 1710 Ludolf Küster reprinted Mill's *Testament* at Amsterdam with the readings of twelve additional manuscripts.

Edward Wells (1667-1727) was an English mathematician, geographer, and controversial theologian, who published a ten-part Greek New Testament text with helps for his readers. From 1709 to 1719, Wells produced a critical Greek edition of the New Testament, which was published in Oxford. Some 210 times, Wells would abandon the Textus Receptus, with the vast majority of his decisions agreeing with the critical texts that would come about 150+ years later when far more textual evidence was available. Even though his work got little press, he goes down in history as the first to abandon the Textus Receptus in a complete Greek New Testament text. Wells had used the variant readings that had been collated in the edition of John Mill in the construction of his Greek New Testament text. As was stated above Mill's edition had involved the most thoroughgoing critical apparatus up to its time and would only be outmatched by Tischendorf some 140+ years later. However, as was stated, the actual text was simply a reprint of that of 1550 Stephanus. So, it bears

277

repeating that it was Wells' edition to be the first to give scholars the complete Greek New Testament as he moved away from the Textus Receptus and to what we now consider the standard critical text, such as the Nestle-Aland.

Richard Bentley (1662-1742), master of Trinity College, Cambridge was an English classical scholar, critic, and theologian. In 1716, Bentley sent in a letter to William Wake, Archbishop of Canterbury, announcing his plan to prepare a critical edition of the Greek New Testament. Throughout the next four years, he was assisted by J. J. Wetstein, a prominent biblical critic, he gathered materials for the work that lie ahead. In 1720 Bentley published *Proposals for a New Edition of the Greek Testament*, wherein he gave examples of how he intended to proceed. In the example of the last chapter of Revelation, he abandoned the Textus Receptus in 40+ places. He was determined to compare the text of the Vulgate with that of the oldest Greek manuscripts. Bentley intended to restore the Greek text as the church has received it at the time of the Council of Nicaea in 325 C.E. Bentley's primary foundational manuscript was *Codex Alexandrinus*, which he described as "the oldest and best in the world." Bentley's intention was to supplant the Textus Receptus. However, the Textus Receptus was so revered it would not be so easily displaced.

Johann Albert Bengel (1687-1752) was a Lutheran pietist clergyman and a Greek-language scholar. Bengel's belief in the plenary inspiration of the Bible coupled with John Mill's 30,000 textual variants is what motivated him to investigate the transmission of the text. In 1734, Bengel's edition of the Greek New Testament without the critical apparatus was published at Tübingen and Stuttgart. As early as 1725, in an addition to his edition of *Chrysostoms De Sacerdotio*, he had given an account in his *Prodromus Novi Testamenti Graeci recte cauteque adornandi* (An essay of the New Testament correctly and cautiously adorned) of the principles on which his intended edition was to be based. as he was preparing to get his work underway, Bengel was able to acquire the collations of upwards of twenty manuscripts. However, none of them were of great importance, not having much influence on his decisions. Twelve of them he had collated himself. Then, he imposed on himself the rule of not inserting any variant reading which had not already been used in an earlier printed edition of the Greek text. However, in the case of Revelation, he deviated from his rule because of the text being so corrupt, he chose to insert certain readings based on manuscript authority. Using the first five letters of the Greek alphabet to establish the level of importance, he inserted a selection of various readings in the lower margin of the page: α was used to indicate the reading Bengel felt to be the original reading, even though he failed to put it in the main text; β indicated a reading that was more likely than that in the main text; γ indicated that it was equal to the reading in the main text, and δ indicated readings that were inferior to those in the text.

Bengel's text was followed by his critical apparatus. The beginning of which was an introduction to his analysis of the New Testament. He explained his famous well-known textual principle in the thirty-fourth section *Proclivi scriptioni praestat ardua* (The difficult reading is to be preferred to that which is easy). This sound principle has held on with textual scholars ever since. The next part of his critical apparatus was his observations of the various readings, wherein he gives the reader the evidence for or against the different readings. Bengel was the first to develop textual families. As he had invested these manuscripts, he began to see a certain resemblance of some Greek NT manuscripts, versions, and church fathers, while others had certain characteristics that grouped them together. For example, particular readings might be found in one particular grouping of manuscripts but not the others. While later the manuscripts would be gathered into four different families: Alexandrian, Caesarean, Western, and Byzantine. Bengel broke it down into two families: The African family and the Asiatic family, the former he considered older and the latter he considered of less value or less weighty as we would say. The next to accept families of manuscripts, which they tweaked, were J. S. Semler and J. J. Griesbach. Modern scholars are now trying to move away from the manuscript family theory. Like those who came before him, like Brian Walton and John Mill, he was criticized for exposing the variant readings and point out the differences in the manuscripts. Again, many felt that his exposing these scribal errors was tantamount to undermining the Word of God. On the other hand, J.J. Wetstein accused Bengel of holding back and that Bengel should have leaned into his critical materials even more. Bengel decided to address all these accusations from both sides in his *Defence of the Greek Text of His New Testament*, which he published in 1736. It contained answers to complaints of both sides, but he focused more attention on Wetstein. The text of Bengel may have hit a few speed bumps in his day but scholars since have recognized its value long after his death, even being frequently reprinted.

Johann Jacob Wettstein (1693-1754) was a Swiss Protestant theologian, best known as a New Testament critic and he was one who collated manuscripts for Bentley. Wettstein gave his lifework to the study of the New Testament manuscripts and other sources and his collection of various readings. He put much labor and love into his study of Codex Alexandrinus. Strangely, he was stumbled in his faith in the Divinity of Christ when he discovered in the Codex Alexandrinus with no corrected reading, the original itself the reading (Ὃς ἐφανερώθη ἐν σαρκί) "who was manifested in the flesh" in 1 Timothy 3:16, as opposed to (θεος ἐφανερώθη ἐν σαρκί) "God was manifested in the flesh." In the Alexandrinus Codex, the contraction for "God," formed by two Greek letters "ΘC," appears originally to have read "OC," which is the Greek word for "who." Bruce M. Metzger in his *Textual Commentary on the Greek New Testament* concludes: "No uncial (in the first hand) earlier than the eighth or ninth century (Ψ) supports θεός [theos]; all ancient versions presuppose ὅς or ὅ; and no patristic writer prior to the last third of the fourth century testifies to the reading θεός [theos]. The reading θεός [theos] arose either (a) accidentally, through the misreading of ος as ΘΣ, or (b) deliberately, either to supply a substantive for the following six verbs, or, with less probability, to provide greater dogmatic precision."[10]

After forty-years of laborious research, in 1751-2, Wettstein published ar Amsterdam, the Greek New Testament in two volumes. He too published the Textus Receptus text but within the margins, he placed readings that he thought were original. In the appendix, Wettstein offers his reader the advice "manuscripts must be evaluated by their weight, not by their number." This is our 'manuscripts must be weighed not counted.' Being weighed means assessing the importance of one manuscript over another, especially with a view to a decision of what the original reading is. The thing is, Wettstein had good rules or principles but he did not apply them consistently. Ironically, considering the line of textual evidence that was coming to light up unto his life's work, he seemed to go against Bengel in his belief that the early Greek manuscripts had been contaminated by the Latin versions and that textual scholars should instead rely on the later witnesses for establishing the original readings. Some of his opponents valued his work less because he did not value the Latin versions, as well as group manuscripts into families of manuscripts, which had also been done by Richard Bentley and J. A. Bengel.

Johann Salomo Semler (1725-1791) was a German church historian, biblical commentator, and textual critic who was also known as "the father of German rationalism." Semler adopted Wettstein's manuscript classification into families but took it a little further. He renamed Bengel's Asiatic group "eastern," assigning the origin to the recension of the early fourth century by Lucian of Antioch. He renamed Bengel's "African" group "Western" or "Egypto-Palestinian" and assigned the source to Origen. He had three classifications for the manuscripts: **(1)** Alexandrians from Origen that was found in Syriac, Bohairic, and Ethiopic; **(2)** Eastern that was prevailing in the

---

[10] Bruce Manning Metzger, *United Bible Societies, A Textual Commentary on the Greek New Testament,* Second Edition a Companion Volume to the United Bible Societies' Greek New Testament (4th Rev. Ed.) (London; New York: United Bible Societies, 1994), 574.

Antiochian and Constantinopolitan churches; **(3)** Western that was found in the Latin version and church fathers. Semler thought that the later manuscripts were distinguished by combining all of the recensions.

Johann Jakob Griesbach (1745-1812) was a was a German textual scholar. Griesbach's notoriety comes from his work in New Testament textual studies, in which he introduced a new milestone. He laid the groundwork for all the work in NT textual studies that would follow. He had been a student of Semler at Halle. Griesbach's critical edition of the Greek New Testament first emerged at Halle, in three volumes, in 1774-1775. He used the *Elzevir* edition of the Textus Receptus in his critical text. When he disagreed with the TR, he would place the TR reading on the inner margin along with other readings that concerned him that he printed in smaller type. The readings found in the margins received special markings as to what he felt their probability was. As he weighed these probabilities and investigated the transmission history of the NT manuscripts, he continued categorizing the manuscripts as J. A. Bengel, and J. S. Semler had. Griesbach placed all then known manuscripts into three categories: **(1)** the Alexandrian, **(2)** the Western, and **(3)** the Byzantine recensions. Griesbach was the beginning of the modern era of New Testament Textual studies, which was followed by such scholars as Karl Lachmann (1793-1851), F. J. A. Hort (1828-1892) and B. F. Westcott (1825-1901) AKA Westcott and Hort (WH), Erwin Nestle (1883-1972), Allen Wikgren (1906-1998), Matthew Black, (1908-1994), Barbara Aland (1937-present), and Carlo Maria Martini (1927-2012). Collation in those early days was no easy task because they were working with the manuscripts themselves, not some digitally enhanced copy. Those collating the manuscripts would have to often travel the globe on ships, trains, even by horse. Now, we can turn on our computers and get an enhanced image like the one below within seconds.

Codex Vaticanus (300-330 C.E.) Gospel of John

The Apparatus

19 ᵒ 𝔓⁶⁶ᵏˑ⁷⁵ ℵ C³ K L Wˢ Γ Δ f¹ 565. 700. 892*. 1241. 1424 𝔐

¦ *txt* B C* 33. 892ᶜ it syᶜ⁻ᵖ sa bo (p. Λευιτας 𝔓⁶⁶ᶜ ᵛⁱᵈ A Θ Ψ f¹³ 579 lat syʰ)

⸆ ερωτησουσιν 𝔓⁷⁵ L Wˢ Δ 33. 579

¦ επερωτησωσιν ℵ

20 ⸀ ωμολογησεν C² L Wˢ f¹ 33 it boᵐˢˢ

¦ − ℵ e l sa

21 ⸆ παλιν ℵ Wˢ it syᵖ

⸉ 1 2 4 5 3 A C³ K Γ Δ Θ 0234 f¹·¹³ 565. 579. 700. 892. 1241. 1424 𝔐 lat syʰ

¦ 1 2 4 5 ℵ L a

¦ 3 2 1 4 5 B

¦ 1-3 5 4 Wˢ

¦ 4 5 3 b rˡ co

¦ *txt* (τις 𝔓⁶⁶) 𝔓⁷⁵ C* Ψ 33 (e) ff² l; Or

ᵒ ℵ a b rˡ bo

22 ⸆ συ 𝔓⁶⁶ᶜˑ⁷⁵ (c rˡ)

24 ⸆ οι ℵ² Aᶜ C³ K N Wˢ Γ Δ Θ 0234 f¹·¹³ 33. 565. 579. 700. 892. 1241. 1424 𝔐 boᵐˢ *txt*

𝔓⁶⁶ˑ⁷⁵ ℵ* A* B C* L T Ψ 086 co; Or

Eberhard Nestle and Erwin Nestle, Nestle-Aland: NTG Apparatus Criticus, ed. Barbara Aland et al., 28. revidierte Auflage. (Stuttgart: Deutsche Bibelgesellschaft, 2012) Some of the symbols in the critical apparatus are as follows. The words enclosed between ᵒ and ` in the text are omitted. ¦ Separates different variants referring to the same variation unit. The symbol ⌐ represents the next word in the text is transmitted with variants. The words enclosed between ⌐ and ⌐ in the text are transmitted with variants. The symbol ° represents the next word in the text is omitted. The symbol * identifies the original reading when a correction has been made. The symbol ⊤ stands for the place marked in the text where an addition is transmitted.

Future Work in Collation

> On this, Dr. Don Wilkins writes,
>
> One thing that is immediately apparent for collation from the present onward is that we can say goodbye to much of the tedious work because computers are very good at doing these jobs. We, humans, were created for better things—not that I do not honor and admire the dedication of those who did such work in the past! We cannot eliminate all of the tedium, unfortunately. For example, humans still have to input or at a minimum verify the accuracy of inputting ancient handwritten text into machine-readable form. But once the text is accurately recorded for all time, we can have computers check the texts of different manuscripts against each other for agreements and disagreements and perform most other tasks of collation that previously had to be done by humans.
>
> Now then, if you have purchased NA28 or GNT5 recently and have discovered that only James through Jude has been reedited, you may feel a little short-changed. You probably should not. If nothing else, you at least have a window into the future of collation. What you find in these short books is the result of the ECM2 committee's work applying the massive collation of the Institute for New Testament Textual Research and using the tools of the Coherence-Based Genealogical Method. In the NA28 and GNT5 apparatuses, you have additional citations of papyri, but also the loss of citations of various variant readings, so *do not* throw away your previous editions of these texts unless you also plan to purchase the ECM2 itself.
>
> Permit me to do some forecasting and advisement beyond this. If you want to know as much as possible about the Greek text, and

if NA28 and GNT5 are representative of what the final NA and GNT texts and apparatuses will be (as I suspect they are), then NA28 and GNT5 will be inadequate for you. For a full reporting of the text and accompanying collation in printed form, you will need the ECM2. On the other hand, if you are content with the methods of traditional TC, then NA26/27 and GNT4 will continue to serve you well, and if you wish, you can consult the online CBGM tools or purchase NA28 or GNT5 to see where the editors have changed their previous decisions in the General Epistles. GNT5, of course, will supply the additional information of ratings and have a clearer apparatus, but at the expense of omitting numerous variant readings.

Whether you purchase the ECM2 or not, I *strongly* encourage you to consult the online CBGM tools, which I will discuss in chapter xii. They provide invaluable information and are free to all users, at least for now. These tools are actually much better as a source of information than the NA28 and GNT5 apparatuses, and even extend the usefulness of the ECM2 considerably.

As to other collations, I can hardly think of any organizations more resourceful than Zondervan and the SBL, and so far neither has made any discernable attempt to add collations to their published Greek texts (*A Reader's Greek New Testament* and the SBLGNT respectively). Indeed, as we have seen, they have not even clarified for their readers what individual manuscripts their texts are based upon when they differ from the NA.

The closest thing we have seen to a rival collation, at least in my experience, is Swanson's work. No one has stepped in to complete that project after his death, and for good reason, I think. Swanson had complained about unidentified mixture in base texts, but now what we have with all of our resources and computing power is common material among all the Greek manuscripts in existence. When we had only print resources, using Swanson's interlinear layout was a pleasure compared to the relative eyesore encountered in the NA apparatus, and Swanson had the extant sources accounted for just as well. Now, however, the Institute for New Testament Textual Research (INTTR) has virtually all the Greek NT manuscripts in existence[11] online, and one can easily see clean representations of all the variants and can even choose any variant temporarily as the base text for comparison.

I think it would be impossible to compete with such a resource and organization, at least so long as the organization provides convenient, free access to its sources. It has flaws, certainly, some of which I will point out in the chapter on the CBGM, and we can only hope that these will be addressed. The intention has also been expressed to make the ECM available online, and that has yet to be implemented. So long as the database is properly managed and good access provided, however, I expect that it will be the one everyone uses in place of everything else that may still be available.

Ultimately, then, I foresee everyone who edits a Greek text of the New Testament linking it to the ECM in some way. Today, probably the only way to do this, at least off-site, would be to set up one's preferred readings as the chosen text and copy and record the results from the CBGM tools, variant by variant. It would undoubtedly be better for someone planning a new edition of the Greek NT to do it by consulting the CBGM, taking full advantage of the information available nowhere else.

In the publication of a new Greek text, we should then expect to see some accounting of the sources behind the editor's (or editors') choices relative to the ECM. I do not know what, if any, copyright issues might be involved at present in listing the actual manuscripts, but I would think that at least it would be possible for editors to note that a particular choice was the 'b' or 'c' etc. reading in the ECM.

In closing out this chapter we can again say that the purpose of collation is to acquire all of the information about the manuscripts without ever having the texts of the manuscripts in full. We can compare a family of manuscripts with a standard critical text (TR WH NA THGNT) and then noting all of the significant differences. Or we

---

[11] This includes only a selected group of representative Byzantine manuscripts.

can compare one manuscript against another. The amount of space that we save is enormous.

Before you begin collating the manuscript maybe take some time and collate a couple of the chapters first to get your feet wet and familiarize yourself with the manuscript: handwriting style, odd or unusual feature or habit of the scribe, how the document is laid out. Every textual student or scholar should try their hand at collating. The collation should be done two times at minimum and then compared and even shared with others. Collating is no easy task, so one should not overwhelm themselves by spending hours collating to then get burned out, take a few days off, which has no rhythm to it. Regular and consistent is best, maybe one hour a day in the beginning. Then, gradually increase your time until you reach two hours a day. The work area for the collation should be comfortable but not too comfortable. There should be no distractions like playing music and you should turn off your cellphone. Nothing should distract you from the task at hand. When you are two hours a day, take a 15-minute break in between the hours. As you work do quick reviews along the way to make certain that you have made no mistakes. As you are working your way through the collation take note of how many correctors worked on the copy and how their habits differ from one another and if the copyist himself was involved in any of the corrections.

Bibliography

Aland, K. a. (1987). *The Text of the New Testament.* Grand Rapids: Eerdmans.

Andrews, E. (2020). *FROM SPOKEN WORDS TO SACRED TEXTS: Introduction-Intermediate New Testament Textual Studies.* Cambridge: Christian Publishing House.

Andrews, E. D. (2023). *ARCHAEOLOGY & THE NEW TESTAMENT.* Cambridge, Ohio: Christian publishing House.

Andrews, E. D. (2023). *GOD'S OUTLAW: William Tyndale and the English Bible.* Cambridge, Ohio: Christian Publishing House.

Andrews, E. D. (2023). *HOW WE GOT THE BIBLE.* Cambridge, OH: Christian Publishing House.

Andrews, E. D. (2023). *THE SCRIBE AND THE TEXT OF THE NEW TESTAMENT: Scribal Activities in the Transmission of the Text of the New Testament.* Cambridge, Ohio: Christian Publishing House.

Bagnall, R. S. (2009). *The Oxford Handbook of Papyrology (Oxford Handbooks).* Oxford, NY: Oxford University Press.

Comfort, P. W. (2005). *ENCOUNTERING THE MANUSCRIPTS: An Introduction to New Testament Paleography and Textual Criticism.* Nashville, TN: Broadman & Holman.

Comfort, P., & Barret, D. (2019). *THE TEXT OF THE EARLIEST NEW TESTAMENT MANUSCRIPTS: Papyri 1-72, Vol. 1 .* Grand Rapids, MI: Kregel Academic.

Comfort, P., & Barret, D. (2019). *THE TEXT OF THE EARLIEST NEW TESTAMENT MANUSCRIPTS: Papyri 75-139 and Uncials, Vol. 2.* Grand Rapids, MI: Kregel Academic.

Elwell, W. A., & Comfort, P. W. (2001). *Tyndale Bible Dictionary.* Wheaton: Tyndale House Publishers.

Gamble, H. Y. (1997). *Books and Readers in the Early Church: A History of Early Christian Texts*. New Haven and London: Yale University Press.

Greenlee, J. H. (1995). *Introduction to New Testament Textual Criticism*. Peabody: Hendrickson.

Hixon, E. G. (2019). *MYTHS AND MISTAKES iN NEW TESTAMENT TEXTUAL CRITICISM*. Downer Groves: InterVarsity Press.

Holmes, M. W. (2007). *"The Apostolic Fathers: Greek Texts and English Translations"*. Grand Rapids, MI: Baker Books.

Hurtado, L. W. (2019). *TEXTS AND ARTIFACTS: Selected Essays on Textual Criticism ans Early Christian Manuscripts*. New York, NY: T & T Clark.

Kenyon Sr., F. G. (1896). *Our Bible and the Ancient Manuscripts: Being a History of the Text and Its Translations*. London: Eyre & Spottiswood.

Metzger, B. (2001). *The Bible in Translation: Ancient and English Versions*. Grand Rapids: Baker Academic.

Metzger, B. M. (1964, 1968, 1992). *The Text of the New Testament: Its Transmission, Corruption, and Transmission*. New York: Oxford University Press.

Metzger, B. M. (1994). *A Textual Commentary on the Greek New Testament*. New York: United Bible Society.

Metzger, B. M., & Ehrman, B. D. (2005). *The Text of the New Testament: Its Transmission, Corruption, and Restoration (4th Edition)*. New York: Oxford University Press.

Omanson, R. L., & Metzger, B. M. (2006). *A Textual Guide to the Greek New Testament: An Adaptation of Bruce M. Metzger's Textual Commentary for the Needs of Translators*. Stuttgart: Deutsche Bibelgesellschaft.

Porter, S. E. (2013). *HOW WE GOT THE NEW TESTAMENT: Text, Transmission, Translation.* Grand Tapids, MI: Baker Academic.

Royse, J. R. (1981). *Scribal Habits in Early Greek New Testament Papyri (Ph.D. diss.,).* Berkeley, CA: Graduate Theological Union.

Wegner, P. D. (2006). *A Student's Guide to Textual Criticism of the Bible: Its History Methods & Results.* Downers Grove: InterVarsity Press.